NEW HORIZONS IN COMPARATIVE POLITICS

COMPARATIVE DEMOCRACY AND DEMOCRATIZATION

Edited by Howard J. Wiarda
University of Massachusetts/Amherst

and

**Center for Strategic and International Studies (CSIS)
Washington, D.C.**

With Contributions by

**Steve D. Boilard, Eric S. Einhorn, Peter R. Moody, Jr.,
A. H. Somjee, Anwar H. Syed, Howard J. Wiarda,
Yohannes Woldemariam**

Harcourt College Publishers

**Fort Worth   Philadelphia   San Diego   Orlando   San Antonio
Toronto   Montreal   London   Sydney   Tokyo**

Publisher Earl McPeek
Acquisitions Editor David Tatom
Marketing Strategist Laura Brennan
Project Manager Barrett Lackey

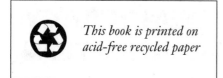

This book is printed on acid-free recycled paper

ISBN: 0-15-507102-5

Library of Congress Control Number: 2001088493

Cover: Graphic World Publishing Services

Address for Orders:
Harcourt College Publishers, 6277 Sea Harbor Drive,
Orlando, FL 32887-6777

Address for Editorial Correspondence:
Harcourt College Publishers, 301 Commerce Street, Suite 3700,
Fort Worth, TX 76102

Web Site Address:
http://www.harcourtcollege.com

Printed in the United States of America

1 2 3 4 5 6 7 8 9 0   039   9 8 7 6 5 4 3 2 1

Table of Contents

Preface

Along with the disintegration of the Soviet Union, the collapse of the Warsaw Pact, and the fall of the Berlin Wall and the reunification of Germany, the transition to democracy in many areas of the world has to be one of the most significant transformations of the late twentieth century—maybe even more important than the others mentioned. Beginning in the mid-1970s in Southern Europe (Greece, Portugal, and Spain), then continuing through Latin America, spreading to much of East Asia, then exploding in Russia and Eastern Europe, and now encompassing parts of Africa and the Middle East, the march of democracy has become a global phenomenon. Sweeping away authoritarian-corporatist regimes on the right and Marxist-Leninist regimes on the left, democracy has now become the only form of government that enjoys universal legitimacy.

The themes and events of these democratic transitions make for exciting reading: the collapse of such long-time dictatorships as those of Franco in Spain and Salazar in Portugal; the sweeping away of authorities who abused human rights in Latin America; the profound transformations, first economically and then politically, in East Asia; the "Moscow Spring" and an earlier, happier vision of Boris Yeltsin holding back the forces of renewed Russian repression; and the early stirrings of civil society, democratic elections, and more participatory politics in Sub-Saharan Africa and the Middle East. All of this is high drama with major issues and major stakes involved, relating to both the domestic politics and international relations of all these areas and the world.

The issues are important both conceptually and for the individual countries and areas affected. How do we explain and account for these democratic transitions? What factors are involved? Are there common patterns of events that these countries and regions have gone through? Have these new democratic regimes been institutionalized and consolidated? Is the process of democratization now complete or might it still be reversible? Do these countries and areas all mean the same thing by "democracy"? What accounts for and what are the implications of the differences? Are these democratic transitions due mainly to domestic forces or to international pressure, or to some combination of both? Does the triumph of democracy worldwide mean that the great systems debate of the twentieth century (Marxism, authoritarianism, or democracy) is over? Has history, as Francis Fukiyama famously argues, ended? These larger issues lie at the heart of the theoretical considerations and the region-by-region analysis in this book and give it both underlying unity as well as the "meat" for stimulating class discussions.

This volume incorporates general theoretical, comparative, and political science approaches as well as proceeding by geographical area. It explores both the general trends undergirding democratization as well as the national and regional variations. It explains the main and global patterns and processes underway as well as the major differences between areas. It utilizes both comparative approaches to democratization and regional and country case studies. The book contains a wealth of factual analyses as well as challenging ideas and brings together a group of experienced, articulate, and well-informed writers.

A special focus of this book is the philosophical, political-cultural, and political-theoretical bases for democracy in different parts of the world. The question is: Is democracy one and universal, largely corresponding to the Western (United States and European) definition of democracy, or is it particular and local with the several cultural areas of the world having their own definitions and practices of democracy? In other words, in addition to the Western model of democracy, is there now an Asian model and theory of democracy, a Latin American version, an Islamic model, and an indigenous or homegrown African model? And what are the implications, both for our understanding of these other countries and areas and for an American foreign policy seeking to advance democracy and human rights, of these distinct meanings and understanding of the key policy terms? Alternatively, is the spread of worldwide communications (especially television), globalization, and the unchallenged power of the United States currently leading to a situation in which these local or regional definitions and understandings of democracy are being overwhelmed by the U.S. and Western conception? These are important issues with major post–Cold War policy implications.

The book begins with an introduction by the editor that sets forth the main themes, introduces the material, and discusses the key issues involved. That is followed by chapters on each of the main geographical areas that have pioneered or have undergone democratization, organized according to the approximate sequence in which democratization occurred: Western Europe, Southern Europe and Latin America, Russia, East Asia, India, the Middle East, and Sub-Saharan Africa. To facilitate comparison and to make the book readable, each chapter will employ, to the extent feasible, a common framework and outline.

Once this factual base has been established, the book introduces some larger comparative themes and ideas. The country and regional chapters are thus accompanied by discussions on transitions to democracy that analyze the main comparative themes involved, the distinct meanings of democracy in different parts of the world, the different levels of institutionalization and consolidation of democracy, and how democracy overlaps with and mixes with local, indigenous, homegrown political processes and institutions. A concluding chapter by the editor ties all these themes together, places the country and regional chapters in a larger context, draws out the comparative implications, and assesses the future of democratization.

There is, surprisingly, nothing comparable to this book in the literature. I say "surprisingly" because, given the importance of the subject and its worldwide ramifications, there still is no textbook that does what this one does. So far we have a number of single country case studies, some devoted to individual regions, and some that are theoretically oriented. Almost all of these were written in the 1980s and early 1990s and are extremely dated, both factually and conceptually. But there is no single book or text that is brief, readable, and well-written, that takes a genuinely comparative perspective on these important themes, that proceeds region by region, that employs a common framework and conceptual design to inform each of the individual chapters, and that also raises major conceptual and theoretical issues for students of political science and comparative politics to grapple with.

This book is aimed at a student audience. It is meant to be a textbook primarily for undergraduates but could be used for graduate courses as well. Instructors, scholars, and general readers will also find its themes of major interest. The book can be used in introductory courses in comparative politics, in courses on developing nations, in courses on comparative social change, and in the mushrooming courses on comparative democratization.

The editor wishes to thank the individual contributors to the book as well as Executive Editor David Tatom and Developmental Editor Stacey Sims of Harcourt College Publishers. It is a pleasure (and rare!) to work with editors who are both thoroughly professional and at the same time extremely pleasant. However, any mistakes of fact or judgment in the book are those of the individual authors and book editor alone.

HOWARD J. WIARDA
Washington, D.C.
Winter 2001

Contributors

Steve D. Boilard
Steve D. Boilard, former Professor of Political Science at Western Kentucky University, is Legislative Analyst at the California State Reference Service. Among other books, he is the author of *Russia at the Twenty-First Century*, also published by Harcourt College Publishers.

Eric S. Einhorn
Eric S. Einhorn is Chair and Professor of Political Science at the University of Massachusetts. A specialist in European politics, the modern welfare state, and particularly the Nordic countries, he is with John Logue author of *Modern Welfare States: Politics and Policies in a Social Democratic Scandinavia*.

Peter R. Moody, Jr.
Peter R. Moody, Jr. is Professor of Political Science at the University of Notre Dame. A specialist on East Asian politics, particularly China and the Confucian tradition, he is the author of *Tradition and Modernization in China and Japan* in the Harcourt College Publishers "New Horizons in Comparative Politics" series.

Margaret MacLeish Mott
Margaret MacLeish Mott is Professor of Political Science at Marlboro College. Her specialties include public law, medieval political theory, and Spain. She is coauthor of *Catholic Roots and Democratic Flowers: Politics and Political Systems of Spain and Portugal*.

A. H. Somjee
A. H. Somjee is Emeritus Professor of Political Science at Simon Fraser University, British Columbia, Canada. A specialist on Indian politics, he is best known for his critiques of political development theory, especially *Political Capacity in Developing Societies* and *Parallels and Actuals of Political Development*.

Anwar H. Syed
Anwar H. Syed is Emeritus Professor of Political Science at the University of Massachusetts. He has written extensively in the fields of international relations, American politics, political theory, and comparative politics. Among his books is *Pakistan: Islam, Politics, and National Solidarity*.

Yohannes Woldemariam
Yohannes Woldemariam was born in Eritrea, raised in Ethiopia, and lived in the Sudan as a political refugee. He is a lecturer in Political Science at the University of Massachusetts and specializes in Africa. He has published in the *African Studies Review* and the *New York Times*. His current major project is a study of peacekeeping in Sierra Leone, Eritrea, and the Balkans.

Howard J. Wiarda
Howard J. Wiarda, the editor of this volume, is also the general editor of the Harcourt College Publishers series "New Horizons in Comparative Politics." He is Senior Associate of the Center for Strategic and International Studies (CSIS) in Washington D.C., Senior Scholar at the Woodrow Wilson International Center for Scholars, and Professor of Political Science at the University of Massachusetts. He is the author of books on comparative politics, American foreign policy, political theory, Latin America, and (East and West) Europe.

1
—

Introduction: Democracy and Democratization— Product of the Western Tradition or a Universal Phenomenon?

—Howard J. Wiarda

Three major types of political systems have been dominant in the world in modern times. These are *liberal democracy*, prevalent in Western Europe, North America, the members of the British Commonwealth (Australia, New Zealand, etc.), and some countries of Asia and Latin America; *Marxism-Leninism* or *Communism*, present in the former Soviet Union, Eastern Europe, and China, as well as North Korea, Vietnam, Cambodia, and Cuba; and *authoritarianism*, often found in developing or Third World nations. The division of the world's political systems into these three major types not only dominated the textbooks most often used in political science courses but also seemed to reflect quite realistically the main political systems by which the countries of the world were actually governed.

However, in the 1970s and 1980s this three-part division of the world's political systems began to change rapidly. First, beginning in the mid-1970s in Southern Europe (Greece, Portugal, and Spain), and then spreading to Latin America, East Asia, and some parts of the Middle East and Africa, a large number of formerly authoritarian regimes began to make a transition to democracy. Second, during the period 1989–91, the Berlin Wall came tumbling down, the

1

Iron Curtain fell, the Soviet Union collapsed along with a host of Marxist-Leninist regimes in Eastern Europe, and a large number of formerly communist countries began transitions to democracy. The results: We saw a *huge* decrease in the number of both authoritarian and communist countries in the world, a large increase in the number of democracies, and the seeming triumph of democracy and the democratic idea as the sole legitimate type of political system[1] (Figure 1-1).

The apparent triumph of democracy globally, however, does not end the debate; history, contrary to author Francis Fukuyama, has not "ended."[2] For one thing, there are quite a number of both authoritarian and Marxist-Leninist regimes still in power, most of which show few signs of disappearing quickly. For another, some authoritarian regimes have instigated just enough "democracy" to earn the world's approval (and qualify for international loans) but not enough to be considered genuinely democratic. More than that, many recent transitions to democracy have been partial or incomplete, leaving mixed or hybrid forms of democracy and authoritarianism in a variety of combinations. But most importantly for the purposes of this book, we have discovered that many countries have different meanings and understandings of democracy, accord it different priorities, and have quite different philosophical underpinnings and institutional arrangements of democracy.

That is what this book is all about. We explore the distinct philosophical, cultural, and political-theoretical bases of democracy in different countries. For example, we know that the philosophical and theoretical bases of American liberal democracy lie in the writings of the English writer John Locke and then in the writings and statements of Thomas Jefferson, James Madison, Abraham Lincoln, Woodrow Wilson, Franklin Roosevelt, and others. But consider Continental Europe, where the basis of understanding derives more from the ideas of French philosopher Jean Jacques Rousseau and not Locke, and where the meanings of terms such as liberalism, pluralism, and democracy are often quite different from in the United States? Or look at Russia, a country that was, and remains, only partly westernized and still seems to want sometimes to follow its own path, or Latin America that has long represented a less-developed, sixteenth-century (scholastic, semifeudal, counter-reformationary) fragment of the West carried over by Columbus and the Spanish and Portuguese conquistadores to the New World.

The issues are compounded when we move to non-Western areas. To what degree is Asian democracy based on historic Confucian theories, or is Asia now, as author Peter Moody argues in Chapter 5, in a "post-Confucian" era? What is the influence of Islam in shaping Middle Eastern democracy (or in explaining the lack thereof), how does one explain the persistence and apparent viability of democracy in India, despite the country's underdevelopment and wrenching social and economic problems, and to what extent does

Figure 1–1 Countries by Level of Democracy, 1996.

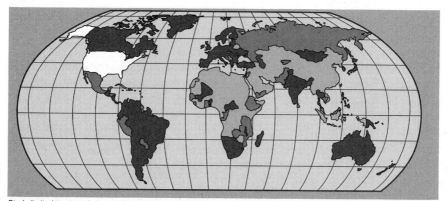

Study limited to states in international system with 1996 populations greater than 500,000; Boundary representation is Eritrea and Qatar inadvertently omitted. Also excludes the United States. not necessarily authoritative.

Full democracies		Partial democracies	Autocracies	
Argentina	Mali	Bosnia and Herzegovina	Afghanistan	Saudi Arabia
Australia	Mauritius	Cambodia	Albania	Serbia and
Austria	Mongolia	Comoros	Algeria	Montenegro
Bangladesh	Namibia	Congo, Republic of the[a]	Angola	Singapore
Belgium	Nepal	Ethiopia	Armenia	Somalia
Benin	Netherlands	Fiji	Azerbaijan	Sudan
Bolivia	New Zealand	Georgia	Bahrain	Swaziland
Botswana	Nicaragua	Ghana	Belarus	Syria
Brazil	Norway	Guinea-Bissau	Bhutan	Tajikistan
Bulgaria	Panama	Guyana	Burkina Faso	Togo
Canada	Papua New	Honduras	Burma	Tunisia
Central African	Guinea	Jordan	Burundi	Turkmenistan
Republic	Philippines	Kyrgyzstan	Cameroon	Uganda
Chile	Poland	Malaysia	Chad	United Arab
Colombia	Portugal	Mexico	China	Emirates
Costa Rica	Romania	Moldova	Congo,	Uzbekistan
Cyprus	Slovenia	Mozambique	Democratic	Vietnam
Czech Republic	South Africa	Pakistan	Republic of the[b]	Zimbabwe
Denmark	South Korea	Paraguay	Cote d'Ivoire	
Dominican	Spain	Peru	Croatia	
Republic	Sweden	Russia	Cuba	
Ecuador	Switzerland	Senegal	Egypt	
El Salvador	Taiwan	Sierra Leone	Gabon	
Estonia	Thailand	Slovakia	The Gambia	
Finland	The Former	Sri Lanka	Guinea	
France	Yugoslav	Tanzania	Indonesia	
Germany	Republic of	Yemen	Iran	
Greece	Macedonia	Zambia	Iraq	
Guatemala	Trinidad and		Kazakhstan	
Haiti	Tobago		Kenya	
Hungary	Turkey		Kuwait	
India	Ukraine		Laos	
Ireland	United Kingdom		Lebanon	
Israel	Uruguay		Liberia	
Italy	Venezuela		Libya	
Jamaica			Mauritania	
Japan			Morocco	
Latvia			Niger	
Lesotho			Nigeria	
Lithuania			North Korea	
Madagascar			Oman	
Malawi			Rwanda	

[a]Congo (Brazzaville)　　　　[b]Congo (Kinshasa)

Source: Daniel C. Esty et al., *State Failure Task Force Report: Phase II Findings* (McLean, VA: Science Applications International Corporation, July, 1998).

Africa have an indigenous or homegrown tradition of institutions that can serve as an African theory of democracy?

The main question we wrestle with in this book is whether democracy is one and universal (similar to the U.S. model) or particular and based on very different local, regional, and cultural traditions and institutions. Is democracy everywhere the same or fated to become that way as countries become wealthier and better integrated into globalization, or is it present in *various* forms depending on distinct philosophical and political backgrounds as well as different levels of socioeconomic and political development? Americans tend to believe that theirs is the best and virtually only form of democracy, but in fact there are many and diverse kinds and foundations of democracy. We need to understand and appreciate these diverse forms not only for a better comprehension of different countries and traditions, but also because many policy considerations having to do with democracy and human rights hinge on whether democracy is everywhere the same or has distinct meanings and priorities in different countries.

This book takes a generally middle and consensus position on these issues. It recognizes realistically that different countries and cultures mean different things by and have different institutions and philosophical foundations of democracy. At the same time it argues that there are certain minimum core requirements, such as competitive elections and basic freedoms, that all countries must have if they wish to be called "democracies." Just because some tyrants call themselves or their systems "democratic" or run rigged elections is no reason why we cannot use more objective standards to verify the truthfulness of their statements. A sense of cultural difference is useful as a way of enabling us to understand diverse countries and cultures, but we also need to recognize a means to gauge whether a country is in fact democratic or not. But then we take the argument a step farther, suggesting that globalization is now forcing *all* countries to come closer to a U.S. or Western understanding and practice of democracy, whether that is in accord with their own philosophical traditions or not. Modern communications (television, satellites, VCRs, etc.) are bringing the advantages of modern Western life, including democracy, into every living room. Democracy and human rights Western-style are now becoming the norm to which all countries aspire—or to which they must conform if they want international aid and investment. The issue is fraught with controversy because it suggests a single standard of democracy—largely defined in U.S. or Western terms and with U.S.-style institutional arrangements—which many countries, because of both a lack of development *and* distinct political traditions, are not able to fully live up to, or which may ultimately destabilize them either because the standard is set too high or because their philosophical traditions are very different from our own.

It is a major issue which speaks to questions of ethnocentrism (whether we can understand other societies on their own terms rather than only through our own rose-colored lenses), whether democracy and the U.S. model are truly universal, and what effects globalization is now having on these controversies.

The Meaning(s) of Democracy

Democracy was born and even "invented" in the West by the ancient Greeks, and it has long been closely associated with the development and institutional arrangements of the West, including both Western Europe and its extension in North America. Democracy, including its several definitions, seems to be a good "fit" in the West, tied in as it is to Western culture and institutions. Implied in the above is the notion that democracy is more than a "mere" set of institutional arrangements (regular elections and the like), which presumably any country could imitate with minimal constitutional engineering. Instead, democracy is embedded in the culture of the West, the society, and the economy, indeed, as a whole way of life. And that makes it much harder to imitate or to reproduce in societies in which history, culture, society, and economic relationships are much different from our own.

It is hard, for example, to conceive of democracy apart from the Renaissance, the Enlightenment, and the sense of individualism, pragmatism, tolerance, and rationality to which these movements gave rise. Similarly, at the social level, it seems hard to conceive of democracy without the presence of some degree of equality or egalitarianism among the citizens. For countries that are deeply riven by class, racial, and ethnic divisions, in which the gaps between rich and poor are so large as to be all but insurmountable, or in which the upper classes do not believe those below them on the social or racial scale are even fully human, it seems hard to imagine that some formula of institutional tinkering (creating political parties or parliaments, for example) could magically transform them into democracies. Democracy, in short, is usually correlated to some degree with a sense of egalitarianism and the rise of a strong middle class.

In the economic sphere, although the correlations are not always one-to-one, most of us understand that at some level freedom in the economic marketplace is related to freedom in the political sphere and that at some points in history the rise of economic individualism, entrepreneurship, and capitalism was and is related to the rise of political democracy. It is possible to have democracy without free and open markets and a system of individual private property rights, but in general a system of strong rights including property rights has served to limit oppressive government and bolster democracy. Parallel comments apply in broad terms to the role of religion; without ascribing any particular good or bad points to any one religion, it seems likely that the rise of a sense of individual choice and responsibility in the polling booth is related to the rise of individual choice and responsibility in matters of religion, to the breakup of the theocracy and absolutist religion of the middle ages, and to the growth of religious pluralism and tolerance that accompanied the rise of political pluralism.

There are other features that need to be emphasized to have a full understanding of democracy and it meaning, as well as its possibilities in diverse societies. For example, can you have democracy in countries in which the levels of literacy or of socioeconomic development are so low that people have no sense of national politics or are so preoccupied with scratching out a daily subsistence that they have no time, energy, or interest in politics? Can you have democracy in countries in which the gaps between rich and poor are so vast that the notions of egalitarianism or one-person one-vote are a laugh, a farce? Can you have democracy when the armed forces or religious authorities intervene in the political process to nullify the popular vote?

In other words, democracy is more than a narrow and particular arrangement of political institutions. It is embedded in the history, culture, sociology, economics, philosophy, and even religion of the West, and it may be inseparable from these. The question, therefore, becomes: If democracy is tied up closely with the history, culture, sociology, economics, and religion of the West, how can the non-West, which lacks the same history and traditions, be expected to develop Western-style democracy? How can societies that never experienced the Renaissance, the Enlightenment, the Protestant Reformation, the Industrial Revolution, the rise of capitalism, the British (1689) or French (1789) revolutions, or the scientific revolution ushered in with Galileo and Newton develop the same kind of democracy as that of the West? If all these ingredients and more were necessary for the growth of Western-style democracy, then surely countries that lack these ingredients will have to enact their own systems of democracy, with their own institutional forms and their own ingredients and priorities.

Democracy, therefore, is not an export commodity; it cannot be transplanted like a rose bush from one cultural flower bed to another. Rather, it requires careful nurturing and adjustment to local conditions. One country can offer to another specific institutional suggestions about electoral systems or parliamentarianism versus presidentialism. But without similar historical, cultural, social, economic, or even religious conditions and philosophical traditions, democracy—and even the possibility of establishing democracy—is going to vary considerably from country to country. Democracy may take many different forms in many different societies—or, as in Haiti, Somalia, or Kosovo, it may be unlikely to flourish at all. We need to recognize these differences realistically, even while we continue to hope and work for democracy's spread.

And yet the familiar definitions of democracy, almost all of which derive from the Western experience, tend to ignore and take for granted the special historical, cultural, and socioeconomic conditions on which Western democracy rests, even while assuming that the West's institutional arrangements can be easily transferred to the non-West. Take Joseph Schumpeter's classic definition of democracy as a system "for arriving at political decisions in which individuals acquire the power to decide by means of a competitive struggle for the people's vote."[3] Similarly, Harvard Professor Samuel P. Huntington in his pathbreaking study of democratization echoes Schumpeter in his emphasis on competitive elections as *the* essence of democracy.[4] Now, of course, competitive and democratic elections are absolutely necessary in any acceptable definition of democracy; the question is: Are they the only thing? And particularly with regard to the Third World, note that the Schumpeter-Huntington definition makes no mention of the particular cultural, social, and other conditions enumerated earlier that make democracy possible. In other words, their definition *takes for granted* the broader Western tradition that allows democracy to flourish and within which a narrow, *institutional* definition of democracy can be offered. But, of course, in the non-West these conditions cannot be taken for granted and, therefore, a broader, ampler definition of democracy would be necessary for it to apply there.

In the political science literature the best-known definition of democracy or what he calls polyarchy, was offered by Robert Dahl.[5] Dahl's definition amplifies that of Schumpeter and Huntington but is very much in the same tradition and, again, closely tied to the Western experience. Dahl's definition emphasizes three aspects: (1) organized contestation through regular, free, and fair elections; (2) the right of virtually all adults to vote and contest for office; and (3) freedom of press, assembly, speech, petition, and organization. Note that Dahl, like Schumpeter and Huntington, also emphasizes competitive elections in his first two criteria, but then expands the definition in his third criterion to include the classic, nineteenth-century Western freedoms. Later, Dahl expanded his definition to include the following eight criteria:

1. Freedom to form and join organizations
2. Freedom of expression
3. The right to vote
4. Eligibility for public office
5. The right of political leaders to compete for support
6. Alternative sources of information
7. Free and fair elections
8. Institutions for making government policies depend on votes and other expressions of preference

No one could quarrel with this broadened definition; the problem is that it still does not go far enough. It is still tied, in its emphasis on elections and political rights, exclusively to the Western tradition, takes for granted once again the broader Western social and cultural tradition that makes democracy possible, and completely ignores non-Western ideas of democracy or the broader non-Western traditions whose ingredients are very different from the West's and that cannot be simply taken for granted.

Let us illustrate these points with some examples from the Third World, reserving a full discussion for later, including the full chapters on each area by our individual contributors. For instance, we all understand that democracy has not often been successful in the Islamic countries of the Middle East. *One* solution to this problem—a not very feasible one, in my view—is to tell these countries to forget about Islam, develop their economies and societies, and become just like us. Of course, that will not work; countries cannot change that fast, dump their entire history and culture, and take up something new, and certainly we cannot tell other countries to forget their religious, cultural, and historical roots any more than they can tell us to do so.

Another solution, therefore, even while encouraging the social, economic, and political development of the Middle East, is to emphasize in the *Koran*, the *Shariah*, and the writings and interpretations of the Muslim clergy those passages that justify consultation between ruler and ruled, the rights of communities and individuals, the necessity of pluralism, honest and responsible government, and democratic representation. These criteria may not fully satisfy Dahl's and others' idea of the strict and narrow *Western* definition of democracy, but they certainly provide a start *and* they have the added advantage of being rooted in *Islamic* culture, history, and beliefs. Such an approach has the benefit of enabling democracy to grow and develop genuinely indigenous roots rather than—as all too often happens—the United States *imposing* its definition of democracy on the region and expecting the Islamic countries to imitate our institutions even though their *entire* culture, history, and tradition are quite different from our own.

Or let us take the case of Africa, another area with only brief and often unhappy experiences with democracy. The solution on the part of the outside powers has usually been to insist on free and democratic elections in the Western fashion—or to wring our hands and ignore Africa altogether. Once again, we all understand Africa's problems: poverty, underdevelopment, disease, the legacy of the colonial powers, ethnic and tribal conflict that sometimes tears society apart, violence, crime, and war. And we all recognize that social, economic, and political developments are absolutely necessary if Africa is ever to achieve stable democracy. But is the way to achieve that to impose prematurely American- or European-style elections on countries that have no such democratic traditions? Would it not be better to build up the African economies and societies, and at the same time—similar to our suggestions for the Islamic countries—try to find in African *indigenous* culture and society institutions and practices that help mitigate authoritarianism, provide for consultation and pluralism, strengthen homegrown civil society, and help deliver sorely needed public goods and services? Meanwhile, we should strive to nudge these countries, if not toward full democracy, at least in a more democratic direction. Such a strategy will obviously not bring instant democracy (impossible to achieve in any case), but it does have the advantage of providing a grassroots and indigenous base on which democratic practices can be nurtured and brought along.

The issue here is not just a hair-splitting definitional one of what we mean by democracy. Nor is it purely a problem of development: the idea that if we provide enough foreign aid, economic growth, and investment, the Islamic world, China, Africa, and other global regions will eventually come to have a democracy that looks just like our own. Nor is it even sensitivity to cultures and societies other than our own, although we should be in favor of that idea, too. Rather, the issue is purely pragmatic: If we are committed to democracy and believe that it is the best system extant for the diverse countries of the world, then what is the best way to achieve that goal? Is it by running roughshod over local institutions, cultures, history, and ways of doing things by imposing our own narrow and particular, U.S.- and Western-based definition and institutions of democracy on countries and areas in which the traditions are different and American-style democracy does not fit very well? Or is it by slowly nurturing homegrown, local, and indigenous institutions, which are often the only viable ones in the society, and carefully cultivating them—meanwhile encouraging economic, social, and political growth—until they have a chance to flower into full-fledged democracy.[6] The latter course, since it implies vast cultural, social, and political change, may require two or three generations—fifty to a hundred years—but it has a much better chance of success than the current policy, which is to try to impose a pure, American-style democracy (Is our own democracy really so pure?) on countries that are ill-prepared for it and whose history and traditions are quite different from our own.

These examples illustrate that the debate over democracy, its meaning(s), and the best way(s) to achieve it is not limited to academic or intellectual debates. Rather, a large part of post-Cold War foreign policy has a democracy component to it; indeed, some scholars and policy activists believe democracy should be *the* basis of U.S. foreign policy. In addition, there are now offices of democracy enhancement in the Department of State, the U.S. Agency for International Development (AID), and even the Defense Department and the Central Intelligence Agency (CIA). Outside the government, but often overlapping with it, the Carter Center in Atlanta, the National Endowment for Democracy (NED), the International Foundation for Electoral Systems (IFES), the National Democratic Institute (NDI), and the International Republican Institute (IRI)—*all* have democracy promotion at the forefront of their agendas. Democracy is, therefore, not just an abstract, theoretical, or philosophical issue anymore; instead, it has become a major policy issue with large interest groups, money, government, bureaucracies, and international actors and personnel involved.

Distinct Philosophical/Cultural Bases of Democracy

Democracy does not have the same meaning, the same socioeconomic, cultural, or institutional base, or the same priority in every society. We believe that there *are* certain universals that democracy requires—regular and competitive elections, political freedoms, periodic changeovers of governments—but at the same time the precise meaning, implications, importance, and cultural understandings of democracy may vary considerably.

In this section we present a summary statement of the main traditions of democracy (or its absence) that are surveyed in this book. At least five agendas or scenarios seem to be operating here:

1. Variations among well-established, democratic regimes; for example, the different types of democracies prevailing in the United States and the countries of Western Europe

2. Rejection of the Western democratic model by a significant proportion of the population, but without a viable alternative—Russia

3. Aspiration for Western-style democracy but a weak socioeconomic base and alternative traditions that may compete with democracy—India and Latin America

4. Successful economic modernizers but now with Western cultural traditions and political systems that are experimenting with their own hybrid forms of democracy for the first time—East Asia

5. Non-Western countries that have neither the socioeconomic base for democracy nor a clear and strong democratic historical and cultural tradition—the Islamic countries and sub-Saharan Africa

Let us take up each of these variations—and the areas or countries represented—in turn.

We begin with American democracy, not only because that is the system most of us know best, but also because the United States is often presented as a model for the rest of the world to emulate, a "beacon on a hill" as Woodrow Wilson put it. However, the American experience is so particular, so unique ("American exceptionalism") that it is difficult to believe our democratic traditions and experiments could be readily exported to the rest of a world that lacks such traditions. First, we are a frontier country that could absorb an expanding population as well as society's discontents. Second, we are a product of religious nonconformity and eventually religious and political pluralism. Third, we are an offshoot of the Enlightenment, the English legal tradition, and the notion of government as a contract between rulers and *consenting* citizens. Fourth, we have multiculturalism and a diversity of racial and ethnic strains. Fifth, although we had slavery in the South, we had no real feudal tradition to overcome to achieve modernity. Sixth, we are a country of enormous wealth, natural resources, and favorable climate and geography. Seventh, we have a homegrown (and constantly evolving) system of checks and balances and representative government. Eighth, as d'Tocqueville demonstrated, we have this incredible infrastructure of grass-roots civil society. Ninth, we are the world's richest and most powerful nation. There are undoubtedly many other unique features of American democracy and doubtless each of us could readily come up with our own list of special characteristics, but the point is how fortunate, and at the same time how distinctive, the United States is. Can any of these beneficial features or combination of features really be replicated in other societies, and is it, therefore, realistic to expect that U.S. democracy can be transplanted in other countries that lack all our advantages?

When we "cross the pond" to Europe, we confront another set of issues. First, Europe is itself exceedingly diverse with many forms and types of democracy in its several countries, so when we speak of "the Western model" of democracy, we will need to know if it is British, French, German, Scandinavian, Italian, Spanish, or another form of democracy we are speaking of. Second, and as implied above, the European experience by itself is the best evidence for the main argument of this book: that democracy can take a great variety of forms depending on time, history, level of socioeconomic development, religion, political culture, institutional arrangements, and international forces.

Third, and as Professor Eric Einhorn's chapter in this book makes clear, the historic tradition and even the meaning of European democracy has evolved over time and is very different from that of the United States. For one thing, Europeans mean something quite different by "liberalism" than do Americans: For Europeans liberalism generally means a nineteenth-century, laissez-faire, economic philosophy akin to that of former conservative British prime minister Margaret Thatcher and with a very small political following that is on the Right of the political spectrum, not the Left. For another, "socialism" or social democracy in Western Europe carries far fewer negative connotations than it does in the United States; the European political and party spectrum is thus generally wider and more to the Left than is that of the United States. Following from the above, when Europeans nowadays speak of democracy, they have in mind modern "social democracy" (the welfare state) and no longer just the formal institutions of democracy. Increasingly, Eastern and Central Europe now aspire to this same social-democratic model.

But as we proceed even farther east in Europe, the issue of democracy becomes more and more problematic. Indeed, some have argued that, while with the end of the Cold War the old Iron Curtain separating East from West in Europe has been erased, a new divide—somewhat farther east and corresponding closely to the borders of the Russia-dominated Commonwealth of Independent States (CIS)—has emerged, separating the democratic (including the newly democratic states of Eastern Europe) from the nondemocratic or only partially democratic. Russia is our primary case in this book, although such newly independent states as Belarus, the Ukraine, Moldova, Chechnya, Georgia, Armenia, Azerbaijan, Turkmenistan, Uzbekistan, Kazakhstan, Kyrgyzstan, and Tajikistan might also be included.

Russia is an especially interesting case for us in this book because, while it is a (mainly) Western country, it has long been isolated from the West and from its key intellectual currents, including the Renaissance, the Enlightenment, and democracy itself. Russia has at present a democratically elected government and many of the classic freedoms, but it also has a powerful antidemocratic and authoritarian tradition, whether that appears in Czarist or Marxist-Leninist versions. Moreover, Russia's attitudes toward the West and Western democracy are ambivalent: At some times (and among some people) it admires the West and wants to imitate and be accepted by it; at other times, it seeks to reject the West and to elevate and laud its own Slavic institutions, sometimes seeking in the Slavic tradition a model of development and governance of its own. Unlike some of the other areas with which we shall be dealing, Russia does not have its own or Slavic theory of democracy, but it is still sufficiently ambivalent about the West and democracy and has such powerful authoritarian traditions that it merits separate treatment in this book.

When we analyze Latin America, we find—and the statement may be surprising—many similarities to Russia. Both are poor, underdeveloped areas, although with many dynamic sectors. Both have long traditions of authoritarianism. In both cases authoritarianism in the political sphere was undergirded by a body of religious beliefs and institutions—in the Orthodox Church in Russia and the medieval Roman Catholic Church in Latin America—that emphasized authority, discipline, hierarchy, and top-down decision-making. Both areas are (mainly) a part of the West but also apart from it, geographically, psychologically, and politically. Russia is contiguous to Western Europe and the latter's democratic traditions, while Latin America is separated from it by thousands of miles of oceans; nevertheless, Latin America's main intellectual and political traditions have been predominantly Western for over 500 years.

Latin America, however, was founded as a *fragment* of the West, circa 1500. That is, it is Western but premodern. Beginning with Columbus's discovery of the Americas in 1492, Latin America was founded on principles and institutions that were feudal, scholastic, and medieval in origins. The

Spanish/Portuguese conquest of the Americas was largely completed by 1570, half a century before the North American colonies were settled on the basis of representative government. In contrast, Latin America emerged from the feudalism of the Middle Ages, from a system that was authoritarian, hierarchical, top-down, elitist, two-class, nonegalitarian, and nondemocratic. Founded on premodern principles and institutions, Latin America did not experience until recently the modernizing trends that we associate with the modern age—the Renaissance, the Enlightenment, the Protestant Reformation, the Industrial Revolution, the rise of capitalism, and liberal, representative government.

Hence, Latin America lagged behind, trapped in the Middle Ages, while the United States forged ahead. Even when Latin America began to move toward independence and republicanism, moreover, it did so on a basis that was different from that of the United States: scholastic rather than empirical arguments, Rousseau rather than Locke (implying heroic "saviors" like Castro or Pinochet instead of democratic elections), Comtean positivism (order and progress) rather than genuine freedom and liberalism. So as Latin America now democratizes, really for the first time, and moves toward a free-market economy, we will want to know if that is genuine liberal democracy as we know it or is it still in keeping with Latin America's own organic, corporate, top-down tradition of democracy. Complicating the issue in Latin America is the emergence of indigenous Indian groups who are increasingly demanding their own system of political organization.

The book now moves from semi-Western areas (Russia and Latin America) to non-Western areas, beginning with East Asia. East Asia, of course, is non-Western and had none of the modernizing, democratizing experiences with which Westerners are familiar: the Renaissance, the Enlightenment, the Industrial Revolution, and so on. Instead, the dominant, historic tradition in East Asia is Confucianism, although Buddhism, Taoism, Shintoism, and other religions are also present and important. Confucianism should be thought of not so much as a religion in the Western sense but as a body of ethical principles: discipline, order, obedience, honor, education, family obligation, consensus, group solidarity, and community. For a long time these principles were thought to be conservative and traditionalist and to hold back East Asian development and democratization. But as, first, Japan took off, then in the "Four Tigers" of South Korea, Taiwan, Hong Kong, and Singapore and eventually in the Philippines, Malaysia, Thailand, and the Asian region as a whole, the principles of Confucianism came to be seen in a new light: as providing the work ethic that undergirded Asian economic development and the consensus and stability that enabled democracy to grow and become institutionalized.

We need to be careful in making these assertions for they do not apply across the board to all Asian nations. First, while much of East Asia has moved toward democracy, Burma is still a military dictatorship and the People's Republic of China, although modernizing economically, is still Marxist-Leninist politically. Second and particularly relevant for our discussion here, the part of Asia that is democratic seems to practice a form of democracy that is different (more Confucian?) from that of the West, with more emphasis on consensus, group solidarity, continuity, and interlocking elites. Third, as Asian nations have developed and become more self-confident, they have asserted the ascendancy of "Asian values" over Western values (which they often see as decadent and distinctive) and expressed resentment over U.S. efforts to lecture them about democracy and human rights. But here again we need to be careful, distinguishing those countries that practice democracy but are nevertheless sometimes critical of the West (Japan, Taiwan, and South Korea) from those countries that hide behind "Asian values" as a way of rationalizing some frankly authoritarian practices (Malaysia, Singapore, and the People's Republic of China).

The book next turns to India. Here we have another fascinating case. First, India is a very old culture and civilization (far older than the United States) with a great variety of religious and ethical traditions: Hindu, Buddhist, Sikh, and Moslem, among others. Second, in large part because of the English colonial legacy, but also by now with India's own institutional development, the country has been a functioning democracy (the world's largest) for over half a century—although we will surely want to know how much Indian democracy reflects that of the West versus how much is homegrown, especially now that the Hindu Nationalist party (BJP), which mixes religion and politics, has taken power. Third, while India is and has been a practicing democracy, the economic model it followed for a long time included central planning, state-led industrialization, autarky, and socialism. Only after the collapse of the Soviet Union and with the incredible economic success stories of Singapore and other East Asian nations in front of it, did India move toward a more open market economy. India, therefore, provides us with an interesting test case, not only of a mix of imported and indigenous elements in Indian democracy but also whether it is possible, for more than the short term, to separate democracy in the political sphere from liberalism in the economy. Keep in mind also that India's democracy is still precarious, that it is an underdeveloped country, and that by mid-century India may surpass China as the world's most populous and "crowded" country.

Next, we take up the Middle East. Here the main question is: Why have so few of the Islamic countries, in contrast to Russia, Eastern Europe, Asia, and Latin America, embraced democracy? Is there something in Islamic culture or religion that retards democratization? Why has the Middle East (except Israel) not become a part of the great wave of democratization that swept over much of the globe in the late twentieth century?

To begin, there *are* powerful admonitions and currents within Islam that seem to legitimize authoritarianism and top-down rule, just as there were in medieval Catholicism. These currents are so strong that frequently the question is raised: Are Islam and democracy compatible? But at the same time, both the *Koran* and the *Shariah* (Islamic law) contain passages that require rulers to govern justly, to consult (elections?) with their own people, and to reflect and respond to the pluralism of their societies—all of which may provide a basis for democracy. Moreover, nowhere in the *Koran* or the *Shariah* is democracy expressly ruled out or prohibited. A third factor to keep in mind is the economic and social underdevelopment of most of the Islamic countries, so that, while democracy there is not widespread now, they may well repeat the experience of other countries: As economic growth and social modernization grow, the chances for democracy to expand are also enhanced. Finally, as with Asia, we need to be careful with our judgments and avoid stereotypes or too-simple assessments, for in predominantly Islamic countries such as Indonesia, Iran, Jordan, Algeria, and Turkey the strength of democratic sentiment and institutions is increasing.

Finally, the discussion turns to Africa. If there is any continent where the prospects for democracy have not been propitious, it is Africa. For one thing, we need to keep in mind the colonial legacy of Africa and its political institutions also imported from the colonial powers that all but guaranteed that Africa's experience with democracy would be less than successful. Second, as with the Middle East, we need to be aware of Africa's incredible poverty and underdevelopment, which suggests that much of the continent lacks the social, economic, and institutional foundation on which successful democracy can be built. Third, there was a time in the 1970s and 1980s when some countries of Africa experimented with indigenous or homegrown models of democracy, but often these were based on naive, romantic, and unrealistic visions that lacked credibility and stood little chance of success. Hence, today, fourth, some of the more grandiose visions have been abandoned and more modest (and realistic) plans put in their place: some decentralization, better human rights, some privatization, investments, greater transparency in the public accounts, education, etc. That is not to say that the goal of democracy has been abandoned (South Africa is a functioning democracy; other countries have had democratic elections), only that a more realistic assessment of democracy's prospects and possibilities is needed and, further, that these more modest steps at present will help lay the groundwork for more solid, more widespread democracy later on.

In each of these country and regional chapters, our authors were asked to follow, as much as feasible, a common outline. Not all countries and regions fit the outline in exactly the same way, and we have allowed our authors to proceed as they see best. At the same time, the use of a common outline helps the reader to think comparatively about the similarities and differences among the several regions. Here, then, are the main subjects readers should be on the lookout for.

1. Introduction: What is unique about this country or region? When did democracy come to this region and in what form?

2. Socioeconomic base: How firm are the foundations for democracy?

3. Institutional changes: Have there been fair and regular elections, new constitutions, the growth of political parties and interest groups, greater freedom, and so on?

4. Changes in political culture: Are the underlying values, beliefs, and behavior patterns changing?

5. Legacies of the past: Are the old, bad, nondemocratic practices and institutions still present, and how do they relate to or interact with democratic practice?

6. Conclusion: How solid is democracy? Is it institutionalized and consolidated? Does it take forms different from those of the West? Are there mixed or hybrid systems?

Some Larger Questions

As we read the chapters that follow, let us also keep in mind some of the broad theoretical and philosophical questions and issues raised here that cut across all nations and areas.

• What is the Western meaning and definition of democracy, and how does the definition used help determine the assessment we reach about democracy in other areas?

• How do other countries' definitions, meanings, and priorities of democracy differ from our own?

• Is a purely indigenous, native, and homegrown model of democracy possible and worthwhile, and what would such a democracy look like in the various countries/areas covered?

• What is the relationship between successful democracy and social and economic development? As countries develop, will their possibilities for democracy also improve?

• A related question has to do with changing power relationships: With the United States now dominant on the global stage and with business groups and the middle class now emerging as dominant in many countries, would that not lead also and increasingly to the dominance of the U.S.-based, or Western, form of democracy?

- With globalization, is it still possible for a country or area to assert its own indigenous model of democracy, or does globalization tend to lead toward a common homogenization of all cultures and areas, including political institutions as well as economic areas?
- How, then, do most countries blend their local and native traditions and ways of doing things with imported models and pressures from abroad; what do the various mixed forms look like; and how are even these changing under the impact of constant new pressures and forces?
- Are those countries with strong cultures (Japan, China, India, Iran, South Africa, Brazil, Mexico, and others) able to sort out, filter, and *selectively* adapt Western influences and accommodate them to their own societies better than small weak countries? Will the latter be able to retain their own cultures under the Western impact?
- What are the varieties of hybrids, mixed forms, halfway houses, and crazy-quilt patterns that are likely to result from this incredible mix of local or homegrown versus international and global forces?
- With such mixed forms, where do we finally come out on the key question of whether democracy is one and universal or particular and reflective of the society from which it emerges?

Notes

1. Samuel P. Huntington, *The Third Wave: Democratization in the Late Twentieth Century* (Norman: University of Oklahoma Press, 1991).
2. Francis Fukuyama, *The End of History and the Last Man* (New York: Free Press, 1992).
3. Joseph Schumpeter, *Capitalism, Socialism, and Democracy* (New York: Harper, 1947).
4. Huntington, *The Third Wave.*
5. Robert Dahl, *Polyarchy: Participation and Opposition* (New Haven: Yale University Press, 1971); Dahl, *Democracy and Its Critics* (New Haven: Yale University Press, 1989).
6. *They Know How* (Washington, DC: Inter-American Foundation, 1977).

2

Liberalism and Social Democracy in Western Europe

Eric S. Einhorn

Introduction

Europe can proudly claim to be the birthplace of the democratic ideal. In ancient Greece more than 2,500 years ago several city-states, most notably Athens, gave suffrage and political power to a substantial number of their male citizens.[1] If we add the liberal principles of freedom, rule of law, and citizenship, the ancient Greeks and Romans certainly thought and wrote about them, as did several non-European classical civilizations. In the tenth century A.D. the Norse settlers on Iceland assembled regional leaders in the valley of Thingvellir to adjudicate and legislate on public matters. Their assembly, the Althing, met for centuries, and as the current Icelandic legislature it can claim to be the oldest in the world. Clearly liberal democracy has ancient roots; it is the pursuit of human freedom with order and of security with participation through constitutional government, social security, and economic justice.

This chapter looks selectively at the current state of liberal democratic politics in the dozen countries of Western Europe in which modern democratic government emerged over the past two centuries. Several modern European democracies in southern and central Europe are treated elsewhere in this book, but they share many of the struggles common to the Western European democratic core. There are numerous patterns to democratic development in Europe and to the content and definition of liberalism. Moreover, there remain subtle but significant national differences within the region and, particularly, important distinctions from liberal democracy in the United States. Ironically, although liberal democracy was under almost constant attack during the twentieth century, it also spread from its American and Western European origins to become a global force while always taking on national variations. Liberal democracy is neither a monolith nor an abstract ideology; comparing its forms and priorities helps to reveal its many facets.

The idea of "Western Europe" has more historical justification than the Cold War (1945–90) divide, but it is a fuzzy geopolitical concept. Moreover, it is difficult to generalize about political development in more than a dozen countries, spanning the slow evolutionary politics of Britain to the dramatic politics of twentieth-century Germany. Yet at the start of a new millennium, political patterns are clearer than they were a generation ago. European democracy rests on three pillars: constitutional political democracy, social democracy of the welfare state, and the relative egalitarian economic democracy of social market capitalism.

There is no single fully accepted definition of democracy, much less its components mentioned above. In his thorough analysis of the myriad aspects of political democracy, Robert Dahl decided to eschew the term in favor of a neologism: "polyarchy."[2] The equally thorough work of Arend Lijphart finds continuing clarity in Abraham Lincoln's "government by the people" with the qualification of "government for the people."[3] Democracy is both a set of institutions and laws and a process and ideology. Liberalism shares the latter aspect particularly in its emphasis on individual freedom and autonomy. Much of the democratic debate in European politics has been over the issue of individual versus collective rights and responsibilities. Moreover, in the long struggle of democratic government in Europe, history has revealed many variations including oligarchy, populism, autocracy, and others. The legacy of history weighs heavily on the European democratic experience.

Three Pillars of Democracy

With its social, economic, and even cultural dimensions, modern European democracy transcends the more narrowly defined American version. European liberalism never focused exclusively on constitutional questions and political forms, but liberalism was profoundly shaped by this debate. In essence then, Europe has a more extensive view of democratic elements, hence the metaphor of three sturdy pillars: political, social, and economic. This perspective largely corresponds to studies of European political development typified by the work of political sociologists Seymour Martin Lipset, Stein Rokkan, and T. H. Marshall.

Political democracy is based on the extension of civil and political rights and the replacement of autocracy with constitutional government. Britain dates this struggle with the *Magna Carta* in the thirteenth century, but there is precious little democracy in that document other than the limits it placed on royal authority and the guarantees of judicial due process. The battles to limit royal authority were fought again in the seventeenth century and culminated in the "Glorious Revolution" of 1688 and the decisive defeat of absolutism in Britain, although "responsible government" (i.e., the subordination of executive power to the will of Parliament) was at least 150 years distant. Elsewhere in Europe absolutism was generally triumphant until the French Revolution. Democracy required civil rights as well as broader political participation and accountability.

Social rights required an equally protracted struggle to end extremes of class privilege and to give ordinary people in industrial urban societies some of the rights and protection that had previously been part of feudal life. Individual security and protection would now be based mainly on egalitarian principles rather than on the rigid hierarchy of medieval society. In Catholic countries the church had remained the main source of social and health services, whereas in Protestant Europe the state had been forced to take on many of these activities. An important legacy was the view that social issues were matters of collective concern and rarely did European liberalism relegate such issues to the "marketplace." What was called "the social question" had grave implications for European societies as social and economic change forced millions from the land to crowded cities or abroad to colonies and immigrant societies. Had not the latter been able to accept Europe's "teeming masses" by the millions, it is hard to imagine that many European countries would have avoided revolutions at least as violent as the French Revolution of 1789.

Economic democracy is a closely related concept that came into focus mainly in the second half of the twentieth century. The principal thrusts here were economic rights, security, and equality. Marxism and other variants of socialism responded to the enormous inequalities and misery of early industrial society. The labor movement and related rural organizations were responses and agents of change, especially when liberalism won them the right to organize and agitate. European concerns about poverty, economic change, and economic security as well as fears of growing inequality remain distinguishing democratic issues.

A Creative Tension

Liberals had sought to free people from the constraints of traditional feudal and hierarchical society. Free citizens would govern themselves without a privileged political class. Yet the original liberals were rarely radicals who wanted to overturn society. They spoke for a growing and often wealthy commercial and professional class (the bourgeoisie) who sought protection for their earned property. Their allies included radicals such as Tom Paine, but their goals were to restrain kings and aristocrats without turning over power fully to the threatening masses. Liberals wanted, in short, "liberty," but that was usually a very concrete and circumscribed liberation from the restrictions that had benefited the great landowners, the courtiers, and those who enjoyed royal patronage. Moreover, during the nineteenth century most European liberals were closely tied to nationalist movements that sought states which would include all of the members of defined historical and linguistic nations. Toward this end they found allies in the traditional civil servants, military officers, and intellectuals. Nationalism shared many roots with liberalism, but nationalism did not guarantee democracy.

Although the French Revolution initially failed—nearly a century would pass before parliamentary democracy took root in France—it unleashed forces that could not be suppressed. By the 1830s Europe seethed with movements seeking a new political order and "justice" for excluded groups. Here demands for social reform and protection and for economic redistribution and regulation and other political demands challenged the libertarian element of European liberalism. Historically European democracy was a liberal idea that benefited from the dedication of generations of liberal political activists, but in the end European democracy would transcend the liberal agenda. Moreover, modern European politics has inherited many institutions and values from its predemocratic era.

The European Democratic Idea

The history of European democratic thought is long, rich, and well documented. This chapter merely recalls some of the principal contributions to the European democratic idea and the institutional forms that it has taken. Since the Renaissance there has been a common European sense that self-government and the rule of law could be traced back to the classical European world of Greece and Rome. Even the notorious fifteenth-century thinker Niccolò Machiavelli could idealize classical politics while calling for the unification of Italy under enlightened and presumably republican leadership. Premodern European "constitutions" were not democratic, but they did recognize fundamental rights and the legitimacy of "pluralistic" divisions of power. The advancing absolutism and the concentration of power in dynastic monarchs challenged these principles. In Britain, the Netherlands, and Sweden, as well as in many smaller city-states, absolutism failed to gain a solid hold, and ancient "estates" divided political power to protect class interests. The British "Tudor Constitution"[4] saw the royal executive share power with the feudal aristocratic elite (House of Lords) and the rising bourgeoisie (House of Commons). It was this divided constitution that the English settlers of North America brought as a "liberal fragment" to provide the germ of American constitutional democracy.[5]

Western European democracy developed in a broad sense three variants or "schools" of thought and practice. *Liberal democracy* originated in late seventeenth and early eighteenth centuries among advocates for political pluralism and religious and later political toleration. Liberal democracy would carry the torch of democratization, but it was not the only agent or road to modern European democracy. *Radical democracy* also appeared first as a marginal body of thought and action, mainly in the aftermath of the English civil war (1641–50). Only with the French Revolution a century later would it return as a political alternative. The third and ironically newest democratic ideology is *conservative democracy*, which emerged first as a social and economic program and then developed political and constitutional perspectives.

Radical individualism was a strong source of European liberalism whose roots can be traced back to Jean-Jacques Rousseau among others. In addition to his philosophical writings, Rousseau gave concrete form to his ideas in constitutional proposals for Poland and Corsica, neither of which was ever implemented. The eighteenth century saw widespread discussions of political reform and rationalism, some of which were often implemented by absolutist regimes (e.g., Prussia and Denmark). With the American Revolution and especially with the adoption of the American Constitution in 1789, liberal democracy turned from philosophical theory into imperfect yet ambitious practice.

The American Revolution may have "turned the world upside down" for the British monarch and his incompetent government, but it was far less radical than the tumult of the French Revolution starting in 1789. Much of the European democratic debate for the following two centuries can be traced back to the issues and themes of that great event.[6] Radical democrats clearly dominated the second (post-1791) phase of the French Revolution. The excesses of the "Terror" and the collapse of the revolution into dictatorship gave the idea of radical revolution a very dark meaning that would be especially prescient for twentieth-century Europe.

Conservative democracy is of much more recent origin in Europe and represented initially an accommodation rather than a political program. Traditional European conservatives resisted fiercely the idea of popular sovereignty, although there was more pragmatism about constitutional government. Britain prided itself on its "mixed constitution" (though largely unwritten) in which the monarchy, aristocracy, state church, and middle classes (commons) had a role. Likewise, the American constitutional order with its balance of individual liberty (excepting slaves of course) and protection of property gave form to a less threatening political democracy than that of the French Revolution. In the nineteenth century a minority of conservatives recognized that constitutional democracy and social reform and regulation could protect their interests better than the doctrines of antirevolutionary reaction. Likewise, nationalism appealed to many conservatives as a means of enhancing loyalty and support from newly enfranchised social groups.

Together the two eighteenth-century revolutions in America and France and the more evolutionary developments in Great Britain established fundamental principles for political democracy. The first is the concept of popular sovereignty: government by the people. It would take several generations for the "people" to include adults of both genders, all social classes, and all ethnic groups, but the idea of government based on the consent of the governed was established. Secondly, governments would require fundamental laws and stable institutions, including an elected assembly with primary power. Parliamentary sovereignty would be Europe's particular contribution to liberal democracy, whereas Americans, inspired by Montesquieu, balanced their executive, legislative, and judicial branches.

Formal political institutions did not in themselves make popular government work. Political parties and interest groups emerged during the nineteenth century as essential elements of political, social, and economic freedom. Informal parties and factions were very much in evidence in the "proto-parliaments" of Britain, Sweden, and elsewhere in the eighteenth century. Only with the rise of mass electorates in the following 60 years would parties take their modern shape. Their role in mobilizing and directing citizen action gave them a central place in European democracy. Likewise, interest groups became a key element of political activity as farmers, industrial workers, and eventually nearly all of the economically active populations congealed into weaker or stronger associations. The experience of medieval guilds meant that for most European countries modern economic interest groups were a continuation of a long "corporatist" tradition.

The main advocates of representative democracy in nineteenth- and early twentieth-century Europe had a roughly similar agenda that historians call "national liberalism." Nationalism challenged and eventually overwhelmed the multiethnic dynastic empires but brought with it war and revolution (1914–18). Popular sovereignty meant not only full citizenship but also the difficult principle of national self-determination, which severely destabilized early-twentieth-century Europe. Where representative government gained a foothold, national tensions were often contained as in Norway, Great Britain, and the Netherlands. Yet even quasi-democratic Britain was unable to manage a peaceful accommodation with Irish nationalism for a generation.

Democratic Development

European democracy took nearly two centuries to turn the ideas of constitutional government into functioning democratic systems. What then are the common principles? Each European country has followed a different road to democracy with some having achieved substantial democratic control by the end of the nineteenth century while others have secured democracy only in recent decades. Analysts of the democratic process have identified several "stages" of democratization that capture well the essence of political democracy.

The first and central principle of European liberal democracy is parliamentary government. Political power is vested in an assembly with constituencies based on geographic divisions and elected periodically by an expanding electorate. The French revolutionary assembly had introduced universal manhood suffrage in 1792, but it spread very slowly. By midcentury most males could vote for at least the Lower House in Scandinavia, the Netherlands, and France (only briefly until the Third Republic was established in 1871). The Reform Act in Britain in 1832 set the precedent of a widening of the electorate roughly once every generation. Women did not get the right to vote until after World War I.[7] Full female suffrage was not universal in Western Europe until after 1945.

Closely related to parliamentary representation was the subordination of the executive to the legislative branch. The British called this "ministerial responsibility," meaning that neither the Cabinet nor any minister could hold office after losing the "confidence" of parliament (i.e., when opposed by a majority of members). Given the evolutionary nature of British democracy, it is hard to set a clear date of when this principle was adopted. Already in the eighteenth century cabinets and ministers had resigned or been dismissed when they lost the confidence of either the monarch or parliament. By the early reign of Queen Victoria (1837–1901), governments lacking a majority in the House of Commons tendered their resignation. By the early twentieth century this was the hallmark of parliamentary democracy as it remains to the present.

Despite different national traditions and historical experiences there has been a remarkable convergence of Western European political institutions and issues. Recently, there has been a move toward decentralization with many European countries adopting essentially federal systems (Germany, Italy, Spain, Austria, Belgium, and Switzerland). Local and regional governments have taken on significant roles as providers of social services. Electoral systems vary, but only in the United Kingdom does the single-member plurality system continue. A consequence of various election rules is a complex multiparty system usually excluding single-party majorities (France with its double election system is the occasional exception). Coalition (multiparty) governments relying typically on small center parties are the European rule. The weakness of such minority or coalition governments and the aggressive use of parliamentary votes of nonconfidence were major sources of political instability and helped undermine Italian and German parliamentary democracy between 1920 and 1933. Other countries have experienced bouts of political instability and stalemate, but minority parties still enjoy representation. Earlier misfortunes have increased the commitment to viable and accountable government.

European parliamentary democracy reflects the culmination of the liberal democratic political ideal. It has taken root on every continent, with necessary adjustment for local conditions and experience. Its achievement between 1850 and 1945, however, nearly eclipsed traditional liberal political parties. Liberal ideology advanced, but liberal parties faced two challenges. First, after 1945 nearly all political parties accepted the democratic political process, but conducted elections by advocating other reforms. Secondly, liberal parties could no longer win electoral support on the basis of earlier constitutional reforms. In a democracy the electorate ungraciously asks, "What have you done for us lately?" or "What do you propose now?"

The adoption of the liberal ideology by conservative, socialist, and a host of other political parties, which were initially skeptical about representative government based on political equality, symbolized the liberal triumph. Conservative democracy was born largely in Britain when Benjamin Disraeli skillfully transformed the old "Tory party"[8] from one of bitter resistance to democratization to one with a more flexible stance. British conservatism embraced the odd amalgam of democratic and nondemocratic elements.[9] In Germany, Austria, and much of the continent, conservative parties resisted change more emphatically, and it really was not until after World War II that conservative democracy emerged. The principles of liberalism were accepted, especially its anticollectivist economic aspects. European conservatives such as Margaret Thatcher (British Prime Minister from 1979 to 1990) became the true inheritors of nineteenth-century liberalism. Other elements are also apparent. Especially in countries with large Catholic populations, there emerged a more centrist aspect of conservative democracy, which accepted liberal forms but favored traditional social institutions—church and family.

Liberal democratic values also became dominant in the political programs of much of the European socialist movement. Originally revolutionary in program, democratic socialism emerged in those countries in which constitutional reforms had opened the way for a "democratic class struggle."[10] By the end of the nineteenth century, many socialists in Germany, Scandinavia, France, and elsewhere adopted a "reformist" approach to social and economic change. Political democracy seemed to be a plausible and preferable way to change society. Given the growing strength of the social democratic and labor movements in Europe at the beginning of the twentieth century, it is entirely conceivable that the alliance of political liberals and social democrats could have completed the journey to parliamentary democracy with universal suffrage without significant violence. World War I and its horrific effects across the continent weakened the growing mass democratic alliance. Revolutions and nationalism swept Central and Eastern Europe and divided reformists and radicals in Western Europe. It took another generation to reconstruct broad democratic alliances in Western Europe and the end of the Cold War to allow similar developments east of the Iron Curtain.[11]

Acceptance of parliamentary constitutional democracy was the first great European political compromise. By adopting a panoply of social security legislation, conservative, liberal, and social democratic governments established the second great democratic consensus. Although government had a natural interest in social affairs long before the democratic era, in the final decades of the nineteenth century several European countries adopted modest laws to protect the growing industrial and urban populations. Ironically the European Welfare State was founded with the unemployment, disability, and old age pension legislation proposed by German Chancellor Otto von Bismarck in 1883. No democrat, Bismarck was a great strategist. Just as he masterminded the unification of most German states under Prussian leadership and secured Germany's borders by complex international treaties, so he sought to win the loyalty of the working classes (and undermine his socialist opponents) through modest but innovative social security programs. It was an example of conservative democratic reform: a program that benefited many people but which kept political power in the hands of traditional political elites. It echoed the British Conservative reformer Disraeli's motto that "if the cottage is not happy, the palace is not safe." Over the following decades most Western European countries adopted similar programs.

Hence the modern and elaborate Western European welfare state has broad support across the political spectrum. Its roots predate the breakthrough of political democracy, but as suffrage spread and mass organizations joined the political fray, social policy—broadly conceived—became the dominant domestic program of most political parties. In particular, the nascent socialist movement, which Bismarck was explicitly trying to undercut with his reforms, moved from revolutionary rhetoric to pragmatic reformism as mentioned above. By the 1930s a "basic" social security system was in place and over the following decades, interrupted by war, programs expanded to provide public support for universal health care, unemployment and economic security, and old age pensions. In the 1960s "social democracy" was no longer predominantly a socialist goal, but rather a broadly accepted response to what had been called "the social question" (poverty, industrial-urban life, and economic inequality). Christian Democrats, social liberals, agrarians, conservatives, and social democrats supported this "post-war compromise."

As economic conditions deteriorated in the mid-1970s, the consensus cracked. A new generation of socialists sought more radical equality and more political control of the economy. They were opposed by "neoconservatives" (in Europe often called neoliberals) such as Margaret Thatcher who sought to privatize state-owned enterprises, shrink governmental bureaucracies, and "roll back" social programs. Politics flourished and "privatization" became a slogan in the 1980s and 1990s, but there were few radical changes in social policy. There were even important expansions including subsidized childcare and other family support measures. The "welfare state" remains a central element of European democracy.[12]

Challenges to Democracy

Modern European democracy has political, social, and economic elements. It is also challenged by domestic, regional, and international developments. Although there are national differences in each aspect, this section will identify the nature, cause, and prospects for major factors challenging European liberal democracy.

There are three broad challenges facing every Western European democracy, although obviously to different degrees. The first is the changing social and economic foundation on which European states (and hence democracy) rest. The second involves domestic political institutions and constitutional forms. The third includes the regional and global policy pressures that will require new democratic forms and procedures. This involves especially the continuing expansion and development of the European Union (EU), which now includes fifteen of the eighteen Western European democracies.

Western Europe exudes a permanence and stability, which can be misleading. Amidst her ancient cities and intensively cultivated verdant countryside the pace of change has accelerated during the past 15 years. Stagnant economies are once again expanding but on the basis of new technologies and a vigorous public and private service sector. Older heavy industries continue to contract, following the American and British pattern, and are being replaced with smaller-scale, highly specialized enterprises. Although in some areas such as telecommunications, media, and pharmaceuticals European technology is second to none, in other areas European enterprises are facing global pressures.

More significant are demographic and ethnic changes. Through the tragedy of wars and nationalist excess, Europe after 1945 became perhaps more ethnically homogeneous and self-contained (i.e., most national ethnic groups lived in contiguous territories) than it had been for many centuries. World War II had, of course, dislocated many people, particularly in Germany, and there were "displaced persons" from all over Europe to be accommodated. Nevertheless, for two decades internal ethnic and national issues abated, and headway toward international reconciliation was made. Europe's interwar demographic problems diminished and birthrates soared during the post-1945 "baby boom."

The steady movement of people from rural to urban areas continued, but a booming economy easily absorbed them.

This placid scene no longer prevails. Europe has become multiethnic once again after more than four decades of immigration have poured non-Western European peoples into her cities. Originally most of the immigrants came to work during Europe's quarter-century economic boom (1949–74) as "guest workers," but in the wake of decolonization they were later to be joined by refugees and permanent immigrants from every corner of the globe.[13] By now as much as 15 percent of the permanent population of Western European countries is nonnative in origin or has descended from post-1950 immigrants. Europe again is multiethnic and in many cases multicultural. Some of these issues are of long-standing historical origin. Everyone is aware of the sectarian strife between Catholics and Protestants in Northern Ireland. What is less often apparent is the general reconciliation of Christian sects across the rest of the continent, including countries such as Germany and the Netherlands in which conflict had long reigned. There has also been a significant improvement in relations between ethnic groups in Spain, Belgium, and elsewhere. The reduction in historic antagonisms is balanced by the new tensions of accommodating hundreds of thousands of new residents, often from very distant cultures. Added to this are mutual antagonisms between immigrant groups (e.g., Turks versus Kurds). Although Europe has never been more tolerant of minorities and religious differences than at present, the cultural "gap" between the majority and the minorities is unprecedented. It is far from certain that this tolerance will continue.

Demographic problems cover many social issues. It has been more than a generation since Western Europe's baby boom (never quite as dramatic as that in the United States) gave way to falling, and in some cases plunging, birthrates. With no significant rural population to draw into urban employment and with resistance to increased immigration (especially from outside the EU area), European populations are aging. In political terms this means that the elderly have a growing impact and may demand additional resources. Given the pressures on public expenditures and social programs in Europe, this could complicate politics considerably. Many are questioning whether the lavish European welfare state can continue to pay for as many social services as in the recent past. In particular, underfunded old age pensions are vulnerable. Additionally, the demographic changes reflect a deeper transformation in the nature of the European family. The plunging birthrates have been especially severe in southern Europe as women abandon their domestic roles and pursue higher education, jobs, and careers. Without adequate childcare facilities, women in those countries may simply abandon childbearing with dramatic long-term demographic and political consequences.[14]

Political institutions and procedures also have changed over the past quarter century. Although some countries have instituted significant constitutional and electoral reforms (e.g., Italy, Belgium, and to a lesser extent France), nearly every Western European democracy has seen major changes in the processes of liberal democracy. These may be summed up as a weakening of traditional political organizations (both parties and traditional interest groups) and the rise of ad hoc and narrowly focused interest groups. Among the most notable changes is the increased use of referenda questions to decide difficult policy issues. European Union questions have been especially prone to referenda. Moreover, increased media access to political proceedings as well as more critical journalism has weakened popular prestige and deference. There is much less interest in arcane political rituals or deference to political leadership. Although the thrust of these changes is both populist and democratic, it has given a raw edge to politics and made personality and media imagery even weightier on the political scales.

Closely related with these changes in European politics and society is the rise of the EU from a narrowly focused economic free-trade area into a broader (geographically) and deeper (policy areas) entity. As the EU has developed into an organization for European cooperation in nearly all policy areas, its governance and administrative structure have become more important for European liberal democracy. The EU has a dilemma: Its basic mission and history have been to strengthen both economic and political liberalism in Europe. This is most obvious in the economic sphere, but its policies have increasingly brought economic and social rights to individual European citizens. Although the evolving treaties, policy directives, and legal apparatus of the EU seem to expand the democratic sphere, the unique political structure of the union provides an unprecedented challenge to European democracy. In simple terms it is a choice between maintaining national states and limiting the EU to intergovernmental affairs as opposed to strengthening the directly democratic participation and accountability of the EU system.

In practice most EU decisions are made by the Council of Ministers upon the recommendations of the European Commission. The ministers represent their individual countries and are democratically accountable at home. But there are significant differences in how this accountability is exercised. In most cases ministers have substantial leeway at Council meetings although they must keep their cabinet colleagues and parliamentary coalition partners "on board." Over the past decade a growing number of Council decisions have been made by "qualified majority votes" where national vetoes are no longer operative. In some countries, such as Denmark and Sweden, domestic parliaments have established strong standing committees to supervise EU policy decisions and keep the national minister closely accountable to domestic democratic control. Generally, however, national parliaments react to EU decisions fairly late in the game.

The European Union has its own parliament, and national constituencies have directly elected members every four years since 1979. Its powers are mainly investigatory although in 1999 the European parliament voted to dismiss the European Commission over financial scandals. Although in limited spheres the European Parliament has genuine democratic powers, it is neither the focus of EU policy nor a significant source of popular sovereignty over the Union's politics. In addition, the EU, headed by the European Court of Justice, has overruled national governments in an ever-wider sphere of issues.

As the European Union institutions "deepen" their role in daily political life, the issue of the so-called "democratic deficit" (the gap between its political power and its democratically accountable institutions) becomes greater. This term is obviously political, but even supporters of "an ever-closer union" (as the EU treaty puts it) worry about balancing national and regional democratic principles. Moreover, Western European states are often entangled in a host of other regional and international organizations and communities that restrict or place obligations on domestic political institutions. The European Convention on Human Rights—very much needed after the gross violations of previous authoritarian regimes in Europe—limits national sovereignty and has overridden domestic legislation. Even technical and "functional" organizations make important decisions without close parliamentary supervision.[15]

Economic Democracy

Liberal democracy has been closely entwined with economic freedom. For more than a century liberals have been divided over whether freedom and democracy are promoted best by minimizing the role of government in the management of the economy or whether individual rights and security require a more active governmental stance. This reflects the division between "classical liberals" (now often called conservatives) and social liberals who have frequently supported Social Democratic governments. In Europe the political center has most frequently promoted the social liberal approach. This has included the "Social Christian," "Christian Democratic," or "Social Market" ideas of the major continental democracies: Germany, Italy, and France.

After World War II many European countries radically increased the role of government in managing the economy. Not only was there a strong consensus that the economic stagnation and crises between 1920 and 1939 had produced unacceptable social and economic hardship, but the failure of laissez-faire capitalism had undermined political democracy. State control, often including public ownership ("nationalization") of industry, finance, and utilities coupled with experiments in large-scale economic planning, was vigorously advocated by the parties of the left and accepted and sometimes even embraced by the centrists and moderate right parties. Europe did enjoy an unprecedented boom between 1949 and 1974; even as postwar economic controls and international trade were liberalized, there was still strong support for state leadership of the "commanding heights" of the economy. In some countries as well there was a desire to increase the role of employees in day-to-day economic and managerial decisions. West Germany pioneered such "democracy on the shop floor" measures by requiring employee representation on corporate boards. How far can "direct democracy" go and still be compatible with liberal capitalism?

The prolonged economic crisis that hit the entire world economy in 1974 produced renewed political tensions over economic policy and finally some radical innovations.[16] The outcome was a radical shift toward economic liberalization together with a "restart" of European integration in the mid-1980s. Although Western Europe remained committed to its "welfare capitalism" model (private enterprise but significant tax-financed public social services), large economic sectors were deregulated and in some cases "privatized" (sold). Even socialist parties and their affiliated labor unions accepted the need for "structural change," which meant liberalizing layers of strict regulation, complex subsidies, and archaic "work rules." None of these changes were easily negotiated, but the fact that labor, management, and government collectively worked out compromises demonstrates that economic democracy, implemented through representative interest organization, has real meaning in contemporary Europe.

European Liberal Democracy: Century Three

Western European liberal democracy greets the new century (and millennium) in good shape. Its twentieth-century ideological rivals are either extinct (Fascism and Marxism-Leninism) or severely discredited (authoritarian elitism). It would be wrong to close the book on democratic development or to proclaim an "end of history" (Fukuyama's term, 1992) or even an "end of ideology" (Bell's term, 1965).[17] Democracy walks on two legs; it is first a set of constitutional rules that guarantees political rights and participation. It is also a set of rules, procedures, and traditions on how to make representative government work. Both are dynamic elements in contemporary Europe for the reasons discussed above.

Western Europeans are no longer willing to rely solely on national constitutions and politics to guarantee their civil and social rights. From the European Convention on Human Rights through the various EU declarations and policies on social and labor affairs, broader continental standards have been set. Both international and domestic courts have used these agreements to enforce individual civil rights even against domestic opposition. This double layer of democratic protections sets a higher standard than the traditional democratic norm. Europeans certainly debate and disagree on some elements of human rights; currently their impact on managing mass political asylum issues is controversial as some European countries feel overwhelmed by refugees, often from very distant cultures. Broad consensus on issues such as democratic governance, civil rights, and limits on national policy (the implicit abolition of capital punishment) are signs of a continental democratic ethos. This is not just theory. The inclusion of the Austrian Freedom Party (FPO) led by the controversial leader Jörg Haider in a coalition government in January 2000 resulted in political sanctions by the 14 other EU states. Provisions in the EU Treaty of Amsterdam (1997–8) that calls for democracy, fundamental freedoms, and human rights in several of its articles justified this.[18]

Western Europe is extending its democratic frontiers into human rights and social and economic spheres. Compared with the United States as well as with several of the newer Asian democracies, Europeans do not draw a rigid line between political, social, and economic democracy. Of course, they debate the limits and contents of each sphere vigorously, but when the dust settles, Europeans have accepted a broader conception of democratic rights, including, for example, social and economic security, than their more liberal (in the classical sense) American cousins. Social and economic equality as well as political and legal equality matters. Skeptics of positive collective action such as Herbert Spencer, Friedrich Hayek, and even Milton Friedman have the respect of liberal intellectuals, but their political impact in Europe remains limited. Certainly the "social Darwinist" current of laissez-faire neo-liberalism, fashionable in several "Anglo-Saxon" democracies, remains discredited in Western Europe by the social and political turmoil of the first half of the twentieth century.

The second element, democratic practice, is more problematic. At issue is the challenge of making representative democracy work in an age of growing individualism and complex interdependence. Democracy is challenged by the citizen's demand for greater autonomy and freedom and the reality of transnational and international politics. The greatest internal danger to representative government has been political stalemate and policy "gridlock." When confronted by political, economic, and social change, government must lead or at least accommodate change. Too much fragmentation or too many "veto points" can cause paralysis. This nearly killed democracy in Europe before World War II and retarded effective responses to various crises in the 1970s. Western Europe has eased some political constraints through deregulation and privatization of some functions as well as the expansion (both geographically and in policy scope) of key institutions of European cooperation. Yet pluralism still confronts dissidents and particularistic elements. Tenacious antidemocratic forces on the political left and right remain active. Liberal democracy invites opposition and dissent and on occasion gets more of each than it can easily handle.

Western Europe is losing its definition as a distinct political region and political culture. This is not meant to condemn or disparage its institutions but rather reflects geographic and political realities. Although Western Europe is not entirely a creation of the Cold War, its definition is changing. Already the Mediterranean members of the North Atlantic Treaty Organization (NATO) and the EU have shown a remarkable convergence toward Western European values and policies. The "new democracies" of Central Europe, perhaps including Russia and other former Soviet republics, are westernizing rapidly. None of this is inevitable or irreversible, but it means that the continent will become more diverse as it becomes more integrated. The emergence of a "European democracy" even without federalization will include forms and institutions not yet apparent.

Western Europe's demographic and ethnic changes cannot be easily reversed and are no less of a challenge. Assimilating distinctive nations and cultures into a multiethnic and perhaps multicultural European culture will be as difficult as it is essential. The new Europeans come generally from cultures and countries without a democratic tradition. Will they adopt the political culture of their new home as they cling to elements of their native cultures? Will Europe's collectivist cultures and social policies accommodate or be overwhelmed by this task?

Can democracy be revitalized? Even in the "old democracies" citizens are less politically active and voting rates have declined (although not yet to American levels). Radical critiques are much less coherent than those of a generation ago, but political violence remains a threat. Or will apathy prove to be the greater danger? In a nonheroic age the strengthening and revitalization of liberal democracy are perhaps the greatest challenges. The development of the European Union requires institutional change and continuous adjustment and reform at both the national and union levels. European liberalism was born to allow citizens the right to cultivate their economic, religious, and cultural interests beyond the political arena. Citizenship cannot abandon politics, but democratic government needs civil society. In its third century European liberal democracy will still be a balancing act.

Endnotes

1. Modern scholars are quick to point out that at no point did such citizenship and participation include a majority of the adult residents; denial of rights to women and the extensive practice of slavery assured that majority rule was impossible. Nevertheless, the idea, if not the practice, of mass government can be traced back to these early European roots.

2. Robert Dahl, *Polyarchy: Participation and Opposition* (New Haven: Yale University Press, 1971).

3. Arend Lijphart, *Democracies: Patterns of Majoritarian and Consensus Government in Twenty-One Countries* (New Haven: Yale University Press, 1984), 1.

4. Compare Samuel Huntington, *Political Order in Changing Societies* (New Haven: Yale University Press, 1968).

5. Louis Hartz, *The Liberal Tradition in America: An Interpretation of American Political Thought Since the Revolution* (New York: Harcourt, Brace, 1955).

6. It is hard to exaggerate the impact of the revolutionary period of 1789–1815, although one may recall the famous response of the Chinese Communist statesman Zhou En-lai when asked about the impact of the French Revolution on world events. In the light of 5,000 years of Chinese history, he replied, "It is too soon to tell."

7. Finland gave women the right to vote in 1906, but was at the time still a semi-autonomous Grand Duchy in the Russian Empire.

8. The British political term "Tory" (ironically derived from the name of Irish horse thieves) originally applied to the eighteenth- and nineteenth-century diehards of monarchical (royal) supremacy and the domination of the state Church of England. American usage applies to the "loyalist" (pro-British) side during the American Revolution (not all of whom would have been British Tories). In Canada, the term combines elements of both but, like in Britain, has become a somewhat archaic term for conservatism.

9. Samuel Beer, *British Politics in the Collectivist Age* (New York: Knopf, 1965).

10. Seymour Martin Lipset, *Political Man: The Social Bases of Politics*, Expanded ed. (Baltimore: Johns Hopkins University Press, 1981); Walter Korpi, *The Democratic Class Struggle* (London: Routledge & K. Paul, 1983).

11. Almost from the start, there were voices within the socialist movement calling for a "democratic" (i.e., electoral) road to power where constitutional reforms permitted. Even Karl Marx admitted that the parliamentary road was possible in a few cases. By the twentieth century every Western European country had a "democratic socialist" party committed to constitutional and liberal political principles and a "revolutionary" socialist party (after 1920) affiliated with the Soviet Communist party.

12. The inherent "efficiency" of universal public social services may explain conservative reluctance to make radical changes. For example, Britain's

"socialized medicine" (National Health Service) costs Her Majesty's Treasury less (relative to gross national product) than American *public* health care programs (mainly Medicare and Medicaid) cost the federal and state governments and which are less than 50 percent of overall U.S. health care expenditures.

13. "Guest workers" were originally a Swiss concept to relieve shortages of unskilled workers. "Gastarbeitere" received short-term working and residence permits and rarely brought their families. Such seasonal and short-term mobility had been common in Europe before 1914. But as the Swiss writer Max Frisch put it, "We asked them to send us 'labor,' but they sent us human beings."

14. Demographic predictions are notoriously volatile, but see Gosta Esping-Andersen's provocative essay on the familial and domestic consequences of these changes. "After the Golden Age: The Future of the Welfare State in the New World Order," *Desarrollo/Económico*, 36 (July-Sept., 1999) 523-44.

15. Functional organizations facilitate technical cooperation between states. Many agencies of the United Nations fall into this category, as does the Organization for Economic Cooperation and Development with membership of about 30 countries with the most advanced economies and, more controversially, the World Trade Organization with more than 100 members and the power to adjudicate very sensitive trade disputes.

16. The global economic difficulties after 1973 were often blamed entirely on the "oil crisis," referring to the quadrupling of petroleum prices by the Organization of Petroleum Exporting Countries (OPEC) cartel. Although the oil crisis did contribute sharply to the problems, the world economy had been staggering for several years, stemming from the breakdown of the "Bretton Woods" currency exchange rate regime, the chronic balance of payment deficits or surpluses in major trading countries, and generally accelerating inflation. The crisis cannot be compared to the Great Depression of the 1930s; however, the loss of control in managing national and global economies led many to express severe pessimism for the prospects of democratic government (Huntington et al. 1974).

17. Francis Fukuyama, *The End of History and the Last Man* (New York: The Free Press, 1992); Daniel Bell, *The End of Ideology* (Glencoe, Ill.: Free Press, 1960).

18. The Freedom Party, ironically previously seen as a "liberal" party, received 28 percent of the popular vote in the 1999 Austrian general elections. J. Haider, governor of the Austrian state of Carinthia and leader of the party until April 2000, has made many statements sympathetic to

some aspects of Austria's Nazi past and his rhetoric condemns liberal immigration and refugee policies. For a preliminary analysis of the EU sanctions, see Stephen Hall, "Tales from the Vienna Woods: EU Constitutional Law and Democracy in the Member States," *Challenge Europe* (2000). Available at http://www.theepc.be/Challenge_Europe/text/memo.asp?ID = 90.

Suggested Readings

Held, David. *Models of Democracy*. Stanford, CA: Stanford University Press, 1996.

Kirschner, Emil J., ed. *Liberal Parties in Western Europe*. Cambridge, UK: Cambridge University Press, 1988.

Klausen, Jytte. *War and Welfare: Europe and the United States, 1945 to the Present*. New York: St. Martin's Press, 1998.

Luttwak, Edward. *Turbo-Capitalism: Winners and Losers in the Global Economy*. New York: HarperCollins, 1999.

Pinker, Robert. "New Liberalism and the Middle Way," in *British Social Welfare in the Twentieth Century*. New York: St. Martin's Press, 1999.

Rhodes, Martin, Paul Haywood, and Vincent Wright. *Developments in West European Politics*. New York: St. Martin's Press, 1997.

Tiersky, Ronald, ed. *Europe Today*. Lanham, Md.: Rowman and Littlefield, 1999.

Wallace, Helen, and William Wallace. *Policy-Making in the European Union*. Oxford, UK: Oxford University Press, 1996.

Zelikow, Philip, and Condolezza Rice. *Germany Unified and Europe Transformed*. Cambridge, UK: Cambridge University Press, 1995.

3

Democracy in the Catholic South: Iberia and Latin America

Margaret MacLeish Mott

Introduction: A Doctrinal and Institutional Approach

The European countries of Spain and Portugal and the twenty Latin American countries,[1] stretching from the United States' southern border to the tip of South America, may not be connected by land mass nor by a common location or geography, but scratch a few hundred years beneath the surface of these varied nations and one will find a common political unit: the Catholic Hapsburg Empire. This political phenomenon emerged on the Iberian mainland with the marriage of Ferdinand and Isabella in 1479 and the consolidation of political power under a Catholic banner. With the expansion west to the New World, beginning in 1492, the nations of Spain and Portugal and their overseas colonies were joined at the soul. Political power may not have been limited through U.S.-style liberal methods—there was no separation of powers and no formal system of checks and balances—but it was often constrained by natural law and the writings of theologians. In much the same way as a written constitution controls the actions of elected leaders, this Catholic Hispanic Empire was constrained by religious

37

doctrine. In addition, in much the same way as the judicial branch of government supervises the efforts of the executive and legislative branches, the political actors of the Hapsburg Empire were supervised by the various institutions of the Church, particularly the Pope, the Inquisition, and, by extension, the Catholic-based agencies and practices of the two mother countries.

Although the Hapsburg Empire was considerably weakened by the end of the eighteenth century, the Catholic system of rules, laws, norms, and governance continues to influence political actors and institutions. Understanding the values and reasoning of that earlier period increases our understanding of current political behavior in this transatlantic region, including both Iberia and Latin America. Religious doctrine and ecclesiastical institutions alone do not explain certain patterns within Iberic-Latin politics, nor are these values unchanging. External factors, ranging from foreign debt to U.S. intervention, and internal factors, ranging from natural resources to economic development, play a large part in the formation of political institutions. Yet the meanings and goals attributed to political behavior tap into foundational beliefs and fundamental values that can be traced back deep into Spanish and Portuguese history. Although all twenty-two of these Iberic-Latin countries have found their own unique expression of *government*, many of the *principles of governance* can be traced back to Catholic political thought.

The democracies that have flowered in the Catholic South have their roots in a very different tradition than those that blossomed in the more Protestant soil of Northern Europe and North America. The former followed the political blueprints of St. Thomas Aquinas, Francisco Suárez, and Jean-Jacques Rousseau; the latter modeled their institutions on the architectural designs of John Locke, James Madison, and Thomas Jefferson. The former stressed unity of faith, universality of membership in the Catholic body politic, and a corporate system of government (i.e., one arranged hierarchically and functionally in which the constituent units were groups). The latter stressed personal conscience, an unmediated relationship to God, and a limited political body (i.e., one arranged horizontally in which the constituent units were individuals). These fundamental differences affected not only the nature of governmental institutions but also their function in society.

The Tale of Two Foundings

When the Spanish and Portuguese explorers arrived in the New World, they not only brought with them the trappings of the Hapsburg empire—priests and prayer books, soldiers fresh from fighting the Moors, and the official seal of the Catholic Monarchs Ferdinand and Isabella—they also brought sensibilities firmly rooted in the medieval world. They looked at the people and institutions of the Mayan, Aztec, and Incan civilizations with an imagination shaped powerfully by medieval Catholicism; whatever they saw was given a religious interpretation. Conquistadors saw a "natural" slave class (the Indians) who could be incorporated into the new hierarchy. Priests looked at the practice of human sacrifice and concluded that the devil had arrived before them. Missionaries compared the plight of subjugated Indian tribes living under the Aztec emperor to the persecution of early Christians living under the terror of pagan Roman rulers. In the eyes of the interlopers, the civilizations of the New World desperately needed the Roman Catholic Church. Only the Church could rid the New World of idolatry and tyranny and bring this new "meek of the earth" to the blessings of Christian salvation. Although greedy conquistadors, eager to capture gold and silver, may not have consistently aided in this effort, the early theologians involved in the incorporation of the New World into the Old World did not see that effort as conquest but as *población* and *civilización* (i.e., the making of Indians into Christian citizens).

From the point of view of the indigenous population, the experiences of Anglo-American conquest and Ibero-American conquest were comparably destructive. Both groups brought European diseases to a world with different immunities, decimating much of the indigenous population, with most of the Indians dying before actual encounters. From the point of view of the respective conquerors, however, the visions and understanding of the enterprise were considerably different. The early settlers in North America intended to live outside the reach of the Anglican Church. Many of them had left England in search of religious freedom. Instead of extending the official church's power, they were hoping to avoid it. Nor was there any concerted effort to incorporate the indigenous population into the blessings of Puritanism. The founding families' imaginations in North America were not Catholic but nascently liberal. Rather than building an organic government that extended its reach into the human soul, the founders of the thirteen colonies wanted what the political theorist John Locke had promised: a government that protected the rights and property of the hard-working individual, one of those protected rights being the right to be left alone.

Although the material conditions of colonization were similar, the natures of the citizens' relationship to the central government in North America and Latin America were entirely different. The former was born out of Protestant nonconformity and rebellion; the latter was an extension of medieval Catholic conceptions of power. The extension of Protestantism brought into existence in the United States a nation even more resistant to centralized power than the English mother country. The extension of Catholicism brought into existence in Latin America a smattering of nations often even more enamored of medievalism, feudalism, and Hapsburgian governance than their Spanish and Portuguese ancestors.

Catholicism and Democracy?

According to many Anglo-American accounts, Catholicism (in its historic or medieval form) and democracy were mutually exclusive belief systems. Democracy required independence of thought, whereas Catholicism demanded obedience to the Pope; democracy assumed that all men were equal, whereas Catholicism accepted a social hierarchy; democracies allowed for a written law open to individual interpretation, whereas Catholicism maintained a tight control over the interpretation of sacred texts. For much of the modern era, democracy was defined using the terms of a Protestant belief system in explicit opposition to the so-called antidemocratic practices of neighboring Catholic countries. Both the United Sates and Northern Europe improved their domestic image by presenting their mode of governance as superior to that of their "superstitious and irrational" neighbors to the south.

Because democracy came to be associated with expressions of Protestant nationhood, Catholic versions of democracy have been largely overlooked. Democratic practices in Spain, Portugal, and all of Latin America were only recognized insofar as they conformed to Protestant orthodoxy. If politicians invoked John Locke, that was significant. But if Spanish or Latin American lawmakers cited St. Thomas Aquinas or Francisco Suárez, few Protestant observers understood or took note. A Catholic source was considered an undemocratic source. Regardless of the existence of constitutions, representative parliaments, or popular elections, countries of the South, inasmuch as they were Catholic, were often regarded as *incapable* of being democratic.

A second factor that complicates a full understanding of Catholic expressions of democracy, particularly in Latin America, is the hegemony of the United States in the Western Hemisphere. To qualify for foreign investment and international funds, countries in Latin America have needed to prove the strength of their "reformed" democratic faith. They must now talk about democracy in terms that the Protestant North can hear, using words such as "pluralism," "civil society," "political parties," and "interest groups." Before extending the carrots of international investment, the United States often coerced its Southern neighbors into correct "democratic" behavior through military interventions and clandestine coup d'etats. Throughout the nineteenth and twentieth centuries, the U.S. government engaged in some highly questionable foreign policies, all of which were conducted under the banner of "democracy." Manifest Destiny translated over time into Cold War necessity. Whether we were annexing Texas or helping to overthrow the Allende regime, the moral high ground taken by the United States was always framed as salvation through democracy, regardless of the degree of popular support for the government we were undermining. Of course, many Latin Americans also favor democracy, independent of U.S. pressures, but the *kind* of democracy they favor tends to be quite at variance with that of the United States, as will be discussed later.

Both of the positions examined above, the first anti-Catholic and the second reductively imperialist, obscure the existence of a different brand of democracy, one that follows a Thomistic, Counter-Reformation tradition. Even in countries in which the Roman Catholic Church was dismantled, such as Mexico after the 1917 constitution, Catholic values and beliefs continue to play a large part in the formation of society. The Mexican Catholic Church had no legal standing from 1917 until 1992, yet in a poll taken in 1994, three-quarters of Mexico's population described themselves as practicing Catholics, attending mass on a weekly basis.[2] The massive demonstrations of support for the Pope when he visited Cuba in 1998 point to the enduring social power of the Catholic Church even in the face of Marxist-Leninist political intolerance. Regardless of the political situation and even in the present context of rising secularism, Iberic-Latin society still understands itself and much of its mission largely in terms of a Catholic system of belief.

Democracy viewed through a Catholic belief system looks very different from democracy viewed through a belief system with Protestant roots. The Protestant version (now understood to be secular and pluralist) emphasizes equality, a limited government, and inalienable individual rights, in the tradition of John Locke. The Catholic version stresses compatibility, organic unity, and interdependence over equality and individuation. Far from the limited government, whose primary functions are coercive and distributive, the Catholic conception of government is authoritative and directive; separation of powers and checks and balances have seldom operated there. Instead of a society in which all members are equal and therefore those who are not equal are not members, the Catholic vision of society considers membership as universal and, at least historically, inequality as natural. Whether the system is just or not depends less on the mechanics of the system and more on the virtue of the leader.

Because of this fundamental acceptance of social inequality, some have argued that the Thomistic tradition (following St. Thomas Aquinas) is inherently undemocratic.[3] Equality being an essential component in the political theory of John Locke, Thomas Hobbes, and John Rawls, a political theory that accepts inequality, therefore, must not be democratic. This argument is very different from the anti-Catholic rhetoric discussed earlier. When Thomas Jefferson surmised in 1813 that "[h]istory . . . furnishes no example of a priest-ridden people maintaining a free civil government," he was making an argument based on prejudice, not reason.[4] The critics of a Thomistic version of democracy, on the other hand, are using a *particular* definition of democracy to support their critique. Indeed, if we define democracy in terms of a limited government, where the office holder is not as important as the office itself, then many of the governments of Latin America do not look very democratic. But if we take democracy in terms of its social impact, (i.e., as an increased sense of participation in public life, a regime that seeks social justice and that offers protection to its people), then the theories developed by Thomists offer a radically different political model by which we might come to understand the corporate unit known as "the people."

The Metaphysics of Political Participation

To consider any group of individuals as a unified whole is to enter into the realm of poetry and metaphysics. The agents of the U.S. Constitution and the Declaration of Independence (i.e., The People), are something we understand but cannot see. That we are able to feel included in a group of nameless individuals points to our capacity to be absorbed into a collective whole. Even groups who were disenfranchised at the time of the constitutional convention (i.e., blacks, women, and indentured servants), invoke that document to demand their civil rights. The eternal rallying cry of mass movements—"The people united can never be defeated"—expresses the basic hope that individuals can come together as one and effect a desired change.

The poetics of absorption varies depending on one's brand of metaphysics. Puritan John Winthrop of Massachusetts, a unique figure in American political thought because many of his ideas were closer to the Catholic tradition, speaking in 1629, called for his followers to conceive of themselves as "members of the same body."[5] With the rise of Lockean liberal theory, that organic conception of society was displaced by an ideology that favored a limited government and an individualistic, pluralist society. Without the authority of a Puritan government behind him, Winthrop's corporate and organic model gave way to the needs of a nation primarily composed of diverse Protestant sects whose rule of law (i.e., the Constitution) was forced to compromise on the issue of slavery and other matters.

In contrast, in the Catholic nations of Spain and Portugal, the Christian metaphor for the body of believers was institutionalized by the Catholic Monarchs, Ferdinand and Isabella. Through diplomatic skills and religious orthodoxy, the Catholic Monarchs joined the diverse regions of the Iberian peninsula under one central government. The various members of the body—the independent kingdoms, the guilds, the autonomous town governments, and the military and religious orders—were all united under one political head, responsible for guiding the body politic down the path of Catholic virtue. These groups or corporate bodies served to check absolutist power and prevent tyranny, but the system was still authoritatively led from the top, from above, ultimately in accord with God's will and law. The people united did not lead the government, as conceived in the Protestant tradition, but were led to salvation under the omniscient reasoning of a responsive head—not government *by* the people, but clearly understood as government *for* the people.[6]

Sources of Catholic Democracy

The use of the human body as a political metaphor finds its source in the New Testament.[7] It is from these Biblical sources, as well as from the pronouncements of the Church fathers, that the nature of Catholic political authority derives. In his letter to the Corinthians, St. Paul likened the early Church as members of a body in which Christ ruled as the head. "Now you are the body of Christ and individually members of it" explained Paul. Yet not each member was expected to be the same. "If the whole body were the eye, where would be the hearing" If the whole body were an ear, where would be the sense of smell?" All could participate, yet their participation was specific to the laws of their particular organ. A foot should not try to think. A head should not spend much time on the ground. Social distinctions were consistent with natural laws.

Christianity, explained Paul, was broad enough to encompass all types of people. "For by one Spirit we were all baptized into one body—Jews or Greeks, slaves or free—and all were made to drink of one Spirit."[8] Difference was not something to be erased, but a natural condition. Differences between social classes were as natural as differences between Jews and Greeks or between slaves and freemen. Although the spirit would change through the process of conversion, the material conditions would remain the same. Christianity did not materially disrupt the social hierarchy established in the ancient world, but gave the believer a method to spiritually transcend it. Like the parable of the laborers in the vineyard, in which those who worked for an hour were paid as much as those who had "borne the burden of the day and the scorching heat," equality was an internal matter like the one Spirit that all were made to drink from.[9] The payment of one coin to those who arrived in the eleventh hour, as well as those who had toiled all day, signaled a new economy. No longer was the law a matter of simple arithmetic: an eye for an eye, a tooth for a tooth. The spirit of God was beyond contractual understandings, beyond a purely secular procedure, such as checks and balances. The worth of the payment was tied to the virtue of the donor; it was no longer tied to the efforts of the donee.

When the Roman Emperor Constantine converted to Christianity in 312 A.D., the Christian Church gained political authority. The spiritual authority held by the Pope now had a secular arm to assist in the spiritual needs of the community. This doctrine of the Pope holding "indirect power" over the secular head of state was clarified in the thirteenth century by St. Thomas Aquinas and further refined during the Protestant Reformation and the "defection" of the British monarchy from the Roman Church in the sixteenth century. The Neo-Thomists of the Counter-Reformation published treatises in which they argued on philosophical, theological, and biblical grounds the rational, natural, and divine reasons why the head of state, albeit supreme in temporal matters, was ultimately subject to the Church. Francisco Suárez, a Jesuit theologian, one of the key architects of the Spanish conquest of the Americas, described the king as just one more sheep in the flock of the Church. His royal soul, just like every other soul in Christendom, was the concern of the Pope. His royal powers, on the other hand, were, within the temporal sphere, absolute.

The duties and responsibilities of Catholic governance were discussed in great detail in St. Thomas Aquinas' primer on kingship, *De Regimine Principum* ("On Kingship") written between 1265 and 1267. The ruler is like "the head or heart that moves all the others." This is not just simple poetry as Aquinas used analogy as a critical method of reasoning. The head that moved all others suggests two important functions of governance: monism (a single authority) and animation (the ability to get people to move). Although he wrote almost 750 years ago, Aquinas remains *the* philosopher of the Catholic tradition, serving as the legitimator of both authoritarian governments and social movements. Particularly since Vatican II, in the 1960s, when the Church shifted its focus to issues of poverty and social justice, his work continues to be cited as a critique of unjust laws (i.e., laws not in accordance with God's will).[10]

That one person should have complete executive powers over all the other members seemed perfectly natural to Aquinas:

> For if many men were to live together and each to provide what is convenient for himself, the group (*multitudo*) would break up unless one of them had the responsibility for the good of the group, just as the body of a man or an animal would disintegrate without a single controlling force in the body that aimed at the common good of all the members.[11]

A single controlling force was necessary to constrain the activities that individual members or interest groups might find convenient and to aim the body politic in the direction of the common good. The single controlling force also transformed the society's members into a single, mystical body, the *corpus mysticum*. Without the leader, the various members would go their own way, the assumption being to their perdition. By virtue of obeying one person, the various subjects became as one, not at all the goal of American-style pluralism.

If we reduce Catholic political theory to a secular framework, then, on the surface, it looks like a recipe for tyranny. The single controlling force conjures up images of leaders—such as Francisco Franco of Spain and Alfredo

Stroessner of Paraguay—who ran their countries into the ground because their power was not constrained. However, according to Church doctrine, political power was always constrained by natural, divine, and eternal law, the Church being the final word on the last two. The effect of this hierarchy of laws was that both political powers and spiritual powers were politically constrained. The monarch was restrained because he or she served the higher purpose of the Church and God's will. The Pope was constrained because his concerns were beyond politics.

For this system to work effectively, the participants needed to believe in a greater world, not just in terms of a teleology of Christian salvation, but because politics itself had to be recognized as a limited activity. Otherwise, this hierarchical arrangement would lead to tyranny. Because of its limited place in the supernatural order of things, Catholic politics had to be authoritative, if not authoritarian, but never totalitarian.

The king and his agents were understood to be the secular arm of the church. Yet it would be a mistake to understand that function in terms of a separated power, something akin to the executive branch, which could be compartmentalized. Although the office itself was compared to the head of the body politic and the arm of the Church, Aquinas referred to the *duty* of kingship in terms of "the soul in the body."[12] "Soul" in this case does not refer to a strictly religious term but to the Aristotelian concept of the animating principle. The soul is what actuates the body, giving the body understanding and consciousness.[13] For the king to act as the soul in the body is to give the king the responsibility to actuate his kingdom and to animate his subjects, each one according to his station in life. But actuate means more than just being alive. According to Aristotelian conceptions of actuality and potentiality, all beings were capable of becoming more perfect versions of themselves within the confines of their social position. The king, therefore, was responsible for bringing all members of society to their full potential, with the understanding that potential was specific to the type of member.

The King's Position in the Hierarchy of Law

Besides the single controlling force animating the body politic, Aquinas likened the role of the king to "God in the world."[14] God in the world was a supernatural figure in a natural environment. The creator of the world and its natural order, He was also endowed with the capacity to change that order. In the four-tiered system of law—divine, eternal, natural, and human—only God was above both human and natural law; only He could effect social and political change.

Natural law is the law evidenced in nature, both in the natural world and in human nature. We might think of it as common sense, a belief that one would naturally come to through reason or instinct based on Christian values. It might also be thought of as the status quo, the default position of enduring values. Through the doctrine of proportionality—in which the laws of God were reflected to a lesser degree in the laws of nature, which in turn are reflected in the laws of man—natural law offers a bridge between the human and the divine. By observing the laws of nature, humans might come to understand God's will. But, as Aquinas explains, "man needs to be directed to his supernatural end in a higher way. Hence there is an additional law given by God through which man shares more perfectly in the eternal law."[15] Miracles and revelations are methods by which God pierces the laws of nature and makes his will known to man.

By granting these supernatural powers to the executive officer, Aquinas is giving legitimacy to an absolute leader to change the status quo. Like God, the king may alter the course of nature so that his people may more perfectly share in eternal matters. Like God in the world, the king becomes *the* agent of social change. Only a king can decide when custom and convention no longer serve the needs of his people. Like God in the world, the king can make the laws and then break them. Above the human law and subject to the divine law, the king's power is not constrained by human law, such as constitutions, but by divine law, the law that only the Pope and his ecclesiastical hierarchy could interpret with any authority.

The Inquisition's Role in Limiting Political Power

In the fifteenth century, Ferdinand and Isabella, "the Catholic Monarchs," were engaged in unifying Spain and Portugal into a single political unit. At the time, corporate groups, such as military and religious orders, as well as towns and regions, held considerable autonomy. Each group had its own traditions, its own legal status, and its own set of rights and privileges (known as *fueros*), all of which threatened the unity of the emerging nation. Ferdinand and Isabella were able to present their authority as the natural complement to these various corporate groups by working in close alliance with the Church, hence their title as the "Catholic Monarchs." To remain on the peninsula, every inhabitant had to swear allegiance to the one, true faith of Catholicism. The Jews were expelled, the last Moorish stronghold, Granada, was overthrown, and those who had been baptized, along with those who had converted, were expected to uphold the principles of the Catholic faith. The first institution created in the newly unified Spain was the Holy Office of the Spanish Inquisition. *Fueros* may have kept the monarchs' agents from intruding into the workings of a particular town or religious order, but no *fuero* could stop the reach of the Holy Office.

The Inquisition is perhaps the defining example of Catholic intolerance. If we associate democracy with religious pluralism, then the extended presence of the Holy Office in Catholic society presents a serious obstacle to any notion of Catholic democracy. But if we consider the function of the Holy Office as an institutional check on political power, then its place in the Catholic tradition makes more sense. For not only did the Inquisition prosecute Lutherans, crypto-Jews, and idolaters, but it also went after the clergy and the political elite who abused the powers of their offices. Colonial authorities in the New World might think twice before taking advantage of their distant posts. Priests who propositioned women in the confessional and conquistadors who raped Indian women were brought before the Inquisition and punished for their misconduct. The inquisitors took their spiritual roles seriously; not only were they the strict shepherds of a largely landless flock, but they also zealously guarded the souls of the political elite. Although there were numerous instances in which their spiritual supervision was used for political purposes, procedural guidelines, for the most part, ensured the apolitical nature of the work. Everything that the colonial inquisitors did was noted meticulously by a squadron of scribes and sent to the home office in Spain for approval. The Holy Office's presence made clear the limit of politics within the concerns of the supernatural state.

To put the function of the Holy Office in perspective, we might liken heresy to the secular crime of treason. Catholic political theory allowed for brutal methods to exterminate seditious beliefs. Liberal political theory is equally severe when it comes to treason. Every nation needs to balance universal participation with the unity of the central ideology. Early American Federalists who defended the supremacy of the constitution were also the authors of repressive antisedition legislation. Every nation depends on a foundational belief in the unity of that nation to survive. However, too much repression restricts the perfection of the individual members. Pragmatic inquisitors would often look the other way, knowing that too many demands could break the spirit of the community.[16]

The Emergence of Community Consent

A healthy respect between ruler and the ruled is implied in the bodily images used by St. Paul and Aquinas. Sixteenth-century Catholic theologians made that mutual relationship more explicit. Suárez argued that it was "in the nature of things [that] all men are born free." Through a "special volition, or common consent" these free men gathered together into "one political body through one bond of fellowship and for the purpose of aiding one another in the attainment of a single political end."[17] To function, the one political body needed a single head, a "common power which the individual members of the community are bound to obey." In a slight shift in the theory of political actuation, the community actuated the ruler who in turn actuated the individual members. The power to actuate was also the power to depose. This power of consent, argued Suárez, authorized the people to depose a ruler who had fallen into heresy.[18]

Democracy, in the Suárezian sense of "community consent," retained its cohesive character. On the surface it looked the same as a medieval monarchy. In fact, it often operated that way. Yet, on a "constitutional" level, the power to lead resided not in the absolute ruler but in the collective power of the community, bound in fellowship. Democracy, in other words, became the natural expression on a community united in Catholic faith—not a rigid, repressive system, but a transformative arrangement in which obedience brought political as well as spiritual fulfillment. The success of that arrangement depended largely on maintaining a natural order of obedience in which the people obeyed the king and the king obeyed the Pope. Of course, this ideal was often abused in both Spain and Portugal, as well as in Latin America by absolutist kings, viceroys, and conquistadors. Yet that should not keep us from seeing that the bases and fundamentals of Iberian and Latin American democracy would be quite different from those in the United States.

Writing against the "heretics" in England, the monarchs who had disrupted the natural order by establishing a political church, Suárez compared the British system under James I to a "mutilated and monstrous organism."[19] The perfect community, on the other hand, would have "some supreme power in its order, such as the Pontiff in the Church and the king in his temporal reign."[20] That the pontiff was the supreme power was the distinguishing characteristic of Catholic governance. Political power may be supreme in temporal affairs, but when it came to spiritual issues, the council of the king must give way to the council of those more in tune with God's will (i.e., the Church).

The people benefited by living in such a perfect society on two levels: the natural and the divine. The natural law theory of Thomism pointed to the spontaneous emergence of a political leader through the process of group living. That naturally occurring leader would in turn benefit from the divine wisdom channeled through the Catholic Church. The natural process of governance would be perfected through the grace made visible by the ecclesiastical hierarchy. Using one of the basic premises of Thomistic thought, that grace does not destroy nature but perfects it, the Counter-Reformation theologians were able to present their Church-dominated politics as more perfect than the flawed "monster" to the north. By subjugating the Church to the will of the Crown, as Henry VIII and his successors had done, the Church was no longer able to perfect the political sphere. In the Counter-Reformation system, grace, as represented by the Church, was in a position to perfect nature, as represented by the Crown.

Progress in the Secular Mode

In the New World the Spanish and Portuguese conquistadors found a climate even more hostile to democracy than that which prevailed in the mother countries. Vast distances, huge empty territories, high mountains and impenetrable jungles, and sometimes hostile natives seemed to call forth the need for strict, top-down, hierarchical, and authoritarian rule. Greed, a get-rich-quick mentality, and vast territories and native "peasants" (the Indians), seemingly there for the plucking, also helped tip the balance toward authoritarianism instead of the carefully modulated balance between central authority and community consent set forth by the Catholic fathers such as Aquinas and Suárez. Plus, in the New World, there were no "natural" or customary corporations (independent town, military orders, or guilds) to serve as brakes on royal authority. Only the Inquisition acted as a brake on political power. In Latin America, it was the close-knit, absolutist, and authoritarian colonial state of the Hapsburgs that triumphed and not the authoritative but just model that Aquinas had set forth.

Unlike the United States' War of Independence, which brought a more liberal form of government into existence, the wars of independence in Latin America were generally fought for the cause of conservatism, dressed up in republican and even revolutionary language. The embodiment of the revolutionary spirit was not a Thomas Jefferson or a George Washington, but a Napoleon Bonaparte or Simón Bolívar, someone who promoted progress through top-down reform. Like God in the World, Bonaparte represented a power capable of reforming the mercantilist, inefficient policies of the past. He was the spokesperson for what Rousseau had labeled "the general will." He knew what the people needed, even before they had voiced it. A secular version of the Thomistic king, Bonaparte animated the social body to bring it along the path of modernity. No social revolution or liberal triumph accompanied the independence movements in Latin America.

Simón Bolívar, known as the "great liberator" of Latin America, modeled his campaign of independence on the successes of Napoleon. The liberator of Venezuela, Colombia, Ecuador, and Peru, Bolívar used Rousseauian political theory to destroy the legitimacy of the aging colonial empire. Social contract theory and the general will became the battle cries for the emerging republics; yet when asked about the efficacy of constitutional government, Bolívar responded, "The only method of governing in the Americas is personal influence. The laws are worth nothing in the eyes of our people who don't understand what they mean."[21]

Rousseau was not the only theorist to drive the liberators of Latin America. Much of the constitutional language used in the new nations was lifted word-for-word from the U.S. Constitution. On the one hand, the spirit of John Locke or James Madison seemed embedded in the development of a new, republican system of government; indeed, many of the provisions appear, at least on paper, to embrace American-style liberalism. On the other hand, the actions of the government constituted by this liberal language suggested a different interpretation, one that was based on the historic Catholic tradition and emphasized unity, organicism, and corporate privilege over individual worth or checks and balances. This discrepancy between rhetoric and procedure and between appearances and substance has prompted one writer to label Latin American democracy as "magical liberalism—a highly fanciful semblance of the spare, elegant system imagined by a John Locke or a James Madison."[22] During much of the nineteenth century Rousseau's emphasis on heroic leadership triumphed over Locke's system of careful, procedural democracy; the positivist idea of Auguste Comte—"order and progress"—with its similarly elitist, top-down, and authoritarian implications also had a powerful influence on Latin America, further preventing the growth of liberal, more participatory democracy.

Old World Dictators and New Euro Kings

The Portuguese dictator, Antonio de Oliveira Salazar, who ruled Portugal from 1928 until he was incapacitated in an accident in 1968, had been trained in Catholic political theory, particularly the works of Suárez. Salazar consciously used Suárez' theory to support his regime. Some of his repressive policies contributed to discrediting Catholic political theory in Portugal as a viable expression of democracy, yet some of his economic and social policies deserve attention. Through corporatist policies reminiscent of those of the Catholic Monarchs, Salazar was able to coordinate a number of economic and political interests under one authoritarian rule. Salazar's integrated, organic systems of rule provided a model for many Latin American countries. He also snuffed out the liberal and democratic currents that had been building for some time, causing Portugal to revert to that earlier authoritarian model.

Following the guidelines established by Suárez, which were updated in two papal encyclicals, *Rerum Novarum* (1891) and *Quadragesimo Anno* (1931), Salazar sought to forge a third way between the then-prevailing ideologies of Marxism and capitalism. Instead of falling into the apostasy of capitalism, with its disregard for the social conditions of workers, or the heresy of Marxism, with its disregard for private property, Salazar followed a Catholic system that favored harmony over class conflict and coordination over a separation of powers. Rather than treating labor and capital as divergent interests, Salazar organized them within hierarchical groups on a per industry basis. Wine producers were expected to represent the interests of laborers in the vineyard; fishing industry executives were expected to represent the interests of the workers on the boats. Horizontal alliances, such as trade unions, were abolished or coopted into the corporatist system. Salazar turned back the clock to the closed, top-down, sixteenth-century model of the Hapsburgs.

Salazar replaced a fragmented, and increasingly violent, liberal experiment with a unified, hierarchical, monist system consistent, in many ways, with the terms of Catholicism. Like the Catholic Monarchs 400 years earlier, Salazar had a modern version of the Holy Office at his disposal: the Portuguese secret police. It is here, however, that Salazar falls out of line with precedent. Rather than being constrained by the ecclesiastical tribunal, as was the case with political powers in the past, the secret police became the coercive conscience meeting purely secular ends. Eventually, as the regime gained political and social legitimacy, those repressive tactics were relaxed. In the middle years of the regime, when the Portuguese community was benefiting from a rapidly growing economy and relatively generous social programs, Salazar's approval ratings went up. It was only when extended wars in the African colonies caused the killing of young Portuguese soldiers that Salazar's system (then ruled by his successor, Marcello Caetano) came under attack. The People, as represented in this case by the progressive, populist military class, withdrew their consent and the dictatorship was deposed in 1974.[23]

Both Salazar and Francisco Franco in neighboring Spain were products of the widespread popularity and revival of corporatism of the interwar (1920s and 1930s) period. Both Franco and Salazar used Catholic theory to legitimize their top-down, corporatist, authoritarian regimes. Both Franco and Salazar were creating Catholic communities: those who subscribed to the "one, true faith" were members of the community capable of giving consent. The "heretics" (i.e., the Republicans, liberals, and Marxists who preceded the two regimes), were "outside" of the community of believers. They had no standing to voice their discontent. Tolerance implied a recognition of functionally distinct groups, at least those that could be coopted by the state; bankers or workers in a government-run trade union could be allowed the special privileges suitable to their industry. However, tolerance was never extended to those who had betrayed the faith or those who had threatened the unity of the community through the application of "foreign" ideas, such as a secular, limited government, let alone a Marxist regime.

The corporatist systems developed by Salazar and Franco became the blueprint for government in much of Latin America during this period. Liberalism seemed to have failed in Latin America as much as in the mother countries. Hence, dictators and generals, favoring bureaucratic, authoritarian systems of government, traveled across the Atlantic to learn how to reproduce the Spanish and Portuguese miracles. With economic growth rates of up to 8 or 9 percent a year and stable governments, the Franco and Salazar governments provided attractive solutions to the turbulent conditions in contemporary Latin America. They also provided legitimacy for the severe handling of political dissent. Loyalty to the regime became an essential ingredient of retaining one's citizenship. Authoritarianism seemed to have triumphed again; democracy appeared vanquished.

Neither Franco nor Salazar was elected, nor did they promote democratic institutions. Indeed, they were opposed to democracy and the fragmentation it set loose. What they did was create unity where there had been a fractured society. Both Franco and Salazar cited Catholic political theory to legitimize their efforts, and in large part, the Catholic episcopacy agreed with them. After the changes instituted by Vatican II, however, which favored universality over unity of faith and social justice over a strict orthodoxy, these regimes lost their Catholic stamp of approval, at least in international circles.

Unfortunately, Franco and Salazar, along with their authoritarian brethren on the other side of the Atlantic, contributed to the general feeling that Catholicism and democracy are mutually exclusive. Yet in Thomistic terms, these regimes failed in the virtue of governance. The repressive forces of Fulgencio Batista in Cuba and Rafael Trujillo in the Dominican Republic and those of numerous other strong-arm dictators destroyed the possibility of democratic participation. People went along with their leaders not because of any passion or faith but because the alternatives, that is, torture, imprisonment, and death, were unspeakably unpleasant. The constitutive elements of Christianity (i.e., charity and justice) were missing. The metaphorical constraints of the corporeal metaphor were inapposite. This was rule by coercion, not by consent. In the Thomistic/Suárezian conception, tempered and just authoritative rule was acceptable but not bloody tyranny that violated all proprieties.

Yet the activities of a Franco or a Stroessner, whose regimes went beyond the pale, should not discount the possibilities of a special kind of democracy within a Catholic context, (i.e., with a strong controlling force). The current king of Spain, Juan Carlos I, wields a power that, in good Catholic fashion, is largely animating. The King rules alongside of and overlaps with a democratic structure that has recently grown up in Spain: political parties, elections, parliament, public opinion, and European-style democracy. The fact that the king is *not* an elected official, however, contributes to his virtue. Unsullied by partisanship and political matters (the Spanish Constitution accurately describes the strength of his power as symbolic), he is able to invoke patriotism without what Aquinas called "the scandal of coercion." Leaders from across the political spectrum point to his ability to hold the country together through aristocratic charm, military discipline, and popular good will. Like the soul in the body, he animates the various interests, coordinating Basque separatists and Catalonian bureaucrats in the best interests of Spain. As political power in national governments is eroded throughout the world under globalization, ceremonial leaders such as Juan Carlos may come to have more importance. Devoid of much political power, these charismatic leaders may be able to guide the people toward a common good instead of xenophobic nationalism. They represent an older, but often still important, organic tradition in Iberia that has recently been blended with newer democratic currents.

Latin American Democratic Liberation

Many of the leaders of Latin America are in a situation similar to those in Spain and Portugal forty years ago. Their older institutions have crumbled, but the newer democratic ones are unconsolidated; fragmentation, division, and discontent prevail. Social change has accelerated, and the people have acquired heightened expectations of convenience and modern luxuries. Faced with a crushing foreign debt, largely created by the questionable lending practices of first-world banks as well as their own corrupt and bloated bureaucracies, the countries of Latin America have been forced to produce rapidly growing economies or else default on their loans and suffer a complete devaluation in their economy. Globalization, privatization, and neoliberalism may all be necessary in the modern world, but they also serve to tear their countries apart. The success of Latin America's efforts to achieve development while also preserving stability will depend largely on the ability of each nation's leader to implement some difficult economic programs.

When President Alberto Fujimori of Peru suspended the Constitution in 1992 he was, to a certain extent, following the duties of the Thomistic king. Following in the tradition of earlier Rousseauian authoritarians, Fujimori instituted austerity measures that fueled the economy rather than protecting civil liberties. He also took sometimes harsh actions against Peru's violent Sendero Luminoso insurgency. During the 1997 Summit of Ibero-American Heads of State, Fujimori explained his actions in terms of economic development and the needs of the poor. "Democracy," he wrote, "should provide a context for sustained and firm development." Rather than worrying about the legal implications of ignoring a constitutional provision, Fujimori declared that "we have to defend the economic basis of democracy." As far as he was concerned, governance was less about following a constitution and its separation of powers, than about providing an "umbrella or parasol that protects as well as permits the development of a recovered Peruvian democracy."[24] Where St. Thomas Aquinas might have inserted the term "Christian faith," Fujimori used the more secular term, "macroeconomic policies." Yet the two are not entirely comparable. Catholic doctrine would insist that *all* members of society are moved toward their respective perfection. A rising gross domestic product alone would not legitimize the executive actions.

In an article filed with the news agency Agencia EFE on December 6, 1999, President Hugo Chávez of Venezuela similarly vowed to lift Venezuela out of poverty through "God's help." Divine assistance may be necessary as almost 80 percent of Venezuelans are living below the poverty line. Even with substantial revenues from oil exports, Venezuela is tottering on the brink of financial ruin. Speaking at a ceremony at the Miraflores Palace, one year after what he called "the peaceful Bolivarian revolution," Chávez called on Venezuelans to celebrate the victory of "the people" over rival political parties.[25] Political parties, a crucial component of Anglo-American democracy, are here depicted as a virus, capable of dividing society and destabilizing the health of the body politic.

Chávez legitimizes his political actions by referring to Bolívar and Rousseau. He calls himself a "Rousseauian democrat," in the tradition of Bolívar; there is no Locke or Madison here. Within one year of being elected, Chávez had abolished the congress through an extraconstitutional constituent assembly. The Supreme Court felt obliged to resign nine months into his administration. Even the constitution was rewritten to permit his reelection. Chávez claims that he is doing all this for the poor and, indeed, according to press reports the poor have, in the absence of repressive tactics, generally supported these measures. Again, it is not necessarily the structure of government that creates social discontent, but the type of governance. Making drastic changes to political institutions does not provoke immediate public fury, but using that power to repress the polity is rarely tolerated.

Both Fujimori and Chávez instituted programs that support urban entrepreneurship and family businesses. In much the same way as Franco and Salazar incorporated business and labor into a state-controlled corporatist system, Fujimori and Chávez incorporated street venders and small business entrepreneurs. Micro-credit lending practices encouraged Andean weavers to set up home businesses and the legalization of street vending turned the streets of Lima into open air shopping malls, where everything from Apple computers to toilet seats were for sale; not as an expression of laissez-faire capitalism but as an extension of state-sponsored activity, or, as in the political sphere, some combination of these two, often competing, systems.

From an institutional perspective the changes in Peru and Venezuela may look less democratic than those of their multiparty, constitutionally consistent predecessors. Yet, in many of Latin America's democracies, corruption and patronage, not democratic accountability, lubricated the mechanisms of government. The hard-driving policies of leaders such as Fujimori and Chávez are often resisted by other members of the political elite because they demand an efficiency and accountability that was often missing in the past. In this sense, what on the outside might appear as a shift from democracy to autocracy may actually be just the reverse. Following St. Thomas Aquinas and then Rousseau, the defining indicator of whether a government is capable of good governance has less to do with the institutions themselves than with the governments' success at incorporating and animating all members of society.

When President Chávez spoke to the Venezuelan people in December of 1999, he warned them that they would not feel the benefits of their labors for ten or twenty years, and even then, he did not promise luxuries or great wealth. Even through hard work and stoic sacrifices, Chávez could only promise a life of honesty and humility. But, he told his listeners, you will have dignity. The state would work to provide full access to education, health care, housing, and social security—what Chávez considered basic human rights—but he never promised them the luxuries associated with modern consumer life in the United States, nor did he promote partisan activities (the old, corrupt, divisive party system has been largely destroyed) or promise to imitate the institutional features and practices of American democracy. In essence, all he asked for was faith in his ability to rule the country away from poverty and toward a healthy economy. Chávez and his Latin American counterparts may, in their own eyes, not be *abusing* the constitution, they may be *transcending* it. Rather than finding the voice of the people on the printed page, as is the myth of constitutions, these leaders may be creating a cohesive popular unit á la Rousseau through the very act of taking the law into their own hands.

Conclusion

Given all this extralegal activity in Latin American politics, what constrains political power? If, as I have argued, the politics of Spain, Portugal, and Latin America are operating in a Catholic culture, then the spiritual demands of Catholicism, or a more secular natural law, are the indigenous methods of restraint. Indeed, the Church, in much of Latin America, has been a constant critic of dictatorships. The liberation theology movement has worked to animate the people, sometimes to the point where, in good Thomistic fashion, they work to depose the tyrannical head. International human rights tribunals have also limited the powers of the political sphere, wielding a greater conscience over the excesses of despotic rulers. The transnational quality of the many church groups involved in Latin America as well as the International Human Rights Commission hearkens back to the medieval arrangement of Christendom, when the Pope acted as conscience for the many Christian kings.

The implications of this analysis are that (1) government will be more organic and unified and there will be less emphasis on the maintenance of a separation of powers or a federalist system; (2) the church will play a bigger role in politics than that envisioned in the United States with its separation of church and state; and (3) human rights, based on group or corporate rights, will be conceived differently than in the United States with its emphasis on individual rights. Unlike the Protestant, liberal arrangement in which government is restrained by internal checks and balances, the Catholic, corporatist arrangement has traditionally depended on external, transnational restraints. Democracy, in other words, can occur in the Catholic South, but *democratization* may be less reliant on the trappings of a liberal democracy—elections, constitutions, parties, and interest groups—and more reliant on the presence of an external, apolitical force, something larger than life: the Church, a moral force, or heroic leadership. Although corporatist governments may be structurally more in need of a guiding conscience, because in these governments power is not limited from within, perhaps we can see how all governments might benefit from such a body: something that reminds the corporate body of the needs of *all* of its citizens and of the bigger picture in which the limited business of politics occurs.

There are difficulties in this formulation, of course. First, Iberia and Latin America are much more secular now, and far less Catholic, than they were in the past. The old values, institutions, and ways of doing things no longer work as well. Second, the pressures for liberal-style participation and democracy, emanating from both the outside world and Latin America's own citizens, are intense. Third, every country in the region is different, and increasingly more so, with the result that there are degrees and gradations of democracy/authoritarianism, varying from country to country. Uruguay, Costa Rica, and Chile are by all accounts full-fledged democracies; other governments are often confused, conflicted overlaps of democracy with the Iberian authoritarian heritage. However, in *all* of these we need to take into account some at times uncomfortable facts: Latin America is animated by different values and ways of behavior than the United States, Latin America's Catholic–Thomistic–Suarezian–Rousseauian–Comtean traditions often produce different political outcomes than American Lockean liberalism, and *every* Latin American government now reflects an interesting, sometimes viable, sometimes dysfunctional, blending of the historic Catholic tradition with the newer pressures of individual participation and American-style democratization. If we wish to advance democracy in Latin America, we need to comprehend and come to grips with both these differences and the similarities.

Endnotes

1. Included under the umbrella term Latin America are Argentina, Bolivia, Brazil, Chile, Colombia, Ecuador, Paraguay, Peru, Uruguay, Venezuela, Costa Rica, Dominican Republic, Cuba, El Salvador, Guatemala, Haiti, Honduras, Mexico, Nicaragua, and Panama.

2. Roderic Ai Camp, *Politics in Mexico*, 3rd ed. (New York: Oxford, 1999).

3. Paul J. Weithman, "Complementarity and Equality in the Political Thought of Thomas Aquinas," *Theological Studies* 59 (1998): 277–97.

For arguments supporting the democratic nature of Aquinas see Brian Tierney, "Hierarchy, Consent, and the 'Western Tradition'," *Political Theory* 15 (1987): 646–52; and Mark Murphy, "Consent, Custom and Common Good in Aquinas' Account of Political Authority," *Review of Politics* 59 (1992): 353–76.

4. Cited in Peter H. Smith, *Talons of the Eagle: Dynamics of U.S.-Latin American Relations* (New York: Oxford University Press, 2000): 44.

5. John Winthrop, "A Model of Christian Charity," *American Legal History: Cases and Materials*, edited by Kermit L. Hall, William M. Wiecek, and Paul Finkelman (New York: Oxford University Press, 1996): 12–13.

6. The author wishes to thank Professor Neal Weiner of Marlboro College for offering this lucid distinction.

7. 1 Cor. 12:12–31.

8. 1 Cor. 12:13.

9. Matt. 20:1–16.

10. For instance, Christian Democrats operating in Chile during the 1960s formed a "communitarian" form of socialism that found its basis in Thomistic natural law reasoning. See Jaime Castillo, *The Ideologies of the Developing Nations*, edited by Paul E. Sigmund (Westport, Conn.: Praeger Press, 1967).

11. Aquinas, "On Kingship": 15.

12. Aquinas, "On Kingship": 26.

13. Aquinas, "Life, or Soul and Its Abilities," *Aquinas: Selected Philosophical Writings* (New York: Oxford University Press, 1993): 121.

14. Aquinas, "On Kingship": 26.

15. Aquinas, "Treatise of Law," *St. Thomas Aquinas on Politics and Ethics*, edited by Paul Sigmund (New York: Norton, 1988): 47.

16. See Richard Kagan, *Lucrecia's Dreams* (Berkeley: University of California Press, 1990); Richard E. Greenleaf, *The Mexican Inquisition of the Sixteenth Century* (Albuquerque: University of New Mexico Press, 1969).

17. Francisco Suárez, "Political Authority and Community Consent," *St. Thomas Aquinas on Politics and Ethics*, edited by Paul Sigmund (New York: Norton, 1990): 148–51.

18. Bernice Hamilton, *Political Thought in Sixteenth-Century Spain* (Oxford: Oxford University Press, 1963): 62.

19. Antonio Molina Meliá, *Iglesia y Estado en el Siglo de Oro Español: El Pensamiento de Francisco Suárez* (Valencia, Spain: Universidad de Valencia, 1977): 97.

20. Ibid.

21. Cited in O. Carlos Stoetzer, *El Pensamiento Politico en la America Española Durante el Periodo de la Emancipacion (1789–1825)*, translated by author (Madrid: Instituto de Estudios Politicos, 1966): 86.

22. Tina Rosenberg, "Latin America's Magical Liberalism," *Wilson Quarterly* (Autumn, 1992): 60.

23. See Howard J. Wiarda, *Corporatism and Development: The Portuguese Development* (Amherst, Mass.: University of Massachusetts Press, 1977).

24. Alberto Fujimori, "Noticia de la Cumbre," *VII Cumbre Iberoamericana de Jefes de Estado y de Gobierno* (Nov. 1997). Available at: http://www.cumbre.ve/pg-d17.htm. Downloaded: 1/13/00.

25. "Chávez Promises to Lift Venezuela out of Poverty," *Agencia EFE* (12/06/99). Available at: http://library.northernlight.com. Downloaded: 1/5/00.

Suggested Readings

Dealy, Glen. *The Public Man: An Interpretation of Latin American and Other Catholic Countries.* Amherst: University of Massachusetts Press, 1977.

Hamilton, Bernice. *Political Thought in Sixteenth Century Spain.* Oxford: Oxford University Press, 1963.

Madden, Marie. *Political Theory and Law in Medieval Spain.* New York: Fordham University Press, 1930.

Morse, Richard M. *New World Soundings: Culture and Ideology in the Americas.* Baltimore: Johns Hopkins University Press, 1989.

Veliz, Claudio. *The Centralist Tradition in Latin America.* Princeton: Princeton University Press, 1980.

Wiarda, Howard J. *The Soul of Latin America: The Cultural and Political Traditions.* New Haven: Yale University Press, 2001.

Wiarda, Howard J. and Margaret MacLeish Mott. *Catholic Roots and Democratic Flowers: The Political Systems of Spain and Portugal.* Westport, Conn.: Greenwood Press, 2001.

------ (eds). *Politics and Social Change in Latin America: The Distinct Tradition.* Westport, CT: Greenwood Press, 2001.

4

The Shrimp That Whistled: Russia— Democracy Waylaid

Steve D. Boilard

Those who wait for [the Soviet Union to reject communism] must wait until a shrimp learns to whistle.
–Nikita Khrushchev

There was a time—a very long time—during which Russia and democracy were considered to be mutually exclusive terms. For centuries tsarist Russia was ruled by men (and some women) who wielded absolute power, attained through a combination of birthright, manipulation, and murderous intrigue. Although the Soviet government that emerged out of the 1917 Revolution claimed to be democratic, the evident hypocrisy of that claim made the government even more reviled among democrats. In fact, for many the Soviet Union came to represent precisely the antipode of democracy.

And yet the collapse of that government in 1991 and the emergence of a new Russian Federation that disavowed its Soviet history triggered a fundamental reassessment of whether Russia could indeed become a genuine democracy, and if so, how?

The case of Russia raises interesting questions not just about the Russians but about democracy itself. Is it simply a matter of setting into place the proper institutions, laws, and leaders? Or does it require a particular mindset on the part of the people or preexisting economic conditions? Can it be imposed from without, or does it need to arise from within?

59

Modern social scientists owe a debt of gratitude to the Bolshevik revolutionaries who created the Soviet Union some eight decades ago. The Bolsheviks (later Communists) seized the largely agrarian, authoritarian Russian state, attempted fundamental changes to the very identity of the peoples in the Russian empire, managed to industrialize major sectors of the economy, amassed one of the most powerful military forces the world had ever seen, and then, after seven decades, vainly attempted to shift the basis of their governmental authority from coercion to popular consent through a series of desperate "reforms" that in 1991 resulted in the collapse of the Soviet state. This history, partly chronicled by the state's fastidious (though ideologically tainted) record-keeping, provides rich material to elucidate any number of theories of political and economic development.

Moreover, out of the collapse of the Soviet Union emerged a new experiment—a postcommunist "transition to democracy." Immediately after gaining independence, Russia's post-Soviet leadership took pains to distance itself from the old regime. The banishment of the Communist Party, President Boris Yeltsin's public commitment to democracy and capitalism, and the country's close cooperation—even friendship—with its erstwhile adversaries in the West all forced a rapid and thorough reevaluation of Russia's essence. In the first heady days of the post-Soviet era, it was tempting to be optimistic. To many it appeared that the crude and heavy blanket of Soviet Communism had been pulled back to reveal a relatively sane society and leadership. Perhaps Russia could be a functioning democracy after all.

That optimism was soon and severely tested. Soviet totalitarianism had collapsed, yes, but Russian democracy had not yet fully materialized. During its first decade of post-Soviet independence, Russia repeatedly strained the definition of democracy. Yeltsin's unconstitutional dissolution of the Parliament in 1993 raised questions about the principle of rule of law in Russia. The forced resignations of a pro-Western foreign minister and promarket economic advisers in 1995 undermined the government's commitment to reform. The Duma's symbolic efforts to restore the old Soviet Union in 1996 suggested imperialist ambitions. The protracted economic crisis in the late 1990s weakened the state and exacerbated crime, corruption, and poverty. Military attacks against a secessionist province smacked of ethno-chauvinism and a bunker mentality in Moscow. Most importantly, the Russian people began to evince an atavistic longing for the ghosts of the past: through substantial electoral support for Communists and nationalists, through violent hostility toward successful entrepreneurs, and through renewed cynicism about government and politics. It was as though the hard lessons learned throughout 75 years of Sovietism (and centuries of tsarism) were forgotten with the passage of a few months and years. Perhaps the Russian people really were undemocratizable.

Cold War–Era Thinking on Democracy

For much of the twentieth century, thinking about democracy and democratization was filtered through the lens of the Cold War. For mainstream Western thought, democracy was understood to mean a form of government in which the citizens—the "governed"—were the source of the government's power, and the government acted on behalf of the governed. Governmental power was derived from the citizens (i.e., with the consent of the governed) and was circumscribed by a constitution (i.e., limited government). The relationship between the citizens and their governmental leaders thus was a contractual one.

The debates focused on which governments were truly democratic. Contrarian left thinkers argued that the putatively democratic Western countries—including the United States itself—were in some ways antidemocratic, which of course was a technically accurate, if not very meaningful, criticism. But at the same time many of these same critics held up communist dictatorships such as the Soviet Union and Cuba as "true" democracies, in which the governments putatively acted in the interests of the people, albeit perhaps not with the formal mechanisms of competitive elections. Mainstream Western thought, in turn, rejects the suggestion that government elites could know the interests of the people better than the people themselves. Thus, without some provision for the people to continuously register those interests and to periodically replace leaders whom they feel have failed to promote those interests, democracy is impossible.

In one sense, the collapse of the Soviet Union exposed the fundamental flaws—the internal contradictions, if you will—of Marxism-Leninism: as an economic system it was a failure; as a political system it lacked legitimacy; as an ideology it fatally misread human nature. Once freed of their well-founded but now obsolete fear of the communist state, Russians demanded Western-style democracy and economic opportunities. And this is what the new Yeltsin-led government promised.

Russia's commitment to democratization, along with similar pledges by most former Soviet-bloc countries, spurred a small academic industry on postcommunist transitions to democracy. Social scientists and politicians alike grappled with the question of how to create democracy in an industrialized, urbanized, sprawling multinational power with a seventy-year history of Marxism-Leninism. Could such an effort succeed? Although the post-Soviet era is barely a decade old, it can be instructive at this time to assess Russia's experience in attempting this transition. The balance of this chapter will briefly review Russia's historical absence of democratic institutions, recount the circumstances surrounding Russia's emergence as a post-Soviet state, examine the main governmental institutions of post-Soviet Russia as well as the five national elections held since independence, and evaluate public attitudes that can indicate support for, or at least tolerance of, the difficult reforms that can lead to democracy.

History

Russia does not have a democratic tradition. Its roots can be traced back some 1,000 years to tribes of Slavic peoples scattered in a region between the Ural mountains and the Black Sea. These peoples were collected under a growing empire that came in the seventeenth century to be dominated by the Romanov dynasty. The tsars were monarchs who ruled with absolute authority. Under this authority, Russia grew in strength and size until, by the eighteenth century, it had become one of Europe's great powers. But the forging of this Russian empire came at great human cost, provoking a series of disjointed but persistent opposition movements.

Public unrest was exacerbated with the onset of Russia's industrial revolution in the last decades of the nineteenth century. Exploitive and unsafe working conditions, food shortages, and urban overcrowding comprised a new category of grievances beyond the now familiar authoritarianism of the regime. By the time the last tsar, Nicholas II, assumed power in 1894, living conditions in the cities were so intolerable that the burgeoning urban population became a fertile recruiting ground for the growing reformist and revolutionary groups. This "proletariat," as the Marxist revolutionaries called it, assumed a pivotal role in the revolutionary events which were to transpire. It was on this proletariat's behalf that a growing revolutionary group, the Social Democratic Labor Party, putatively would fight.

The Russian Revolution

On Bloody Sunday in 1905 the slaughter of more than a hundred unarmed protesters by guards at the tsar's Winter Palace knocked out one of the regime's few remaining props: the popular belief that it was governmental underlings and renegades, rather than the tsar himself, who were responsible for the people's privations. In the following months, demonstrations, riots, and assassinations would collectively constitute the 1905 Revolution, and by October Nicholas conceded and agreed to establish the trappings of a constitutional monarchy. Within a year, however, the tsar had reneged on most of his promised reforms. General public dissatisfaction with the regime persisted, and increasingly radical revolutionary groups continued to agitate against the government.

Then, in 1914, Russia was drawn into war against Germany in defense of its Slavic ally, Serbia. The resultant World War I created conditions for a successful coup de grace against the tsarist regime. Simultaneously weakening the country and galvanizing public opposition, the war cut the tsar's power base, including his own armies, from under him. In March 1917 Nicholas abdicated the throne, and power was transferred to a Provisional Government. Fatally, the new government refused to remove Russia from the war—perhaps the most important and immediate demand of the disaffected population. Meanwhile, Lenin's Bolsheviks, who were not part of the Provisional Government, established a power base in Petrograd (nee St. Petersburg). Emboldened by the government's disarray as well as by their own successes, the Bolsheviks overthrew the Provisional Government on November 17, 1917.

Although Lenin was successful at toppling the old regime, it would be three more years before the Bolsheviks (now calling themselves Communists) would consolidate power. But after the defeat of Germany and the vanquishing of Lenin's domestic foes, the Communists proceeded to establish Soviet Socialist Republics in neighboring countries such as the Ukraine and Belorussia. Moscow initially maintained that these new republics should be considered independent countries, but by the end of 1922 they had all been absorbed in the new Union of Soviet Socialist Republics. The USSR was born.

The Soviet Union

After Lenin's death in 1924, Josef Stalin had contrived a successful path to supreme power using a combination of political manipulation and ideological contortion. During the time of Stalin's rule, the Soviet Union pursued a range of effective, frequently harsh modernization and militarization policies. The country's production, investment, and development were dictated by "five-year plans," a testament to the Communists' hubris in harnessing the economy but nevertheless brutally effective. The progress achieved by the interwar Soviet Union is remarkable by a variety of standards: industrialization, mechanization, and urbanization; the building of infrastructure, the creation of a world-class army, the establishment of a complex bureaucracy; progress in science and technology; and increases in literacy and life expectancy. All this was accomplished, while the leadership simultaneously consolidated and centralized power in a totalitarian fashion over a population that could never be considered wholly, or even largely, accepting of the Communist regime.

This last feat reflects the core of what would come to be known as Stalinism: the domination of the population, even of most of the government bureaucrats, by a pervasive system of ideological indoctrination, omnipresent surveillance, and political punishment (including exile, imprisonment, and execution). World War II's demands upon Soviet manpower would require the mitigation of the worst of these excesses, and Stalin's death in 1953 would pave the way for Khrushchev's "de-Stalinization." Yet the core of the Soviet political system continued to rest upon the political neutralization and physical restriction of the hapless population.

The Cold War and Superpowerdom

When the Soviet Union, along with the United States, emerged victorious from World War II in 1945, the Soviets had seized or reclaimed most of the territory between Stalingrad and Berlin. The borders of the Soviet Union itself had been pushed to the Baltic Sea and into eastern Poland and Romania, and the Red Army occupied most of Eastern Europe. British and American forces, now with the assistance of liberated France, occupied the Continent's western territory. The ideological antipathy and geopolitical competition between the Soviet Union and the West—only submerged, but never eliminated during the wartime alliance—returned with a vengeance.

For the next four decades there ensued the Cold War, whose fundamental logic of bipolar competition would largely direct the Soviet Union's development until its demise in 1991. As a superpower Moscow enjoyed an expanded sphere of influence that reached beyond Europe to Southeast Asia, Africa, and even Latin America. Its nuclear arsenal earned Moscow negotiating

leverage with Washington, eventually blossoming into a period of "détente" in the late 1960s and 1970s.

Having secured a measure of international prestige and strategic stability with the West, the post-Stalin leadership permitted Soviet domestic policies to thaw somewhat. The Soviet Union progressively adopted the societal and political trappings of other industrialized states. But at the same time social discipline, industrial strength, economic health, and other vital signs began to decline at an alarming rate. More worrisome still, the USSR's client states in Eastern Europe were experiencing an ominous level of popular protests and dissent.

Gorbachev's Reforms

By the beginning of the 1980s, the declining cohesion of Moscow's empire was witnessed by the rise of the Solidarity movement in Poland and the civil war in Soviet-backed Afghanistan. At the same time Soviet society was displaying signs of social, economic, and environmental decline through such indicators as decreasing life expectancy and diminishing agricultural yields. Brezhnev's own ill health and advanced age prevented his making any substantial course corrections, and the Soviet system was still on the path of decline when he succumbed to a heart attack in 1982. Brezhnev's next two successors died shortly after assuming office and effected few meaningful reforms.

Such was the setting when Mikhail Gorbachev took the post of General Secretary in 1985. Healthy and only 54 years old, Gorbachev was from a younger generation of Soviet leaders. He immediately acknowledged that all was not well with the USSR, and before long he was calling for radical reforms. During his seven years in power, Gorbachev undertook the most far-reaching reforms in Soviet history. He did not initially conceive them as such; he developed his reform program gradually and improvisationally. For all his commitment to reform, Gorbachev remained a socialist to the end.

Beginning with a policy of glasnost ("openness") to renew public faith in the country and encourage greater social discipline, Gorbachev soon recognized that fuller, more structural changes were needed. He began to introduce significant, though limited, market reforms. He moved to partially separate the functions of the Party and the state. He established a new legislature that was filled through secret, multicandidate elections in 1989. Gorbachev's reforms were not an effort to transform the Soviet Union into a true republic, however. Instead, he allowed the people limited (though frequently real) choice in selecting their leaders.

Had Gorbachev democratized the Soviet Union? If democracy is seen as a continuous variable, then certainly it would be fair to say that Gorbachev began to democratize the country. But so many legal restrictions remained on the forming of parties, the qualifications for candidacy, and campaigning for office that the Soviet electoral system, even in the later Gorbachev period, failed to meet the standard of even a procedural democracy. (As will be discussed below, the more difficult standard of substantive democracy would be even more elusive.)

Still, even the very limited transfer of certain electoral powers to the people was enough to undermine the supreme authority of the Party, which was the central support of the Soviet regime. The new legislature soon amended the Constitution to permit opposition parties to form. In a free market of competing ideologies, the Party's days were numbered.

Meanwhile, the Eastern European peoples interpreted Gorbachev's domestic reforms as a tacit endorsement of democratization movements in their own countries. Protests and demonstrations became more fervent, and by the fall of 1989 virtually all of the East European countries had overthrown their Communist governments. These successful revolutions in turn provided powerful inspiration for the nationalist forces within the USSR. By allowing the countries of Eastern Europe to break away from the Soviet sphere of influence, Gorbachev lent credibility to the growing belief that Moscow as unwilling to use military force against its own secessionists.

In reality, the Soviet leadership was sharply divided over the question of how to respond to domestic demands for popular sovereignty and national self-determination. Gorbachev encountered increasingly hostile opposition from other Party elites who thought his reform agenda was foolishly defeatist. These conservatives insisted that the Soviet Union could be preserved only by maintaining one-party rule and a unified state. Then, in August 1991, with Gorbachev on the verge of signing a treaty with the country's fifteen constituent republics that granted them unprecedented political and economic autonomy, a small group of conservative party and military leaders staged a coup attempt. Gorbachev was placed under house arrest, and the coup leaders created an eight-man committee to rule in his place.

For all its drama, the coup collapsed after three days. A variety of factors contributed to its failure. Most importantly, the coup leaders failed to detain Boris Yeltsin, the popular elected leader of the Russian Soviet Federated Socialist Republic (RSFSR) and vociferous critic of the conservatives. Yeltsin proclaimed his own control of the RFSFR and called for general strikes and public resistance. Yeltsin also called on the military not to obey the "usurpers." Most military units heeded this call, and the coup fizzled.

The Demise of the Soviet Union

The coup attempt was the climax of the Soviet Union's demise, and the denouement would be over in just four more months. The reformist image of the Party nurtured by Gorbachev was now destroyed by the coup attempt, and even Gorbachev himself was ultimately forced to renounce his party membership. In practical terms, the coup attempt catapulted to completion the disaggregation of the union. Republics that only days earlier were prepared to voluntarily sign a treaty proclaiming their ultimate allegiance to Moscow in exchange for greater latitude under that tutelage now balked at such a stingy offer. Now was the time to break free of the Soviets' deadly embrace. Before the end of the year, all the Soviet republics—including even Russia—would be reconstituted as sovereign states.

The breakup of the Soviet Union was occasioned by two revolutions. National revolutions, fought on behalf of the republics' titular nationalities, caused the Soviet Union to divide along its internal provincial boundaries. At the same time, a democratic revolution destroyed the Soviet state itself. Yeltsin's government symbolized Russian national self-determination, as well as anticommunism and popular sovereignty.

Underlying these revolutions was a current of consumer dissatisfaction. Bolstered by less-sanitized economic and social data made available by glasnost, the long-time dissatisfaction with the quality and variety of consumer goods, the condition and reliability of transportation, the allocation of living space, and other aspects of living standards was channeled into the campaigns for national self-determination and popular sovereignty.

The formal dissolution of the USSR was marked by Gorbachev's resignation speech on Christmas Day, 1991, and on the next day, a formal legislative action by the Soviet Parliament. The Soviet Union had succumbed to both aspects of revolution—territorial secession and political rejection. But the fifteen new countries that stood in its place now faced the tasks of recreating territorial and political states and of satisfying their populations' expectations for improvement in living standards.

The Reemergence of Russia

A sardonic joke from the time of communism's collapse in Eurasia asserts that communism is the long road from democracy to democracy. This may have been the case for some Eastern European states, but the people of Russia, as we have seen, had not been burdened with the responsibilities of citizenship in a functioning democracy. With the emergence of an independent Russian state in 1991, however, Russians began to feel their way into this unfamiliar territory.

The post-Soviet Russian Federation was born as something less than a genuine democracy. Yeltsin was ruling the country by emergency powers granted by the Russian Parliament after the August 1991 coup attempt. The country's bureaucracy and economic institutions were largely under the control of Soviet-era apparatchiks. Serving as the country's constitution was the heavily-amended version of Soviet Russia's 1978 constitution. And only the most rudimentary forms of political parties and interest groups struggled to aggregate and articulate the people's post-Soviet interests. Although state sovereignty had been secured, achieving the goal of popular sovereignty was only beginning, and the objective of improved living conditions, by some measures, was losing ground.

Although the Soviet Union's seven years under Gorbachev largely validated the thesis of the Soviet state's irredeemability (it could not be reformed, only destroyed), it undermined the conception of Russians as a passive people. But given the preconceptions developed during the Soviet period, it is not surprising that most Western governments and universities, as well as Gorbachev himself, did not every really understand the enormous power of the newly liberated citizenry until after the entire Soviet edifice had collapsed. The Soviet Union was not conquered by the West as a culmination of the Cold War, although its collapse was hastened by pressures from the United States and elsewhere. Instead, it was brought down by its own people, infused with a sense of self-determination and liberated by a regime that had lost the ability, or the willingness, to continue oppressing them.

Democracy, of course, is more than the absence of oppressive government. It involves the establishment of democratic institutions such as representative bodies and a legal system. It also requires certain attitudes, values, and beliefs—that is, a suitable political culture—among the citizens. Democratic theorists continue to debate whether political institutions give rise to the political culture or vice versa. Russia began its post-Soviet era with neither.

Democratic Institution-Building

Under Yeltsin, Russia worked quickly to establish the formal trappings of democracy. Central to this effort was an all-new Russian constitution, adopted in December 1993, which formally established and conferred authority to Russia's political institutions, bureaucracy, and legal system.

The new constitution came about under less than auspicious circumstances. During its first two years as an independent state Russia retained a heavily amended version of its Soviet-era constitution. Some of these amendments sought to eradicate Marxist-Leninist principles, but others resulted from the parliament's desire to reduce Yeltsin's power. For his part, Yeltsin conducted several efforts to create a new constitution from scratch. A constitutional crisis mounted until the fall of 1993, when Yeltsin issued a decree suspending the parliament, establishing a new legislative body, and calling for new elections in December. The parliamentary leadership responded by declaring that Yeltsin had forfeited the presidency and swearing in the vice president, Aleksandr Rutskoi, as Yeltsin's replacement. With Yeltsin and Rutskoi both claiming to be the real president, Yeltsin ultimately called in Russian troops to storm the parliament building. After a brief battle the remaining parliament members surrendered. Now, with his major governmental rivals suspended, in prison, or dead (more than 100 people died in the "October events," as they came to be known), Yeltsin made a final push to establish a new constitutional order. A new draft constitution, tailor-made to suit Yeltsin's vision for his country and his rule, was put before the voters at the same time as the already scheduled parliamentary elections in December 1993. The constitution was approved with 58 percent of the votes cast.

Unlike the U.S. Constitution, the Constitution of the Russian Federation is detailed and specific, comprising 137 separate articles. A mix of old (Soviet) principles and specifically anti-Soviet ones, the Yeltsin Constitution specifies a separation of state power into three branches, ensures "ideological plural-ism" by proscribing any state-sponsored ideology, and maintains a separation of church and state. Forty-eight articles grouped as "Human and Civil Rights and Freedoms" provide a liberal and expansive, even majestic, expression of human rights. The listing of affronts to human rights that are proscribed by this chapter serves as a catalog of the various abuses practiced by the Soviet state: diminution of human dignity, prolonged detention without judicial ac-tion, invasion of privacy, forced renunciation of opinions, censorship, and many others.

More prosaically, the Constitution describes the specific powers and re-sponsibilities of the major offices and institutions of the Russian Federation.

The Presidency

The Yeltsin Constitution designates the president as the head of state. Like the president of France, however, the Russian president possesses powers far beyond the ceremonial role that "head of state" implies. In this sense, Russia has an "executive presidency." The Russian president appoints the prime minister (with the parliament's consent), appoints governmental ministers (after vetting by the prime minister), and nominates justices (for approval by the parliament). He or she may call referenda and grant pardons.

The Constitution also grants to the president the power to issue decrees and directives, which are legally binding throughout the country so long as they do not contradict the constitution or federal laws. Although this power is potentially enormous, it is limited by the willingness of the federal and local bureaucracies to implement the decrees. Throughout the 1990s, Yeltsin's de-crees were regularly ignored by many of the regional governors and even cen-tral government bureaucrats.

Although the ability to effect substantive change in the bureaucracy is limited, the president wields considerable power over the federal parliament and cabinet. The president has the power to dissolve the Duma and call new elections. If the Duma passes a vote of no confidence in the government, the president may either dissolve the Duma or dismiss the government. The president may introduce martial law and declare a state of emergency, but while either of these is in effect the president may not dissolve the Duma. A new (or, one supposes, renewed) government must be appointed only when a new president takes office.

The president also wields formal power over the regions of the Federation—power which was consolidated in 2000 by President Putin. The Constitution permits the president to use "reconciliatory procedures" to settle differences between the federal and regional authorities. The president also may suspend acts of the regional executives if he or she finds that they contradict the federal constitution or federal law, until "the appropriate court" decides the question. As noted above, the president may declare states of emergency and martial law in particular regions.

The president takes the lead in conducting Russia's relations with other countries. The president is commander-in-chief of the armed forces and is generally responsible for conducting the country's foreign policy. He or she appoints ambassadors and other diplomats. The Constitution affords the president the power to approve the country's military doctrine, although numerous informal and formal structures are involved in the drafting of military and foreign policy. The president conducts international negotiations and signs international treaties (which require ratification by parliament) and recognizes foreign diplomats.

Overall, the distinction between the president and the "government" (i.e., the prime minister and the cabinet) is vague, given the president's influence over the makeup and actions of those offices. Yet when it suited him to do so, Yeltsin blamed social and economic problems on the actions of "incompetent ministers." Under Yeltsin, continuous cabinet reshuffling handicapped the state's ability to effect long-term policies.

The Government

Although the president's decision-making powers are enormous, the Constitution formally places executive power in the government. "Government" is defined in the European sense, meaning the prime minister (formally called the chairman of the government), deputy prime ministers, and federal ministers. Collectively, the federal ministers compose the cabinet. In its capacity as the executive branch, the government is charged with carrying out the laws and policies of the Russian Federation. The government also submits a federal budget to the Duma and oversees the implementation of the final budget.

The Duma's powers over the government are complex and heavily checked by the president. A simple majority of deputies may pass a vote of no confidence in the government. The president may either accept the Duma's vote, in which case he or she announces the government's dissolution, or reject the vote of no confidence. If the Duma's vote is rejected, the Duma may pass a second vote of no confidence within three months of the first. In this case, the president must either announce the government's resignation or dissolve the Duma.

The Legislature

Like most democratic governments (and some nondemocratic ones), Russia's legislature takes the form of a bicameral parliament. This Federal Assembly, as it is known, is charged with the usual representation and lawmaking tasks, as well as providing certain checks on the other branches of government. It is, however, significantly less powerful than the Gorbachev-era Congress of People's Deputies which it replaced.

The upper house of the Federal Assembly is the Federation Council, and in several ways it resembles the U.S. Senate. Like the Senate, the Federation Council is constituted on the basis of equal geographical representation. Each of Russia's 89 regions sends two representatives to the Federation Council, for a total of 178 members. And, like the Senate, the Federation Council ratifies treaties (along with the Duma) and possesses the power to impeach the president. The Federation Council holds powers relating to the Russian Federation's justice system, including approving and dismissing the prosecutor-general and approving or rejecting the president's nominees for justices on Russia's three high courts. In addition, the Federation Council approves internal border revisions, approves presidential decrees of martial law, and "decides the possibility" of deployment of the military abroad.

Half of the Federation Council (one of each region's two seats) is to be composed of regional governors. As regional executives, these governors have tended to be more loyal to the federal executive (that is, the president) than members of the lower house. The other half of the Federation Council is made up of regional legislative leaders. The two representatives from each region are not "elected" to the Federation Council; rather, they automatically become deputies of the Federation Council by virtue of their regional offices. As a result, these regional leaders split their time between their regional and federal positions, making the Federation Council a part-time body.

As is true for many parliamentary systems, Russia's lower house, the State Duma, is the more powerful of the two chambers. Because its 450 deputies are directly elected as representatives to the federal parliament, the Duma enjoys a stronger mandate than the Federation Council. The Duma is the more important and more powerful chamber in the making of legislation, as it initiates all legislation and can override a rejection of a bill by the Federation Council. The Constitution also provides for the censure of the government by the Duma. The term of office for Duma deputies is four years. The Duma elects a speaker to preside over the body.

The Constitution reserves for the Duma various powers: approving the president's nominee for prime minister, deciding votes of confidence, appointing and removing the chairman of the Central Bank, appointing and removing the officer for human rights, initiating articles of impeachment against the president, and issuing declarations of amnesty. The Duma used this last power shortly after it convened in 1994, granting amnesty to the leaders of the 1991 attempted coup against Gorbachev and the 1993 "October events" against Yeltsin. In 1999 the Duma's communist leadership attempted to impeach Yeltsin, but votes on all five of the indictments failed.

Legal System

The institutional structures created by the Constitution and the body of laws passed by the legislature amount to little without a concomitant commitment to the principle of rule of law. The significance of a law-governed state is not simply that it has working laws, but that in the final analysis, it is laws, and not politics, personality, or naked power, that regulate the actions of society and the government. The Soviet Union, like tsarist Russia before it, observed no such principle. The Soviet regime was not bound in any meaningful way by an enforceable constitution, and laws affected the general population in an arbitrary and capricious fashion. In short, law in the Soviet Union was subordinate to the regime.

The Yeltsin leadership set itself upon the task of reforming the legal system with the same ambition, and perhaps with the same lack of preparation, as it did upon the task of reforming the political system. Few legal procedures and institutions were left untouched by the reform program. Some of the reforms simply applied international norms to the Russian legal system; for example, there was a requirement that all laws be published. Others filled large voids that the Soviet legal system had never had reason to address—consumer protection requirements and laws protecting intellectual property, for example. But the most important reforms concerned limitations on state power.

One of the most important bulwarks of a law-governed state is an independent high court with jurisdiction over constitutional issues. Through the 1993 Constitution Yeltsin sought to recast the Russian Constitutional Court as such a body. The Constitution of the Russian Federation grants to the Constitutional Court the power of judicial review: to determine whether laws and governmental actions conform to the Constitution. The Court also decides questions of competence between the central governmental bodies. In addition, it is charged with resolving disputes between the central and regional governments.

The Yeltsin Constitution established two additional high courts. The Supreme Court of the Russian Federation is the highest court of appeal for civil, administrative, and criminal law. In matters of impeachment, the Supreme Court must verify the Duma's findings of presidential criminality, and the Constitutional Court must verify that the proper impeachment procedures are followed. The Supreme Arbitration Court of the Russian Federation is the highest court of appeal for cases concerning economic matters. The Russian judiciary system includes a network of courts of arbitration, which settle economic disputes. However, it is widely understood that the rich and persons with political influence are able to either bypass or manipulate this system, at least at the lower levels.

To help isolate the courts from political pressure, judges in Russia are immune from criminal prosecution. It is a difficult and important provision, given the Party's co-optation of the courts in the Soviet period and also the incidents of bribery and other forms of corruption in the post-Soviet court system. Of course, the power of courts depends on whether the government is willing to follow their decisions. Still, the creation of a formally independent judiciary is a central pillar of Russia's procedural democracy.

Overall, Russia's Constitution would appear to create, on paper, a government that could properly be called democratic. It limits the powers of the government, separates the powers of government into distinct branches, provides for the government's accountability to the voters, and establishes inviolable rights for Russia's citizens.

Development of Parties and Interest Groups

Real electoral choice is the heart of genuine democracy, and well-defined, responsible parties are especially well suited for facilitating that choice. The success of Russia's transition from authoritarianism to liberal democracy, if it occurs, will depend in no small measure upon the creation of viable, distinct parties and the conducting of periodic, fair elections.

The Soviet political system was frequently described as a "one-party" system. Yet the Communist Party of the Soviet Union (CPSU) was never a political party in the Western sense of the term. The 1977 constitution called the CPSU "the nucleus of [the Soviet] system," and post-Soviet Russian critics have labeled it a quasi-state organization. Its contrast with the democratic ideal of a political party is stark. The CPSU did not so much aggregate group interests as it sought to indoctrinate Soviet subjects. Rather than putting up candidates to acquire governmental power, the Party was practically indistinguishable from the government. It did not offer alternatives to governmental programs; it dictated those programs. The Party sought above all to mobilize, co-opt, and control the 10 percent of the population who joined its ranks often in search of the concomitant privileges that a party state afforded.

After three-quarters of a century under such a system, Russians can be forgiven some hesitation in warming to the practice of multiparty democracy. Thus, the bitter reply to Gorbachev's unprecedented introduction of multiparty elections in 1989: "Isn't one Party bad enough?" Like the founders of the United States two centuries earlier, the leaders of post-Soviet Russia initially eschewed political parties as distasteful, divisive, and even antidemocratic entities. Throughout his tenure as Russia's president, Boris Yeltsin would not formally associate himself with any political group. He conceived of the presidency as properly above the squalid business of party politics—a sentiment earlier held by other notable figures such as George Washington and France's Charles de Gaulle. Although the virtue of the Russian presidency nevertheless suffered without the connivance of party affiliation, it is clear that the development of parties in Russia has indeed been a chaotic affair that has enmeshed many of its advocates.

Once the CPSU's monopoly was broken in 1990, thousands of new groups sprang up to fill the void. Yet few, if any, of these groups could immediately be considered parties. They were too small and amorphous, and they lacked any clear role in the political system. They were given to factionalism, and many were geographically isolated. In Gorbachev's final year, the Soviet Union was transformed from a one-party system not to a multiparty state, but to a no-party state.

Even after the collapse of the Soviet Union and the establishment of the Russian Federation as a sovereign country, Russia's political landscape was fractious and anomic. For the first several years of Russia's independence, nascent party organizations were short-lived—dividing, combining, dissolving altogether, and reemerging with new ideological foundations. Their development and behavior more closely resembled narrowly defined interest groups than political parties.

Not only were Russia's political groupings being narrowly segmented along functional or interest lines, but they also tended to be defined along regional lines. The vast geographic and cultural differences among Russia's disparate peoples provide fertile ground for regional parties, and this in turn may threaten the viability of the Russian Federation as a cohesive political entity.

The post-Soviet government scrambled to adopt regulations, registration procedures, and electoral laws to structure the emerging multiparty system. (Even then, a law on presidential elections was not adopted until 2000.) A fluctuating number of factions and blocs developed within the Congress of People's Deputies. One year after the collapse of the Soviet Union, about two dozen parties were formally registered in the Russian Federation. A much larger number of political organizations—by some counts more than 1,000—

did not formally register, but in one way or another had surfaced as country-wide political groups. By the end of 1992, there were more political organizations than there were seats in the Russian legislature.

The first post-Soviet Russian elections, in December 1993, forced some discipline upon the chaotic and amorphous congeries of party groups. By the time of the September 1993 deadline, 140 national groups had registered. Only 35 of these managed to submit the requisite number of signatures to participate in the elections. Consolidation and invalidation reduced voters' choices still further, with 13 "electoral associations" ultimately appearing on the ballot. Of these, only 8 managed to obtain the 5 percent of the vote required to gain Duma seats allocated through proportional representation.

Russia's party system was finally beginning to coalesce. As the first Russia-wide elections to be held since the demise of the Soviet Union, the 1993 parliamentary elections infused the victorious parties with a certain legitimacy and credibility that theretofore had been unknown in Russia. The performance of these parties in the newly constituted parliament helped establish a legislative record by which they could be distinguished. And the procedural requirements imposed by the new constitution nudged the parties to take up the arcane democratic arts of compromise and coalition building.

The Russian Duma was now dominated by fewer than a half-dozen parties. But what could be said about the ideologies they represented?

Evaluating the general political philosophies of Russia's political parties presents frustrating conceptual difficulties. Post-Soviet Russia lacks a meaningful left-right political spectrum. The West's Cold War-era practice of defining "Communism" as the left end-point of an ideological spectrum offers little assistance in post-Soviet Russia. If "conservative" and "orthodox" are characteristics of the right side of the ideological spectrum, where should one place the revolutionary Communists of contemporary Russia who long for a return to the old (Soviet) order? Should "reformists" be placed leftward on the familiar Western continuum (with progressives) or rightward (with laissez-faire capitalists)? Other issues on which Russia's emergent parties can be distinguished do not lend themselves to the traditional left-right spectrum. Nationalism and imperialism are two critical issues coloring Russian politics at the dawn of the third millennium, but they are not easily placed on the familiar left-right continuum. The task becomes even more difficult with the unusual combinations of values that are amalgamated within some party platforms.

This is not simply a methodological problem. It illustrates the amorphous nature of contemporary Russian politics. In the first months of the 1996–99 Duma, coalitions were built between "reformers" and Communists against nationalists. Similar coalitions among ideologically strange bedfellows were created to run in the 1999 Duma elections. Such alliances resulted more from political expediency than from any harmony of fundamental values.

The subordination of ideology to short-term tactical gains becomes especially clear when one recalls that the Communists and nationalists were frequently allied against the democrats in the 1993–95 Duma. In other words, the coalition building in modern Russian politics resembles the forging of alliances in nineteenth-century Europe's balance-of-power system. In both systems, ideology matters less than political survival.

Elections

Elections are a common and typically well-documented political activity that is crucial to meaningful democracy. In its first decade as a post-Soviet state, Russia held two presidential elections and three countrywide parliamentary elections. Although the elections have been marred by biased coverage on state-operated media outlets, as well as instances of outright fraud, in general, election results have been accepted by the contenders and the public in general.

Presidential Elections

Post-Soviet Russia's first presidential campaign was held in June 1996—five years after Yeltsin became president of the Russian Soviet republic. Of the 78 presidential candidates that registered, 11 met all the requirements to participate in the election. The candidacies that attracted the most attention were those of Yeltsin (as the incumbent), the Liberal Democratic Party's Vladimir Zhirinovsky (as the most controversial), and the Communist Party of the Russian Federation's (CPRF) Gennady Zyuganov (with the greatest support of potential voters in the spring of 1996).

The 1996 presidential elections were simultaneously a referendum on Yeltsin's leadership (including his handling of the war in Chechnya), a test of the democrats' ability to unite behind a single candidate, and a gauge of the Communists' resurgent strength. Yeltsin was shameless in his election-season populism, making reckless promises about new affluence and governmental accountability. Although few accepted these at face value, Yeltsin's firm verbal commitment to political and economic reform played well with the country's new elites. Yeltsin, with the support of the major media outlets, cast Zyuganov's platform as a return to the stagnation and oppression of the Soviet period under Stalin and Leonid Brezhnev. For his part, Zyuganov portrayed Yeltsin's leadership as misguided and inept, facilitating the decline of Russian prestige and the increase of crime and inequality.

Zyuganov's initial commanding lead waned as the election date approached. It became clear that Russian voters were less concerned about ideology than about their personal living conditions. Many voters said that their decision on whether to support Yeltsin hinged on their assessment of whether he could ensure that salaries and pensions would be paid on time and whether he could restore their lost savings. In the first round, Russians cast the plurality of their vote (35 percent) for Yeltsin. Zyuganov came in second with 32 percent. Immediately afterward Yeltsin appointed the third vote-getter (Aleksandr Lebed) to head the Russian Security Council, and Lebed returned the favor with an endorsement for Yeltsin in the runoff election. Yeltsin made a number of other personnel changes, presumably devised to bolster his reformist credentials.

In the final days of the runoff campaign Yeltsin's health became a major issue. He abruptly canceled campaign appearances and did not show up at a scheduled public appearance on voting day to cast his ballot. Yeltsin had had a history of heart problems, and his time in power had been marked by periodic mysterious absences. Nevertheless, Yeltsin won the second round handily, with 54 percent of the vote to Zyuganov's 40 percent.

Yeltsin's reelection ensured a precious measure of continuity in the morass of post-Soviet Russian politics. Yet it also postponed for another four years a scheduled opportunity to infuse the presidency with a more vibrant, effective leader. Yeltsin's second term ended six months early, however, when he unexpectedly resigned on the final day of 1999. Power passed to the prime minister, Vladimir Putin, in the country's first constitutional transfer of executive power.

Putin's election as president was never seriously in question. As the acting president, he had the advantage of an incumbent. Still, he had genuine opposition and had to run a campaign that spoke to the interests and concerns of the people (which focused on protecting the freedoms that had been won since the Gorbachev period while reducing the social disorder and inequality that had plagued Yeltsin's era).

Putin was elected president in his own right on March 26, 2000. Receiving almost 53 percent of the vote, Putin gained the majority necessary to avoid a runoff election. His nearest competitor was CPRF chairman Zyuganov, who earned about 29 percent of the vote. Although the usual charges of media bias and even instances of voting fraud were made by Putin's opponents, Putin's margin of victory was so large that he almost certainly earned the support of a large plurality of the voters. Perennial democratic opposition candidate Grigory Yavlinsky captured less than 6 percent of the vote, and Vladimr Zhirinovsky earned only about 2.5 percent. Finally, Russia experienced its first peaceful and democratic transfer of executive power—albeit not to an "opposition" candidate.

Parliamentary Elections

Russia's parliamentary elections also reflected the country's success in establishing procedural democracy. Many races were highly competitive, and the results of the elections ensured that a broad range of interests were represented in the state Duma.

Not everyone was pleased with the election results. In 1993 almost a quarter of the popular vote went to Vladimir Zhirinovsky's ultranationalist Liberal Democratic Party. Another 12 percent went to the Communists. But what was most important about Russia's founding election was not so much the distribution of political power that resulted, but the establishment of the principle of popular sovereignty. The general population, the state bureaucrats, and the various parliamentary contestants all accepted the electoral outcome.

The next parliamentary elections, which incorporated new registration procedures, occurred two years later. About 8,000 candidates and 43 parties were registered. But despite the political and geographical fragmentation evident in post-Soviet Russia's first years, electoral politics now seemed to be solidifying around a handful of viable parties. Indeed, over half the deputies elected in 1995 had served in the first Duma, and all but 4 of the 43 parties vying for "party list" seats failed to secure the 5 percent of the vote required to be awarded seats.

This time it was the CPRF that won the largest number of votes cast. And in the words of the British magazine *The Economist*, "Nobody could sensibly accuse Russians, of all people, of voting for Communists in ignorance of the possible consequences." Or could they? The meaning of labels such as communism, reformism, and conservatism had been contorted and twisted during the campaign, throughout the perestroika era, and indeed throughout the Soviet era. And yet the high proportion of votes going to the Communists suggested, at the very least, that a substantial segment of the Russian population desired to balance the presidential "party of power" with opposition forces.

Russia closed out its turbulent and often tragic twentieth century with its third election to the Duma. On December 19, 1999, Russians finally appeared to give the government a working majority in the Duma. Although the CPRF still won the largest number of seats, its percentage of Duma seats had dropped by a third. The number of parties appearing on the ballot had dropped from 43 (in 1995) to 26, and four-fifths of the party votes cast went to the 6 parties that cleared the 5 percent threshold (compared with only one-half in 1995). Clearly the consolidation of Russia's political landscape was continuing, although this landscape had by no means stabilized.

Voter Participation

The final point to be made about Russia's elections is the relatively high level of participation, which ranged between 60 and 70 percent. This is considerably below official participation levels during the Soviet period (which by some accounts exceeded 100%!), but still well above that of many Western democracies. In an era marked by increasing apathy and cynicism about many aspects of their lives, Russians have continued to place value in their hard-won franchise.

Public Opinion

We now return to the question of whether Russia's prospects for achieving democracy depend on the effects of newly created democratic institutions upon the political culture or on the political culture's ability to sustain democratic institutions.

The establishment of democratic political institutions is a necessary but not sufficient condition to create true democracy. For that, the citizenry must accept their government as legitimate, actively convey their interests to the decision-makers, and participate in the selection of their leaders. We have already observed Russians' participation in elections. But how do Russians feel about their government? More importantly, how might the government's ability or inability to address major economic and social conditions affect Russians' support for the government?

Without an appropriate political culture, even democratic institutions can produce very illiberal and antidemocratic policies. Particularly when weakened by public cynicism and resentment brought on by poor living conditions and pervasive malaise, even democratic mechanisms can fail. Weimar Germany is the classic example, and in the early 1990s the economic and societal problems in Yeltsin's country gave rise to the term "Weimar Russia." Even Putin's election in 2000 has raised concern among some observers who fear that Russians are coming to believe that only "strong measures" (generally meaning some curtailment of civil liberties and expansion of police powers) can keep the specter of chaos at bay. There are indeed significant domestic problems that Russian must overcome. Since the collapse of the Soviet Union, male life expectancy has dropped to about 57 years, once-eradicated diseases have reemerged, many basic consumer goods are unaffordable or in short supply, and drug abuse is rampant. Enormous inequality in the distribution of wealth is starkly evident. And intractable ethno-regional and nationalistic conflicts threaten to divide the country's population.

Public opinion about living conditions is sobering. In the summer of 2000, almost a third of Russians indicated that living conditions are "unbearable" and half labeled them as "difficult but endurable." Moreover, almost 90 percent of Russians believe their incomes are not adequate to cover basic needs. Assessing the direction of change, 17 percent of Russians believed that their material well-being was improving, whereas 39 percent believed it was getting worse and 43 percent thought it was not changing.

These attitudes affect public behavior, threatening to create a vicious circle. With public cynicism and frustration on the rise, the Russian state has had difficulty consolidating its authority over its citizens. With about half of Russian citizens refusing to pay taxes, the state cannot collect enough revenue to fund its operations. The state is politically unstable, with various groups and regions threatening to secede and with major constitutional conflicts festering within the government. Extraconstitutional activity by business tycoons, criminal syndicates, military officers, and religious leaders challenge the authority of the state. It will take time, wise policies, and a good measure of luck before the Russian state emerges from its crisis.

While material living conditions are the subject of widespread concern, Russians generally look favorably on the concept of Western-style democracy. In fact, at the opening of the twenty-first century almost 90 percent of the population considers democracy to be a desirable goal. But do Russians believe this is being achieved? Looking retrospectively shortly after Yeltsin's resignation, about a quarter of Russians identified "democracy, political rights, and freedom" as a positive result of Yeltsin's tenure. Smaller percentages of Russians identified outcomes such as the restoration of private property and the improvement of relations with the West. At the same time, 46 percent could not name any positive result from Yeltsin's tenure.

Although Russians generally support democracy in the abstract, their opinions about particular issues suggest that they either support other values (such as order) more than democracy, or perhaps they have a view of democracy that is quite different from that in the West. On the subject of civil liberties, a June 2000 poll found that 43 percent believed Russia had no or only limited freedom of speech, 25 percent thought the country's level of freedom of speech was normal for a democratic country, and 22 percent believed there was too much freedom of speech. Similarly, about half the population was against limits of speech, whereas about a quarter believed speech limits can be good, and 18 percent were apathetic to the topic. A majority also seem to believe that it might sometimes be necessary to rein in fundamental democratic principles to contend with other issues. For example, the percentage of Russians agreeing that the president should have the power to suspend the parliament and rule by decree rose from 51 percent in 1993 to 67 percent shortly after Putin's election in the spring of 2000.

Crucial will be the public's future willingness to tolerate the hardships associated with the transition to democracy and capitalism—or, conversely, its willingness to support leaders and policies that sacrifice democratic ideals on the altar of "social order" or "economic stability." One of the greatest causes for hope in Russia's successful transition to democracy lies in demographics. The "democrats" and "reformers" tend to be younger as well as better educated and urban. There is also a strong correlation between support for democratic reforms and improving living conditions—where, at the present time, most Russians do not find themselves. This highlights the important linkage between economic conditions (or the results of economic reforms) and political conditions (or the support for democratic reformers). This chicken-and-egg conundrum is exacerbated by two legacies of the Soviet era: a high level of public mobilization and an expectation that basic needs will be assured.

Timing is everything. When he first assumed power, Yeltsin argued that Russia could make the transition to democracy and capitalism in a few years. When he resigned seven years later, he admitted that he had been too optimistic. If Putin slows the pace of reform any further to minimize short-term pain, he risks public fatigue with a process that shows few results. Yet his mandate appears not to be one of instituting shock therapy. The next decade will be crucial. A poll in early 2000 found that 87 percent of Russians believe that Russian society is not "normal," requiring changes in economic security, governmental stability, social conditions, and other factors. More than half of these expect such changes to be accomplished within six to ten years; however, almost 30 percent believe Russian society will never become "normal."

Conclusion

Russia's history, demographics, economic infrastructure, and culture affect how it fares in its quest for democracy. Russia's political development, as halting and problematic as it had been, was hijacked in 1917, and the ensuing Soviet period created political and social abnormalities that were not faced by many other democratizing countries. These factors present very little in the way of resources for a successful transition and much in the way of obstacles.

Although the Russian people clearly prefer democracy to the alternatives they have experienced in the past and while Russian leaders have managed to establish formal, structural democracy in the country, Russian democracy nevertheless remains exceedingly weak. The economy performs poorly, corruption is widespread, civil society and other democratic institutions remain tenuous, the leadership is thin, and government has proved inept at delivering goods and services to the population. Nor is it clear how deeply and thoroughly democratic sentiments (support for rule of law, egalitarianism, fairness, and justice) have infused the political culture. The weakness of democracy and democratic institutions and their failure to deliver help account for the continuing popularity of antidemocratic politicians, such as the "new" communists, as well as demogogic appeals and popular disillusionment with democracy itself.

And yet we have not seen in Russia, as seen elsewhere in this book, either a wholesale rejection of democracy or an attempt to develop a new, indigenous, *Russian* theory of democracy. We do see widespread resentment of the West, some bitterness, some nostalgia for the old Marxist-Leninist regime, and sometimes the assertion of "Slavophile" values over Western ones. These sentiments typically manifest themselves in calls for stronger government, greater discipline, nationalism, and more authority—often reminiscent of the czars or the old Communist regime. So far, however, these sentiments have neither implied the formulation of a new antidemocratic ideology nor presented an alternative to democracy.

Like many new or emerging democracies, Russia still has a long way to go in developing and consolidating its democratic institutions, and it will continue to show strains of the older authoritarianism. Russia is thus a "mixed" system—a weak and underdeveloped democracy—but it shows few signs of completely abandoning the democratic path in favor of some other option. The greater threat is that, lacking improved success in the medium term, a progressive deterioration of the economic and political systems could undermine the foundations of Russia's fledgling democracy and create conditions for an antidemocratic putsch. The coming years will be critical indeed.

Suggested Readings

Aron, Leon R., *Yeltsin: A Revolutionary Life*. London: HarperCollins, 2000.

Boilard, Steve D., *Reinterpreting Russia: An Annotated Bibliography of Books on Russia, the Soviet Union, and the Russian Federation, 1991–1996*. Lanham, MD: Scarecrow Press, 1997.

Boilard, Steve D., *Russia at the Twenty-First Century: Politics and Social Change in the Post-Soviet Era*. Fort Worth: Harcourt Brace, 1998.

Braginskii, Sergei., *Incentives and Institutions: The Transition to a Market Economy in Russia*. Princeton, NJ: Princeton University Press, 2000.

Cox, Michael, ed., *Rethinking the Soviet Collapse: Sovietology, the Death of Communism and the New Russia*. New York: Pinter, 1998.

Field, Mark G. and Judyth L. Twigg, eds., *Russia's Torn Safety Nets: Health and Social Welfare During the Transition*. New York: St. Martin's Press, 2000.

Gaidar, Egor. *Days of Defeat and Victory* (tr. by Jane Ann Miller). Seattle: University of Washington Press, 1999.

Hancock, M. Donald and John Logue, eds., *Transitions to Capitalism and Democracy in Russia and Central Europe: Achievements, Problems, Prospects*. Westport, CT: Praeger, 2000.

Husband, William B., ed., *The Human Tradition in Modern Russia*. Wilmington, DE: SR Books, 2000.

Nagy, Proska, *The Meltdown of the Russian State: The Deformation and Collapse of the State in Russia*. Cheltenham: Edward Elgar, 2000.

Nichols, Thomas M., *The Russian Presidency: Society and Politics in the Second Russian Republic*. New York: St. Martin's Press. 1999.

Nicholson, Martin, *Towards a Russia of the Regions.* New York: Oxford University Press, 1999.

Riasanovsky, Nicholas V., *A History of Russia*, 6th ed. New York: Oxford University Press, 2000.

Robinson, Neil, ed., *Institutions and Political Change in Russia.* New York: St. Martin's Press, 2000.

Shaw, Denis J. B., *Russia in the Modern World: A New Geography.* Oxford: Blackwell, 1999.

Shleifer, Andrei, *Without a Map: Political Tactics and Economic Reform in Russia.* Cambridge, MA: MIT Press, 2000.

Silverman, Bertram, *New Rich, New Poor, New Russia: Winners and Losers on the Russian Road to Capitalism.* Armond, NY: M.E. Sharpe, 2000.

Treadgold, Donald W., *Twentieth Century Russia*, 9th ed. Boulder, CO: Westview Press, 2000.

Ulrich, Marybeth Peterson, *Democratizing Communist Militaries: The Cases of the Czech and Russian Armed Forces.* Ann Arbor: University of Michigan Press, 1999.

Weigle, Marcia A., *Russia's Liberal Project: State-Society Relations in the Transition from Communism.* University Park, PA: Pennsylvania State University Press, 2000.

Woodruff, David, *Money Unmade: Barter and the Fate of Russian Capitalism.* Ithaca, NY: Cornell University Press, 1999.

Yeltsin, Boris, *The Struggle for Russia.* New York: Times Books, 1995.

5

East Asia: Democratization from the Top

Peter R. Moody, Jr.

Even if the crisis of 1997 put the "East Asian economic miracle" into a more realistic perspective, the region as a whole has still met the challenges of modernization more successfully than any other non-Western area and may have handled the social and cultural pathologies of modernization better than the Western heartland.

In this chapter East Asia is viewed more as a cultural concept than a geographical one. It is a synonym for the "post-Confucian" societies: China, Taiwan, Japan, Korea, Vietnam, and, at a stretch, Hong Kong and Singapore. "Post-Confucian" may not be the ideal term, but it does no harm if used carefully. Before their incorporation into the contemporary global economy by Western imperialism in the 1800s, the elite cultures of these societies were based upon variations of the Chinese model and accorded legal and social approbation to loose congeries of ideas, practices, attitudes, and texts, which can be classified under the rubric "Confucianism."[1] The "post" indicates that if Confucianism (in some way) can be said to characterize these societies in precontemporary times, they are no longer Confucian in precisely that way. These societies have sufficient similarities among themselves and sufficient differences from other societies to allow useful and interesting comparative analysis.

During most of the final quarter of the twentieth century these societies enjoyed vigorous economic growth when they had a strong central government and a nonsocialist economic system (or a socialist system that had become highly attenuated, as in China in the 1980s and 1990s and Vietnam during the early 1990s). If democracy is considered the heart of political modernization, the record is more mixed. China, the largest post-Confucian society, is not democratic, despite evidence of the great social appeal of democracy. Yet Japan seemed to be developing a parliamentary democracy indigenously in the 1920s (a process aborted by military rule in the 1930s) and has been a stable democracy since the late 1940s. During the 1980s Taiwan and South Korea also evolved in a democratic direction, with democracy seemingly solidly established by the turn of the century.

Post-Confucian Democracy

In 1993 Asian countries caucused in Bangkok in preparation for a United Nations conference on human rights. They produced a statement (Japan and the Philippines opposing) on "Asian values." This statement argued that the concept of human rights is not limited to the Western (particularly American) version of it. Its Western version, however, is a product of Western culture and history and cannot be mechanically applied elsewhere. "Asia," the delegates asserted, has its own standards and has no need of lessons from the likes of the United States on how to respect human decency.

At that time most of the Asian states were enjoying an economic boom while America was seen as economically flaccid, its society beset by crime and immorality, yet determined to bully the rest of the world through an unjustified moral arrogance backed up by military threats. The Asian values theme, traceable to the musings of Singapore's elder statesman Lee Kwan Yew, was, understandably, embraced with particular ardor by the more openly tyrannical regimes, such as Burma (Myanmar) and China. Taken as a concept it is incoherent. Asia is a geographic expression and includes an enormous diversity of cultures, many of these differing as much from each other as any one of them may differ from the culture of the "West" (there is perhaps greater resonance between the "values" of premodern Europe and premodern China, say, than between either of them and those of India). Admittedly, persons reared in Asian cultures may well find what they consider the ultra-individualism of contemporary Western (here, too, especially American) society both foreign and distasteful. Dogmatic insistence on Western liberal standards leads to a most illiberal intolerance of alternative and legitimate ways people might prefer to arrange their lives. On the other hand, there is nothing particularly

"Asian" about hard work, respect for parents, or concern for the general good, and one might make a case that the Asian values argument is more validly directed against perversions of Western values than against Western values as such. The financial troubles of 1997 deflated some of the claims about Asian values. But, given all this, some of the Asian value claims seem to be simple truths. The vision of human rights current in the "West" is, whatever its universal validity, a product of particular historical and cultural circumstances, and few would dispute the abstract desirability of most of what was touted as Asian values (e.g., hard work, etc.).

Culture, Values, and Democracy

The analysis of culture is often treated as an explication of values and their supposed consequences for action and behavior. It may be more useful, however, to go a bit deeper to examine the general vision of the world that underpins the values, without necessarily expecting any direct or simple association between political culture and political behavior. The Confucian tradition is sometimes considered (even or especially by persons living in it) an obstacle to democracy, just as a generation and more ago it was considered an obstacle to economic development. The "traditional" Confucian societies were certainly not democratic, no more than were the traditional Christian societies in Europe. There is much in Confucian thinking that emphasized hierarchy and respect for proper authority. As one of Confucius's smugger students is supposed to have said: One who honors his father and mother is unlikely to disobey his prince.

But even in its classic form, Chinese Confucianism, at any rate, never advocated blind obedience to authority. One serves one's prince or one's parents not by obedience but by acting in good faith in the interests of one's prince or parents, and the overriding interest of the prince, his moral imperative, is, whether he knows it or not, to serve the people. Mencius stresses that political authority exists for the sake of the people and is justified only insofar as it benefits the people. Social roles are and must be hierarchical, and moral persons conform to the proper expectations of the roles they acquire. But the hierarchy adheres only to roles, not to persons as such, and every human being has the potential, with proper effort, training, and environment, to become a "sage," the highest development of humanity.

Confucian thinking may have an abstract bias toward democracy, once it has the occasion. This is clearly seen in the Chinese "democracy movement" of 1989 but even in some Confucian commentary from the mid-1800s. One Chinese work of that time (preoccupied with the wickedness of the English, who had just fought and won the Opium War) described how in America George Washington and others of the "local gentry" joined together to defeat the British and gain their freedom. The "multitude" wanted to make

Washington their king, but he said that would be selfish: "The duty of looking after the state should be carried on by those who have virtue."[2]

Democracy, perhaps in a relatively elitist version, may be in the contemporary era the political form most congenial to the erstwhile Confucian mentality. It is striking how relatively much political discontent and instability there was in even the most economically prosperous Asian states in their post–World War II authoritarian phases. One plausible hypothesis is that political legitimacy in contemporary East Asia rests on democracy.

Culture and Structure: The State in East Asia

Just because we value something, however, does not mean that we get it. In addition to stressing the "deep structure" of social values, cultural analysis might also look at "structures" characteristic of particular societies, which help fashion the behavior of persons in those societies—sets of rules, customs, and rituals, explicit or tacit—to which persons must more or less conform if they wish to function in the particular culture.

The most relevant political structure in East Asia is the *autonomous* state.[3] As used here, the term does not mean simply that the state operates independently of social pressures, but that the state shapes the social order. The "paradigm" is the traditional Chinese system, whereby the political elite was selected through competitive state-sponsored examinations, with those who passed the examinations also constituting the social elite.

Such a structure runs counter to Western expectations, where the political system is usually seen as a reflection of an underlying socioeconomic structure. Marx famously considered the liberal state to be the executive committee of the bourgeoisie (to be replaced by the dictatorship of the proletariat), but in broad terms Plato and Aristotle, as well as contemporary liberals, share this vision. For the Greeks, democracy, rule by the "people," really meant rule by the "many," which amounted to rule by and in the interests of the poor. In liberal democracy (considered as an "ideal type"), state policy is a kind of vector sum of various social forces, with the state serving as the umpire of disputes among those forces.

An autonomous state in the sense used here need not be a *strong* state, that is, a state exercising effective control over society (nor need a nonautonomous state be weak). One reason for East Asia's past economic success was that the state in prosperous societies was both autonomous and strong: the state could set policy directed toward its own wealth and power without worrying too much about indulging private interests and could effectively carry out these policies. A consequence of a weak state in East Asia has typically been what the Chinese call chaos, *luan*—a corollary of the dependence of the social structure on the political foundation. None of this should be taken to imply that the various soldiers and technocrats who ruled the autonomous state were always filled with public spirit. Indeed, when the state is weak, corruption, unchecked by mechanisms making officialdom responsible to society, becomes a norm. Rather, they were interested in fostering the power of the state or of those institutions within it to which they belonged, and for much of the Cold War era growth with equity served state interests. Nor should this language imply that the state is a monolithic, single-interest entity. The normal expectation would be a high degree of fractionalization along institutional and personal lines, with state strength checking these tendencies toward fractionalization.

Under these conditions political mobilization tends to occur along lines of personal connections rather than by class or economic interest. Local political commentary focuses on the dynamics of factional alliances and maneuvering in the court of the ruler. The social institutions characteristic of "civil society" tend to be weak. Because social interests are weak and government rule is not based on any particular set of social interests, rulers are often able to co-opt elements of the opposition, so dividing it. The opposition, for its part, tends toward extremism, a radical stance against the rulers serving as (a not always reliable) signal that one has not been co-opted.

This "post-Confucian" pattern implies, given the weakness of social forces generally, that social forces pushing for democracy will be weak, despite the general approbation for democracy by both regime and opposition. The rulers have at least a minimal interest in sticking together against the opposition. The opposition, in the absence of representative institutions, have no such incentive to cohere and often dissipate what strength they have in quarrels among themselves over who is politically the most pure and intransigent.

The 1989 Tiananmen demonstrations in China showed some of these effects. The protesters displayed impressive organizational ability in holding down acts of vandalism, but they had no solid leadership core—indeed, they were afraid that to set up such a thing would lead to their followers criticizing them as undemocratic. As the weeks wore on, newcomers kept streaming into Peking, all eager not to miss out on the action—so that even if those who had spent days and days camped out on the square were longing for more comfortable quarters, there were plenty of others to take their place. As the regime gave increasing signs of turning nasty, those holding visible positions of leadership over the protest hinted that maybe the point had been made and now it was time to back off a little. Other would-be leaders, assured of a receptive audience, then condemned the old leadership group as being weak and cowardly and lacking ideals, unwilling to carry the struggle through to the end. To indulge in too much of this kind of analysis smacks of blaming the victim, and nothing here excuses the brutality of the regime once it did lose patience. But the situation was structured with a bias toward confrontation, not democratic development.

The weakness of social institutions cuts both ways. If social forces promoting democracy are weak, under proper circumstances there need not be many obstacles to democracy. Democracy in East Asia has been a consequence of the adoption of democratic, or more precisely, representative, institutions. There are social demands for democracy, but democracy results from its imposition from the top. Civil society and grass roots activity from below remain weak. The rulers (it is hypothesized) turn to democratic institutions when it suits them to do so: when they need to humor foreigners, deflect responsibility for certain problems from themselves, devolve authority over decisions for the sake of greater efficiency, defuse popular discontent they are not prepared to repress, or deflect support for the opposition, or for other more or less noble or ignoble reasons. In the short term democratization will not threaten the position of the ruling group, although over the longer run, if it is genuine, it should reduce the autonomy of the state, making the state more responsive to social forces.

Japan as a Post-Confucian Democracy

It is sometimes asserted (say, by critics of American moral posturing) that democracy cannot be imposed. A consideration of contemporary Japan refutes this assertion. Since the late 1940s, in no small measure as a result of the American Occupation, Japan has had free and fair elections, full civil liberties, and, at the official and state level, the rule of law.

This democracy was not entirely novel, however, for there had previously been an evolution toward democracy, and a look at "indigenous" Japanese democratic development may give hints into both the prospects and limitations of the process in East Asia. In 1889 Japan adopted a written constitution, the first non-Western state to do so. In form the Constitution was "bestowed" upon the people by the emperor who, in principle, retained full executive, legislative, and judicial sovereignty—delegating these functions to the institutions of the state. In practice Japan was a constitutional monarchy, albeit one with a very strong executive. Behind the forms, actual political power into the early 1900s was held by the state founders (the *genro*) who, a generation earlier, had begun to build Japan's modern political, economic, and social system.

The Constitution provided for a legislature, the *Diet*.[4] The Diet had very limited ability on paper to control the actions of the Cabinet or Government, which on paper was appointed by the emperor and in practice designated by the genro. The Diet served in part as an outlet for public opinion hostile to the genro's modernizing reforms, that hostility coming from both traditionalistic and Western liberal directions. The opposition to the new state had begun to form political parties as early as the 1870s, and despite stringent limitations on the franchise (only very wealthy men were allowed to vote), these parties found representation in the Diet. Although the Government could live with this, things would be more convenient had it some legislative support, and after 1890 some of the genro sponsored a pro-Government party, in effect buying politicians willing to talk and vote the Government line.

Once instituted, the Government party acquired an interest in enhancing its own position in the Diet and the position of the Diet in the political system. By the end of the first decade of the twentieth century the genro were dying off. The emperor, although formally empowered to appoint the prime minister, was supposed to "transcend" all political divisions and not make political choices. The convention gradually emerged that the prime minister would be the leader of the dominant party in the Diet's (elected) lower house—a pattern familiar from British political development.

To the extent that the Japanese parties, really collections of politicians, had a social base, the pro-Government party represented the urban rich and the opposition represented the rural rich. Party government tended to focus on jockeying for positions of personal benefit, with elections conducted on the basis of patron-client ties and personal favors rather than on issues and principles. The party governments mostly took their cues from bureaucratic and business cabals. A favored campaign technique was to hire goon squads to disrupt the rallies of the other party.

Even so, throughout the early 1920s the Diet voted to extend the franchise, so by 1925 all men over the age of 25 enjoyed the vote, regardless of wealth or income. The expectation of whichever party was in power was that the new voters would be grateful to the government which had empowered them. The larger and more diverse electorate raised the possibility that the parties might actually have to address interests not indulged by the ruling establishment—those, say, of factory workers or poor farmers.

This, too, has parallel in the English tradition. The English parties, most creatively the Tories, did adapt to the new conditions by incorporating new interests into their program. The British state, although a relatively strong one, was not autonomous in the sense used in this chapter. It took its cue from civil society. In Japan the state was sufficiently autonomous to spare the parties the trouble of adaptation: Rather than attempting to co-opt potentially radial social forces, it was more convenient to repress them. The extension of the franchise was followed by the passage of the Peace Preservation Law. Democratic forms remained unconnected to a popular base, and Diet legislation that in the 1920s had been used to curb socialists and communists was turned against ordinary people and the party politicians themselves by the military rulers in the ensuing decade.

The Japanese political system in the 1930s took on some of the fascist tone of its German and Italian allies. Among the many differences between Japanese fascism (if that really is the appropriate word) and the European original, however, is the absence in Japan of any mass-based antidemocratic movement. The trouble was that neither was there any mobilization of popular support for democracy. There were, of course, limited opportunities at best for any such mobilization, but as far as the general public was concerned, democracy had come to be identified with self-serving conflicts within a corrupt oligarchy.

Under the American Occupation, Japan rewrote its Constitution, establishing a genuine parliamentary system, with the government selected by and responsible to the Diet. The vote was extended to the full adult population: men and women over the age of 20. With the constitutional guarantees of civil liberties, communists and socialists and other antiestablishment types were able to voice their opinions and organize political parties.

Students of contemporary Japanese politics are familiar with the so-called "1955 system." In 1955 the noncommunist left joined to form a United Socialist Party, setting up the possibility that they might actually capture the government. The conservative politicians, previously organized (so to speak) in various squabbling smaller parties, most of which traced their roots to the prewar parliamentary parties, joined together in the Liberal Democratic Party (LDP), to guarantee a united conservative tendency to face the leftist threat. The LDP kept sufficient strength in the lower house of the Diet to maintain control of the government until 1993, with the socialists permanently in opposition. Over the decades the LDP's share of the popular vote fell, but the defectors went less often to the Socialists (whose popularity declined even more steeply) than to a set of minor parties.

The LDP tended to take its policy cues from the professional civil service (many of its leaders were retired bureaucrats) and its money from big business. LDP control of the Diet meant virtually automatic legislative endorsement for a decision-making system dominated by the bureaucracy, which governed in the interests of business but also kept business subordinated to administrative guidance. Despite the formal (and real) democratic structure, Japan was governed in a way reminiscent of the old Latin American bureaucratic–authoritarian model, albeit without the brutality that term implies.

The Japanese parties were not entirely without social bases. The Socialists received support from segments of organized labor; the LDP was financed by big business and courted votes from farmers and small business (so Japan enjoyed extraordinarily high prices for food and consumer goods). Although the LDP continued to cultivate these interests, during the 1970s it evolved into a catch-all party, addressing whatever electoral concerns it was expedient to address.

This is somewhat misleading, though, because the main LDP appeal to the electorate continued to rest on direct or indirect personal ties. It was not quite the same old patron-client system, since now the politicians had to grovel for votes rather than command them. But votes were solicited less on the basis of appeal to opinion or collective interest than on constituency service—from pork barrel projects to special favors to outright vote buying. LDP politicians worked their constituencies by means of organizations loyal to them personally, not the larger party, and they received less outside support from the party than from the parliamentary LDP faction to which they belonged.

When public discontent with particular social ills (say, pollution) reached a point where it might endanger LDP control of the political system, the bureaucracy and the Diet could deal with these ills (without too much worry about opposition from business interests which might just as soon continue to pollute), but generally there was a lack of connection between political opinion and the electoral process. Party "politics" consisted of LDP factions and faction leaders combining with and betraying each other, maneuvering for positions of government leadership. The process made for interesting and entertaining journalism, but not necessarily for democratic accountability.

The 1955 system collapsed in the early 1990s, a result not of the LDP's being displaced by anything else but, rather, a fragmentation of the party. Problems associated with the breakup included out-of-control corruption (itself reflecting the ever more insatiable need of politicians for money to keep up the nurture of their constituencies) during the era of the bubble economy in the 1980s. Bad feelings left over from earlier fights made it difficult for certain factions to keep up the flexibility in making alliances characteristic of a classical balance of power system and to this were added bitter personal rivalries within the party's largest faction. At the same time, by the 1990s socialism (or any radical break with the existing order) had become irrelevant (the Socialists were reduced to having fewer than 30 seats in the 500-some member lower house), removing the incentive of the LDP to cohere.

At the end of the century the LDP remained Japan's largest party, its major opposition being unstable secessionist fragments of the party. Attempts to join the Socialist and other opposition parties with each other and with different rumps of the LDP had generally failed. To keep power the LDP had to rely on coalitions, some of which were grotesquely unprincipled (at one point there was a coalition of the LDP with the Socialists). In structure the Japanese party system resembled what Giovanni Sartori calls polarized pluralism[5] (as in Italy or Third or Fourth Republic France), without the historical religious, economic, and other social cleavages that underlay the European examples.

Democracy, as mentioned earlier, should theoretically undermine state autonomy, although in Japan it did so only to a limited degree. By the 1990s general prosperity and globalization impaired the ability of bureaucracy to control policy as it previously had. In the 1980s there was academic speculation that Japan was moving toward what should properly be expected of a democracy—political, particularly legislative, control over policy. The evidence, however, to caricature only a little bit, seemed to amount to an ability of Diet members to persuade bureaucrats to direct resources to the members' constituents in such a way as to enhance the members' tenure in office. The new polarized pluralist system and coalition governments are unlikely to enhance democratic responsibility. Initiative is likely to revert to the bureaucracy—now less able than before to exercise that initiative.

East Asian Transitions

At the turn of the century it seems proper to include both South Korea and Taiwan along with Japan as East Asia's democracies. Despite differences from Japan and from each other, these new democracies show elements of the post-Confucian pattern. Both had a strong and autonomous state during most of the Cold War era. Both had vigorous but incohesive opposition movements, with democracy installed from above through the development or activation of democratic institutions. In both countries democratization provided the entrenched authorities a way to resolve certain of their problems without, in the short run, endangering their positions.

Although Taiwan and South Korea had democratic institutions "on the books," in practice, until the late 1980s, both were harshly authoritarian, Korea perhaps more consistently harsh than Taiwan, but also, paradoxically, more tolerant of open political opposition. The Taiwan regime was the remnants of the political system organized by the Nationalist Party (Kuomintang or KMT) and Chiang Kai-shek, expelled from the China mainland in 1949. Rule on Taiwan was based on a combination of the KMT, the technocratic executive bureaucracy, the military, and the political police, coordinated by a strongman leader, first Chiang Kai-shek and later his son, Chiang Ching-kuo. Korea was also governed by a technocracy that held power at the sufferance of the military, the core of the regime being the intelligence-secret police service, first and most famously known as the Korean Central Intelligence Agency (KCIA). As in Taiwan, there was a strongman to coordinate the various institutional and personal forces within the regime, first Park Chung Hee and later, less effectively, Chun Doo Hwan.

It is often asserted that democratization in Korea and Taiwan reflected the power of a prosperous middle class. But the middle class enjoyed prosperity in both polities long before democratization, and elsewhere in East Asia (prominently in Singapore and possibly in Hong Kong) there is reason to believe that the middle class may prefer stability and predictability to democracy. A strong middle class was not a sufficient condition for democratization and may not even have been necessary. This certainly does not mean that the general prosperity of these societies was irrelevant: if nothing less, by the 1980s it had taken off the edge of any appeal to radical alternatives, and so reduced the risk to the ruling elite entailed by democratization. On the whole, however, East Asian democratization may stem from more directly political causes.

On Taiwan, by the early 1970s Chiang Kai-shek was in unofficial retirement (he died of great old age in 1975), and daily control of the regime was exercised by his son Chiang Ching-kuo, the architect of Taiwan's police state. During the earlier part of the transition Ching-kuo was also hailed (especially by the official media) as the architect of Taiwan's democracy. This last theme was more or less ignored during the 1990s, but still has some validity.

By the early 1970s the founding generation of mainlanders was beginning to slide into death and the United States was in the process of abandoning its commitment to Taiwan for the sake of cultivating good relations with the People's Republic of China (PRC). It appears that Chiang Ching-kuo concluded that if the regime were to survive it had to sink deeper roots into Taiwan itself. He encouraged the recruitment of natives of Taiwan province into the party and bureaucracy and also sponsored a limited number of new elections to the national Legislature (which previously had been filled with lawmakers elected on the mainland in 1948). He did not permit the opposition to organize official parties, but tolerated informal collaboration among opposition politicians in the elections and in the legislature.

A decade later Ching-kuo himself, at his best never as healthy as his father, was increasingly incapacitated. Lacking direction from a strong leader the regime began to drift. A confrontational opposition election rally in 1979 grew into a riot (perhaps because of police provocation) and resulted in the imprisonment for sedition of the more outspoken opposition leaders. In the early 1980s there were a series of almost-certainly political murders of figures associated with the opposition, with elements of the regime definitely proven to be implicated in at least one of them. Theretofore respected members of the older generation of the mainlander elite were implicated in a large financial scandal. Rumors circulated that Chiang Ching-kuo was hoping to transfer the leadership to one of *his* sons, and, indeed, that young man (who seemed to have been involved in at least one of the murders) appeared to be trying to carve out a power base for himself in the security system and in the underworld.

To his credit, Chiang Ching-kuo seems to have recognized the basic flaw in the regime setup: no one in the successor generation had sufficient connections in all the regime's bureaucratic and military power bases to serve as a new strongman. His unusually creative response was to further open up the political system, reactivating the dormant democratic constitutional functions. As his last vice president he selected Lee Teng-hui, a Taiwanese technocrat. He further expanded the scope of elections. He sent his son, a scapegrace, into exile in Singapore and made his scariest security chief ambassador to Paraguay. He revoked emergency rule and tolerated the opposition's coalescence into a formal political party, the Democratic Progressive Party (DPP), even though this was still technically illegal.

Lee Teng-hui assumed the presidency in 1988, upon Chiang Ching-kuo's death. It suited both his convictions and his political advantage to work to consolidate the democratic development. Other bureaucratic oligarchs, most of them (but not all) mainlanders, questioned Lee's primacy, so Lee found it expedient to appeal to public opinion and to present himself as the embodiment of a distinctly Taiwanese consciousness. Younger mainlander reformers assisted him in his maneuvers, only later to be abandoned once they had served Lee's purposes.[6] Lee was in no position to be a Chiang-style "strongman," but he exploited to the full the constitutional powers of the presidency to control the army and bureaucracy (leaving former potentates of the police state to whine about his dictatorial tendencies). He continued Chiang's trend of enhancing the role of the elected institutions. The Legislature came to be wholly elected by the people of Taiwan.[7] The Constitution was amended to mandate the direct popular election of the president, replacing the earlier indirect election, in effect both strengthening and popularizing the formal position of the president while enhancing the sense that Taiwan was a distinct political entity, not a "part" of China.

The main obstacle to Taiwan's democratic consolidation is the outside one, the role of China. The PRC implies that should Taiwan continue to refuse to "reunify" peacefully, a resort to force is inevitable. But the more democratic Taiwan becomes, the more tenuous the ROC's political connection with its mainland roots and the less likely peaceful reunification. It might have been thought that fear of war and conquest would limit the consolidation of democracy. But at the turn of the century this was a risk the Taiwan people seemed willing to take, or, to put it another way, the process of democratization had overwhelmed any prudential scruples blocking it.

Political mobilization by the DPP and other popular opposition forces was certainly among the pressures the ruling regime had to meet, but the scope of mobilization was limited by what the regime would at any point tolerate. The regime's freedom from a social base allowed it to co-opt the DPP's positions and, by the turn of the century, there was little real difference between the KMT and DPP platforms. America is often faulted for supporting authoritarian dictatorships such as those in Taiwan and South Korea, although it could equally plausibly be argued that their connection with the United States kept these regimes less repressive than they otherwise might have been. Fear of American abandonment motivated some of Taiwan's earlier transition, and democracy helped keep Taiwan in American favor in times of trade tensions and American desire to conciliate the mainland.

Both social and American pressures may have played a greater role in South Korea's democratization. Korean development strategy stressed the formation of state-dependent big business combinations on the Japanese model but without the Japanese paternalism, and Korean labor tended to be considerably more militant than the Taiwanese. Before democratization, however, most politically relevant protest was conducted by perennially disgruntled students, supported by some religious groups.

Korea has a longer experience of representative institutions than Taiwan and also a considerably more turbulent recent history. Korea has had (in principle) legal toleration of political opposition since the 1940s, but the ruling regimes were seldom shy about suppressing its expression. The old dictator Syngman Rhee was brought down in 1960 by student protests, with the army standing benignly by. A year later the army seized control, in a coup masterminded by a young and ambitious Park Chung Hee, from a disorderly democracy. Park ruled under a few different constitutional forms until his murder in 1979 by his security chief, with labor and student unrest forming the social context for the murder. A brief period of quasidemocratic chaos was ended by another coup by general Chun Doo Huan. Chun's coup was a bloody one, especially in the southeastern city of Kwangju, where several hundred persons were killed by Special Forces troops, and the bloodshed at Kwangju made it impossible for Chun ever to legitimate his rule.

Park consolidated his hold on the regime by having himself elected president in ostensibly competitive elections and his most outspoken critic, Kim Dae Jung, once even came close to beating him. Chun also had himself elected president after his coup. Before Kwangju the sense of disorder was fed by squabbling among Park's older political opponents: Kim Dae Jung (a native of Kwangju), the slightly less confrontational Kim Young Sam, and Kim Jong Pil, the founder of the KCIA, Park's cousin and consigliere, who had fallen out with Park by the early 1970s. The refusal of the three Kims to cooperate with each other left the field open to the existing establishment.

The democratic breakthrough of 1987 came from a split in that establishment. Chun intrigued, in violation of an earlier promise, to extend his hold on power, precipitating student protests, with the students taking heart from the earlier "people power" movement in the Philippines and Chun's ambitious colleagues from the American refusal to back up President Marcos. Chun's deputy, Roh Tae Woo, "capitulated" to opposition demands, rightly confident that once again the three Kims would fight among themselves rather than unite to oppose him. Roh won the presidential election with a small plurality of the popular vote, less than 40 percent, with the Kims splitting the majority among themselves.

This was, however, the first really fair election since 1960, and Roh's authority rested on election rather than intimidation. Kim Young Sam won the next election, allying himself with the Park-Chun-Roh forces to defeat Kim Dae Jung. The next time round Dae Jung won over the old establishment, forming a highly unprincipled alliance with Kim Jong Pil. There was less, perhaps, to this transfer of power to a new tendency than might have been expected, because any populist inclinations Kim Dae Jong might have had were dampened by the 1997 Asian crisis and the disciplines imposed by the International Monetary Fund (constraints that Park Chung Hee, cruel tyrant and generally mean person though he was, would have successfully rejected as contrary to Korean national dignity).

Democracy is probably not yet as solid in Taiwan or Korea as it is in Japan, but there may be better-functioning systems of democratic responsibility. It has become conventional political science wisdom that democracy is more easily consolidated with a parliamentary system than with a presidential one.[8] Where democratic institutions are weak and the rule of law is poorly developed, a president may become little better than an elected dictator. The Japanese experience shows, however, that at least in the East Asian context a parliamentary system may work to keep policy initiative in the control of an unelected bureaucracy, deflecting the politicians to fights among themselves for office and spoils. Chun in 1987 and Lee Teng-hui's opponents in the early 1990s persuasively argued the merits of a parliamentary system. The concentration of authority in the president, however, may allow for a democratic "capture" of the system as a whole, bringing the bureaucracy, no doubt with some compromises, into obedience. While both the Taiwan and Korean democracies do show traces of executive arrogance, on the whole presidentialism seems to have helped democratic consolidation.

Democracy in East Asia

Japanese democracy in the 1920s and especially since the 1980s has been associated with money politics, and money plays a perhaps inordinate role in Taiwanese and Korean democracy as well. Electoral politics everywhere, of course, is notoriously expensive. Democratic politics taken in itself reduces state autonomy, making the state more responsive to social interests and opinions. As power in the state shifts to those who hold authority because they win elections, the state might well become more responsive to those who provide the money. Whether coincidentally or not, democratization in East Asia seems associated with declining income equality.

The East Asian democratic transition more or less coincided with the onset of "globalization," so the effects of the two are not easy to distinguish. Democracy makes politicians vulnerable to donors, while pressures of globalization make it more difficult for technocrats to dictate to business. The combination of these elements may have contributed to the Asian crisis: the sweetheart arrangement between the state and business persisted into the democratic era, but the state was no longer as able to impose discipline on business. Businesses could continue to pile up debts without much worry about how they might be repaid, assuming that the bureaucrats and politicians would take care of things.

The corruption that seems to accompany democratic politics has led some theorists to wonder whether developmental theory has paid too much attention to elections at the expense of the inculcation of a rule of law. They used to adduce the example of Hong Kong, which under the British had no democracy to speak of but whose residents enjoyed prosperity, security, and liberty. But Hong Kong also shows the limitations of a disregard for democracy. The Hong Kong public had no say at all over the return of the colony to China, whose People's Republic had a tradition of rule of law less venerable than that of England. The Hong Kong democracy movement grew in the wake of the 1984 agreement to return sovereignty to China, gathering strength especially after the tragedy of 1989. Democracy, in effect, was a way to protect the people from a state not committed to liberty. Chinese hostility, exacerbated by the well-intentioned but tactless attempts by Governor Chris Patten to foster a democratic system, left the movement impotent, divided, and confused. In the meantime, Hong Kong's big money had early on shifted its allegiance to the Peking authorities.

What, then, are the prospects for the democratization of the big one, China itself?[9] If democracy in East Asia comes through decisions at the top, it is not clear that democratization would solve any problems for China's turn-of-the-century rulership. The "critical juncture" was probably 1989. Had events gone differently (and there was considerable sentiment for the students not merely in society but among the Party and the military), China might have moved toward democratic evolution. After 1989 any nondemocratic regime will continue to be of questionable legitimacy, especially as the good times cease to roll (or American arrogance abates). But it will probably continue to be easier to suppress than to co-opt opposition.

The PRC is no longer a totalitarian regime, but continues to bear some marks of totalitarianism. The opposition does not have even the limited opportunities for expression that it had in Korea or Taiwan. Regime persecution in 1999 of the new religious sect, the Falun Gong, shows that the party is unwilling to tolerate even ostensibly nonpolitical popular social activity it cannot control.

The state in Taiwan and Korea was not only autonomous but strong, and state strength was itself a factor allowing democracy to take hold. The Chinese state is largely autonomous but possibly not that strong and not always able either to enforce policy or to control the behavior of its own functionaries (as manifested in widespread corruption—a phenomenon, then, evidently not restricted to new democracies). The economic reforms may have weakened the state without enhancing civil society or reducing state autonomy. Political institutions themselves are weak, with the leader, whether Mao Zedong or Deng Xiaoping, able to bypass or override institutions. There were signs by the late 1990s of enhanced central state authority, which may mean strengthened dictatorship or, not so paradoxically, conditions propitious for democratization. A so-called neoconservative tendency has argued that democracy must rest on a strong middle class; this middle class is created by economic development, which in its turn rests on economic freedom. The state, then, should do all it can to guarantee economic freedom while restricting political participation, repressing the discontents which are the inevitable, hopefully temporary by-products of economic liberalization. More than democracy, China needs a strong state and a rule of law.

Democracy someday, but not now: This should comfort those in power. The analysis in this chapter implies that neoconservatism is flawed as a theory of democratization, but it still has some merit. Should China develop a genuine rule of law, binding both rulers and ruled, and be able effectively to enforce that law, perhaps the issue of participation would take care of itself. The rulers could no longer claim that the alternative to autocracy is chaos—a claim that, if one thinks about it, any ruling group should be ashamed to make.

Concluding Thoughts

The tone of this analysis may seem hostile to East Asian democracy: it encourages corruption; it favors the rich; it may not be a country's most pressing need; and other defects might well be identified. Democracy anywhere is bound to be a defective system. Americans, so eager to commend their own ways to others, loudly complain about the palpable defects of their own democracy. Democracy in practice certainly does not routinely address itself to what is most noble in human nature: We are encouraged to sell our votes to those who will most gratify us. Scholarly writing, which in some of its aspects shows the sometimes sordid realities of democratic politics, also often treats democracy as a synonym for everything good, so that to dismiss a policy or practice it is sufficient to label it "undemocratic."

To paraphrase Winston Churchill's familiar dictum: Democracy is certainly an imperfect system—but compared to what? To set the bar very low: Democracies rarely torture or even imprison those with different ideas, but this is a very big deal for those who once lived under autocracies. Democracy may encourage corruption, but other types of systems may also be corrupt, and democracy provides ways of holding the corrupt responsible. Democracy usually avoids the worst kinds of corruption: A democratic China would certainly have had no great Leap Forward or Cultural Revolution.

Without democracy the post-Confucian regimes have been of questionable legitimacy. This generates a certain bias for democratization. Where democratization has succeeded there have been vigorous opposition movements, but the initiative has come from the existing elites, who have controlled the timing and approach. Democratization entailed the development of the functions of existing formal institutions, however much these functions or the institutions themselves may change in the process. The East Asian experience corroborates the as-it-were rational choice approach of the transition theorists of the 1980s: Democratization solves problems for those in charge. It is undertaken when the benefits exceed the costs. It comes from the top rather than the bottom.

A central hypothesis, formulated with some reluctance, is that in East Asia a strong state is a necessary condition for democratic transition. State strength reduces the risks of democracy to the rulers. There may be at least partial validity to the neoconservative thesis that democracy will be possible in China once that country develops an effective rule of law and an honest, effective, predictable administration. However, democracy in East Asia is also related to modernization and overall development. In its early stages—such as in the West—authoritarianism reigned in East Asia. But as economic development accelerated and social pluralism grew, elites found it useful to democratize—both as a measure of growing self confidence and as a pragmatic response to new pressures both internal and external. Democracy in East Asia is thus a product of both history and culture on the one hand, and institutional changes on the other, including outside intervention. Whether China follows this pattern is still an open—and hotly debated—question.

Endnotes

1. Objections to the application of the term are not entirely pedantic. There is, obviously, much more to these societies than Confucianism, and much of the modernization process in these societies may derive from non-Confucian or anti-Confucian elements in them. And the term itself is controversial. Lionel Jensen, in *Manufacturing Confucianism: Chinese Traditions and Universal Civilization* (Durham, N.C.: Duke University Press, 1997) argues only partly perversely that Confucianism is a Western construct.

2. From an 1848 discourse on western geography by Xu Jiyu, as cited in *China's Response to the West: A Documentary Survey, 1839–1923*, edited by Ssu-yu Teng and John King Fairbank (Cambridge, MA: Harvard University Press, 1965), 44.

3. The thesis presented here is couched in a dogmatic rather than a critical form, without nuance, qualification, or consideration of alternative explanations. This reflects constraints of space and a need to get on with the overall theme of the chapter. If possible, the various cocksure apodictic assertions in this chapter should be treated as hypotheses, suggestions, and conjectures. For more of an attempt to argue the

"theory," see Peter Moody, *Political Opposition in Post-Confucian Society* (New York: Praeger, 1988).

4. The Japanese term means National Assembly. The term *Diet* is used in the English translation. I think, because that was the English translation of the term for the Prussian parliament, and Japan's Constitution was modeled on that of Prussia.

5. Giovanni Sartori, *Parties and Party Systems* (Cambridge, UK: Cambridge University Press, 1976), 132–40, 145–71.

6. As the saying goes, once the clever rabbit has been caught, the hunting dog goes into the pot.

7. To be pedantically precise, the Republic of China (ROC) electorate consisted of the inhabitants of the island of Taiwan (which, administratively, includes Taiwan province and the "special municipalities" of Taipei and Kaohsiung); those of various outlying islands, which are part of Taiwan province; and the inhabitants of the islands of Quemoy and Matsu, which are part of Fujian province but have been under Nationalist or ROC control since 1949.

8. See, especially, *The Failure of Presidential Democracy*, edited by Juan Linz and Arturo Valenzuela (Baltimore: Johns Hopkins University Press, 1994).

9. To be thorough but extremely brief, the Vietnamese experience will probably approximate a combination of that of Taiwan and China, whereas for North Korea there are simply too many unknowns and contingencies to allow for speculation.

Suggested Readings

Curtis, Gerald. *The Logic of Japanese Politics: Leaders, Institutions, and the Limits of Change.* New York: Columbia University Press, 1999.

De Bary, William Theodore, *Asian Values and Human Rights: A Confucian Communitarian Perspective.* Cambridge, Mass.: Harvard University Press, 1998.

Hall, David, and Roger Ames. *The Democracy of the Dead: Dewey, Confucius, and the Hope for Democracy in China.* Chicago: Open Court Publishing Company, 1999.

He, Baogang. *The Democratic Implications of Civil Society in China.* New York: St. Martin's Press, 1997.

Hood, Steven J. *The Kuomintang and the Democratization of Taiwan.* Boulder, Colo.: Westview Press, 1997.

Jenson, Lionel. *Manufacturing Confucianism: Chinese Traditions and Universal Civilization.* Durham, N.C.: Duke University Press, 1997.

Lie, John. *Han Unbound: The Political Economy of South Korea.* Stanford, Calif.: Stanford University Press, 1998.

Moody, Peter R. *Political Opposition in Post-Confucian Society.* New York: Praeger, 1988.

Nathan, Andrew J. *Chinese Democracy.* New York, Knopf, 1985.

Pye, Lucian W. *Asian Power and Politics: The Cultural Dimensions of Authority.* Cambridge, Belknap Press, 1985.

Teng Ssu-yu, and John K. Fairbank. *China's Response to the West: A Documentary Survey, 1839–1923.* Cambridge, Mass.: Harvard University Press, 1954.

6

Western Democratic Theories and Non-Western Democratic Experiences: India

A. H. Somjee

Introduction

Democratic theory so far has had only one source, namely, the liberal democratic experience of a few countries of Western Europe and North America. Such a theory, however, is not without its own accretions of the time and place where it was formulated. No social science theory can fully purge its existential source, least of all democratic theory. In its formulations it has very nearly ignored the living *democratic experiences* of non-Western societies without moderating its claims to universality.

In this chapter I underline certain aspects of those experiences that have implications for an inclusive democratic theory. Not to recognize them is to miss out on its testability and inclusiveness.

Several scholars, including Karl de Schweinitz and Barrington Moore Jr., have argued that liberal democracy in the West has been a product of the convergence of a large number of forces; the most important among them was the rise of capitalism. And capitalism itself, as Max Weber, R. H. Tawney, F. Tonnies, F. Braudel, etc. argued, was a product of a complex mosaic of forces, which played their critical part in pushing the countries of the West to build and expand the new form of economic institutions that capitalism provided. So what we have both in liberal democracy and capitalism are the consequences of social and economic forces that were at work in Western countries from the seventeenth to the twentieth century.

Over the period of those three to four centuries, the Western world also produced thinkers who gave the emerging liberal political institutions their normative base. John Locke was one of the earliest thinkers to argue that citizens need to enter into explorations of institutional and practical measures that can make the enjoyment of natural rights a certainty. Over and above normative expressions and institutions, as Alexis de Tocqueville pointed out, a change in political character is also needed to make the operations of liberal democracy a living reality. And in his *Democracy in America* (1889) he paid a rich tribute to the post–Independence War Americans for having responded to it. Later on, the notion of liberal democracy, particularly in the United States, was enriched by thinkers such as John Dewey, who spoke of human potentiality, and John Rawls, who underlined the need to rethink its utilitarian assumptions.

The evolution of the three mature democracies of the world, namely the British, the French, and the American, also underlined the need to strike a balance between what was normatively desirable and politically possible, a balance which needs to be continually redefined and reformulated. They also contributed a great deal to the civilizing of political contests, the opening up of access to political power, and the learning of the difficult art of consensus building. Also of inestimable value was their continuing discourse on the ideal "fit" between public and private interests, to be explored within the framework of legality, propriety, and morality.

Although a large number of these issues have been common to almost all political societies—for example, wanting to introduce, sustain, and develop liberal political institutions—countries such as India have also experienced peculiar problems of their own in their attempt to transplant liberal political institutions from the West and also to sustain them with the help of indigenous institutions. To be brief, democracy in India was not a product of capitalism, as in Western countries, but rather it was introduced by the leaders of the Indian independence movement as the very focus of their struggle against alien rule. As a result, the subsequent attempt to liberalize the economy was not going to be as easy as in the countries of the West. But what puts India in a unique category of its own, in this business of transplantation of liberal institutions, is the way in which its hoary grassroots institutions jived with them, supplied the groundwork, and put them on a firm footing in the shortest possible time.

Then one of the major problems India faced was the growth of the political capacity of its people, particularly in a society with a deeply entrenched social hierarchy. Such a hierarchy was more than that of class and there was nothing corresponding to it in the Western democratic experience. When the democratic process started operating within such a hierarchical society, some kind of *participatory queue* was formed whereby, gradually, different social and economic strata got involved and also gave the democratic process a different operative character.

All these issues have implications for theory construction, regardless of the region in which they occurred. Consequently, any democratic theory that aspires to be truly universal in its claims will have to include them. In the following pages I shall illustrate some of them. This chapter is divided into the following subsections: the changing bases of Indian democracy, the actualities of transition, the growing awareness of how to make democracy produce results, and global norms and definitions.

The Changing Bases of Indian Democracy

Prolonged Exposure to Liberal Political Ideals

As stated before, in Western countries, democracy was created by the rise of capitalism. Entrepreneurial and modernizing forces of capitalism, in search of more profit and wealth, pierced through the obstructive barriers of the preceding feudal regimes and not only made them more permissive of economic entrepreneurship, but also forced them to accept increasingly representative forms of government in which the general population had a say. The success of the capitalist class in forcing representative forms of government also stimulated the growth of an urban propertied class, professions, trade unions, and women, and provided an opportunity for them to have a say in the legislature. Those classes and groups together, over a period of 200 to 300 years, changed the nature of governance in the countries of Western Europe and North America.

On the other hand, India had waged a national struggle for independence for nearly a century, with a focus on the democratic ideals that the colonial regime claimed it enjoyed at home. The Indians now wanted these democratic institutions. If it was an elected legislature to which the executive was answerable, the Indians were for it. If it was civil and political rights that the average citizen of Britain claimed to enjoy, with law courts charged with the responsibility of protecting them, the Indians were eager to have them. Above all, the Indians wanted the colonial judiciary to be as impartial in the administration of justice as the judiciary was in Britain. In short, colonial India was bursting with demands to enjoy all those rights and freedoms that Britain claimed it enjoyed as a developed nation. The response of colonial rulers changed from the Indians not being fit for them to the Indians not yet being ready for them.

In demanding rights and freedoms, the leaders of the national movement, most of whom were trained in British law schools or were well versed in

British jurisprudence, waged a two-pronged battle: one in the streets and fields of India, mostly by nonviolent means, and the other in the colonial law courts. In both of these locations the British were made to feel morally embarrassed. And the person who became the master of moral embarrassment was none other than Mahatma Gandhi himself. No British official cold argue with him to say that he, Gandhi, was not educated, civilized, or morally an appropriate person to enjoy those rights. He almost exceeded them in every department and gave them a sense of guilt to live with for the rest of their lives.

The prolonged national movement also gave the Indian leaders an opportunity to deeply assimilate the significance of democratic ideals and practices. Although those leaders had familiarized themselves with British Common Law and also the constitutional law governing countries such as France and the United States, it was in the streets and law courts that they realized how significant these laws would be if and when Indians emerged as a free people. The national movement then was a struggle against the colonial rule as well as a lesson in learning to live within a democratic polity under the rule of law.

When the Indians finally wrote the constitution of free India, the people who were in charge of its making were not the nationalist leaders as such, but only those among them who were constitutional lawyers steeped in the Anglo-Saxon tradition of liberal democracy. These founding fathers of the Indian republic tried to defy the Indian social and cultural reality of *associated* living and acting and of caste and religious groups, by endowing its citizens with rights as if they were separate individuals and charging the courts with the responsibility of protecting them. When Ghandi, who had returned from British jails, protested against the foreignness of the draft constitution, the only concession the constitutional lawyers were willing to make was that India's hoary institution of *panchayats* (local councils), which were as old as the classical civilization of India itself, should be revamped on the basis of the principle of universal adult suffrage. While the panchayats at the grassroots level had played a much less effective role than was expected, they nevertheless had become important institutions to look after India's grassroots democracy. The point is that with the adoption of the constitution of free India in 1952, India made a radical departure, politically speaking, from its past traditions of governance and yet created institutions which resonated with the changing social and economic realities of the last half-century. Rarely were such institutions found wanting. What was found wanting, repeatedly, was their effective use by a free people.

Socially and culturally speaking, there were two major influences that have shaped the social and religious conduct of Indians: social compliance in cultural matters demanded by caste and religious groups and a wide range of individual choice, for the Hindus, to choose one's deity within the accepted pantheon. Quite often members of the same family, and even husband and wife, may go to different temples and offer their prayers to different deities. And if individuals are philosophically well-versed then they may have their own philosophical interpretations bordering on agnosticism. India's classical civilization and Hinduism in particular, have also allowed intellectual disputations and explorations into different levels of spirituality if an individual so chooses. The point is that while social conformity was prescribed at the level of rituals of caste and religious groups, Indians have also enjoyed individual freedom at the level of philosophical explorations in religion and in choice of gods and goddesses. Such freedom was of inestimable value when the constitution of free India endowed an Indian with several rights, including the right to vote as an individual.

Culturally too, the living experience of having many castes, religions, deities, and holy men and their prescriptions, has made Indians accustomed to living with *plurality*. Although at a philosophical level one may explain it as leading to one god almighty, in Indians' day-to-day experiences they had to live with many different kinds of divinities and spiritualities. Through such a living experience, an individual was inevitably schooled into accepting pluralism as a fact of life. Such a background proved to allow Indians to be receptive to democratic pluralism of parties, candidates, platforms, and different points of view. After that no further justification for plurality was needed.

Diversity in all its manifestations, including pluralism, tolerance, and coexistence, which are all at the heart of democracy are, in fact, a part of the living experience of Indians. In that vast country there are at least 20 recognized languages (not just dialects), with scripts, grammars, literatures, and loyalties of their own. In addition, there is a baffling diversity of social customs, dress, and cuisines. Such diversity also has implications for political institutions of democracy. For one thing, the old-style federation of Indian polity, when towering leaders in New Delhi used to dictate what the distant provinces should do, is gone forever. Also gone is the possibility of what used to be called "all-India" or national political parties. Regional leaders are now altering the shape of the Indian polity.

Students of the democratic process from all over the developing world know that having a plurality of political parties and periodically conducting free and fair elections is the easy part or component of democracy. The difficult part follows in making it work and produce results, which means ensuring the enjoyment of freedom within the rule of law, an electorally mandated legislature and executive, an independent judiciary, freedom of the press, the opportunity to run for public office, the freedom to undertake economic initiatives, and an increasing measure of social justice. Realization of all these noble ideals in India was hindered by the traditional political relationships and attitudes toward authority that were deeply anchored in the hierarchical social organization. The national movement had concentrated only on the alien rule, not on how you behave in a democracy. In that respect everyone had to begin at ground zero. Everyone had to learn democracy by getting involved in various processes of democratic government, which the newly created institutions gave rise to. Whether at the level of village or district or state or union, the citizen of India had to learn the dos and do nots of operating and sustaining the new political institutions on both sides of the political divide. The very competition for public office had to be civilized: Treatment of a political adversary after the contest had to be placed above the zero-sum game temptation, the respect for the electoral verdict had to be created and assimilated, and, above all, the door had to be kept open to others to win public office in future when the current winners' terms came to an end. All these had to be inculcated and their democratic significance grasped.

Assimilation of Liberal Political Ideals by Grassroots Communities

The people in rural, urban, and metropolitan India thus had their own democratic lessons to learn. Here the major cities of India had the initial advantage, which they did not fully cash in on. They had better education, a professional class, transportion and communication facilities, and greater exposure to political activities of the visiting leaders. But they also had the disadvantage of having large numbers of migrants coming from different parts of the country who did not fully identify themselves with the local people and their problems. In election after election, the quality of their democratic involvement, including voter turnout, was not always higher than that of rural India. The real drama, where a difficult transition was made from colonial to democratic governance by stages, took place in rural India. In the postindependence period then, the bulk of the population of India has not only lived in rural communities, but has also continued to depend on the rural agricultural economy for its livelihood.

The initial political change for rural communities, through the democratic provisions of the constitution, gave the impression that they would be transformed from hitherto "harmonious" communities to those that were riven by divisiveness, distrust, and conflicts. Such criticisms often came from families that were entrenched in a position of power as a result of the status of their caste and ownership of land. They did not see the legitimacy of those competing for power who were socially and economically inferior to them but simply enjoyed greater numerical support. The numerical support enjoyed the middle and lower rungs of traditional society helped them to make inroads into the secure power hold of their predecessors.

Initially, of course, the political scene in rural India did not change very suddenly. The village elders from the upper castes, when they found the rough and tumble of democratic politics too much for them, put their sons into the democratic fray to make deals with the lower castes and to hold on to power while they retired to their caste councils. Such a bifurcation of social and political leadership, in the intermediate stages, gave way to still another coalition of the lower-middle and lower castes of India, which could muster political support.[1] Distinguished Indian anthropologist Andre Beteille explained how after India gained independence, one could see that the caste, status, and political power enjoyed earlier by the same group of people, namely, the Brahmins and warrior castes, had begun to be dispersed. The numerical principle introduced by democratic India displaced them not only from political power but also from ownership of large areas of land. Today, in most parts of India, agricultural prosperity is enjoyed by lower-middle castes and also by what is known as the other backward castes. They often group together with castes below them, either scheduled castes or scheduled tribes and enjoy political power and high agricultural income, but not high caste status. At least politically, and also to some extent economically, rural India has been forced to change because of the introduction of the principle of one-man, one-vote. What it has not been able to do, however, is to penetrate the poverty curtain effectively.

The entire drama of the transition to democracy was being played out in the half a million villages of India and there too within their panchayats. With all their imperfect ways of operating, they had become veritable schools for democracy. They came from India's distant past and had enjoyed revenue and judicial powers of different degrees in different times. One thing that was constant in them, however, was their *participatory* character. Although people from the upper castes and those with large landholdings controlled them, whenever lower-caste individuals were involved, they were given a due hearing of a semijudicial nature. One of the greatest democratic transitions was brought about in India when its constitution, framed in 1952, required panchayats to be organized on the principle of one-man, one-vote. From then on there was nothing to stop them from reincarnating themselves into democratic bodies with all their inefficiencies, cleavages and conflicts. Although the majority-minority mechanism introduced by them did not always work for the harmony, clean administration, or economic progress of rural communities, they nevertheless firmly established the principle of electoral legitimacy. After that it was universally accepted that you enjoy political legitimacy only when you have majority support. No amount of scare mongering about impending emergencies, the barrel of the gun, or the incorruptibility of the man in a military uniform could undo that legitimacy.

While the grassroots learning about the operations of democracy began nibbling away at the traditional emphasis on social status and class, it also did not spare familial status and age as the necessary condition for qualifying for public office. None of these could hold out against the massive tide of political power backed by the numerical principle. But what proved far more obdurate to yielding was the primary social cohesion of castes, and in recent years, that of the lower castes. It took at least two decades of elections for panchayats to bring home to rural communities the fact that emphasis on caste cohesions in nontraditional matters, such as elections, merely serves the interests of electioneering politicians. Consequently, they learned to build a patchwork of electoral support cutting across caste cohesion.[2] Although in the bulk of Indian states the pattern that emerged was one of heterogeneity in political choices, in some states cohesion of castes in elections persisted.

What fifty years of democracy in India has witnessed is its working through the traditional *social queue* in a top-down sequence. Initially, the chief ministers of various states and also prime ministers and presidents of India were, by and large, individuals from the higher social background. And as the numerical principle was grasped by those in the middle and lower positions in the social queue, they too used it to their political and economic benefit. The result was that more and more individuals from the lower castes could now aspire to the highest office provided the political arithmatic favored them. But that was not enough. Whereas *as individuals* the representatives of backward groups could get into such positions, their own following did not benefit much. The collective economic benefits that they received were not always commensurate with the individual economic benefits that the political leaders of the backward received.

Despite not being served adequately by Indian development and the democratic process, the backward social groups in India—who constitute nearly one-third of the country and are also considered to live below the poverty line—did not cherish military or civilian dictatorship as an alternative. Such threats came from the top leaders of India, such as Indira Gandhi and her cronies in the Congress party. What the poor nevertheless considered in several states of India was a Marxist alternative strictly within the framework of a democratic polity.

Growing Appreciation of Democratic Coexistence

Given a culturally and linguistically diverse country—with almost all the major religions in it and a highly fractured social organization on the lines of caste—there was a genuine fear that democracy would give Indians freedom to express differences, followed by demand for the creation of independent states. That fear, barring isolated cases, did not materialize. Different states, despite cultural, social, and linguistic differences, discovered more and more advantages of being a part of a country with subcontinental proportions. Well-known Indian journalist Prem Shankar Jha had once described India as having crystallized into "an ethnic federation."[3]

Such a coexistence of a diverse group of states would not have been possible had there been no liberal democracy. Increasingly, Indians discovered that in their peaceful, and even competitive coexistence, democracy is a major precondition. The cultural lives of each state, together with linguistic development, have evolved vigorously in the last half a century. The initial attempts of the *Hindi belt* to dominate the rest did not bear fruit. On the other hand, Hindi films, in their own nonimposing ways, have done much to popularize the elementary Hindi language. But the language of the educated, of interstate administration, and of commerce remains, by and large, English. India, it is claimed by some, has now become the second-largest English-speaking country in the world, next only to the United States, with a distinct possibility of overtaking it.

Furthermore, the Indian federation has given increasing levels of freedom to the states to attract their own investments from indigenous and expatriate sources. In that respect, the states of Gujarat, Maharashtra, Karnataka, Tamil Nadu, Andhra Pradesh, Punjab, Haryana, etc., have moved much faster than the rest. Gujarat is supposed to have attained the growth rate of nearly 12 percent a year, which is twice that of the national average. At some stage, such a faster growth rate will contribute to interstate jealousies, but democratic compromises and learning from others how to accelerate economic growth will ensure a continued coexistence of a highly diverse nation.

Impact of Diversity on Political Institutions

As states become adept in launching their economic initiatives and making a success of them, their commercial and industrial corporations, along with their politicians, became equally important to the center for making policy, preparing a budget, and deconstructing the residual command economy that had condemned India to a growth rate of 2 percent a year for four decades after independence. Simultaneously, regional political parties that showed much greater appreciation of the problems of their states grew into prominence. For a long time national political parties such as the Congress Party and the Bharatiya Janata Party (BJP) refused to accept the fact that they needed the support of regional political parties to run the country. In that respect the BJP was the first to change its position to say that the country had now entered the phase of coalitional politics and one needed coalitions of political parties not only to win elections but also to govern the country. The maturing perception of diversity in India, leading to decentralization of economic initiatives first, then to coalition governments, brought the country closer to the basic realities of democratic politics.

The Actualities of Transition

It was relatively easier to put in place the institutions of liberal democracy, from the grassroots up, than to make them produce the intended results.

Only in actual operations of such institutions did the Indians realize that there was more to democracy than just institutions. For it is one form of government in which people do matter, and they *can* get it to respond to their wishes, needs, and concerns, provided they become actively involved in making it do so. But the process of involvement was itself riddled with problems, some of which were historical and others of which were more recent.

In the euphoric days of the postindependence period, it was difficult to question the decisions of towering nationalist leaders, let alone critically examine them on a day-to-day basis. Their moral stature and sacrifices gave rise to a belief that even in policy matters they could do no wrong. The Indians paid heavily for that slip up in their democratic responsibility.

Stranglehold of State Institutions and Corruption

In fact, Indians lost too much time in waking up to their democratic responsibility—of acting as critics when public policies did not produce the intended results. Such a responsibility was left to rival political parties, the media, and the economists. Initially there were two normative commitments of the national movement: liberal democracy and secularism. To that Nehru added the third one, namely, socialism, which made ample sense in a highly unequal society. Even during the national movement, he had sensitized his colleagues to the need for such an ideology, the main inspiration for which came from British Fabian socialism. His mistake was that without revamping the inherited colonial bureaucracy, given to obstructionist and negative ways, he gave them the responsibility of building a socialist India with the help of various public undertakings. Such a bureaucracy monstrously expanded and became a class by itself. The average Indians toiled, paid high taxes, repeatedly forgave public undertakings for losing money, and bailed them out again and again. For four decades Indians had to be content with an economic growth rate which barely went above 2 percent when that of most countries of Asia was nearing or exceeding 10 percent. Permits were required for everything a person needed, and bureaucrats took bribes to issue them. People got sick of it and called it a *permit-licence raj* (a corrupt payments system). The next group to benefit were the elected officials. So now one had to bribe both bureaucrats and politicians. This situation was then dubbed by the critics as *neta-babuji raj* (politician-bureaucrat regime). The shame of it all was that during the period of the Congress Party's socialism, the incomes of more and more people sank below the poverty line. The Congress party thrived under these conditions. Its politicians, in the name of socialism, got bribes from all those who approached them for permission of all kinds. Bribes were taken in the name of election funds. Because it was a clandestine activity, no one kept accounts. Nothing in India moved unless officials and politicians were bribed. When other parties came to power, they also learned very quickly from the Congress how to enrich themselves. The Congress even introduced the curse of vote buying.

A Nonimplementing Democracy

But that was not the end of the matter. Members of state legislatures and the Lok Sabha in New Delhi would support a public policy with their votes in the house and then offer their services privately to those who wanted to get around it. Individuals who had contacts with high officials and ministers could see that none of the punitive measures of the law applied to them. All they had to do was bribe. In addition, law-enforcing agents could be influenced to delay dispensation of justice. Rarely would a politician in India be punished for taking bribes while helping others to dodge the law, a law that he might have voted for himself in the legislature. A curious situation was thus created in Indian democracy: It became a virtually *nonimplementing* democracy. Everyone had the privilege of electing deputies and making them pass legislation to set certain policies. But that is where it all stopped. After that the bureaucrats, the elected politicians, investigative agencies, and the law courts took over. And the result was that rarely was anyone sent to prison.

The last to arrive on the scene were the individuals with criminal records. In the earlier period of Indian democracy, the politicians who got involved in dubious activity needed the help of strong-arm men. Later on such men themselves sought party nomination and got themselves elected. Indian state legislatures and the Lok Sabha came to have a large number of elected members who had criminal records. In 1995, a highly disturbing government report came out that pinpointed the relationship between criminals and democratic politics of India.[4]

Individuals join the public service for a variety of reasons. Soon after Indian independence, it was very common for these individuals to claim that their motives were purely in the interest of public service and nothing else. However, after fifty years of abuse of the electoral trust, that moral hyperbole is masked somewhat by them saying what they want to see is that their district or state gets a fair shake. The question, then, is how does a democracy defend itself against such abuses when elected representatives, bureaucrats, and the bulk of the law-enforcing agencies, at the slightest opportunity, want to serve only themselves and their families? Making more laws against them, which these very individuals are expected to implement, is not going to help. What is needed is massive involvement, in vigilance and accountability-seeking activity, of the educated Indian middle class. This will then pass on to average citizens the message that they too have to pay a price for the democratic government they opted for.

Decline in Political Involvement of the Middle Class

Middle class apathy is one of the biggest problems that democracy in India is facing today. Along with the deep commitment of a huge group of electorally empowered poor, who stood by Indian democracy, there is also an equally huge group of India's burgeoning middle class, which has a deep appreciation, bordering on pride, for democracy, and would rather let Indian politicians do anything but undo democracy. This group is variously estimated to consist of between 200 and 300 million people. And it has become an engine of India's economic development, pushing the growth rate to between 6 and 7 percent, with a distinct possibility of attaining 8 to 10 percent during this decade. It has put an enormous emphasis on education of its children and made many financial sacrifices to see that they go to the best schools in the country and then abroad. Economic development is now driven by, among other factors, an educated, highly skilled, scientific, managerial, and entre-preneurial English-speaking workforce. This workforce has been successfully competing for employment at home and abroad.

India has always been a land of great contrasts. The latest in this list is the disparity between the two huge segments of its population: one living below the poverty line and the other enjoying the fruits of science and technology that Nehru put in place half a century ago. Such a contrast was effectively pointed out by President K. R. Narayanan on the first Republic Day of the millennium as follows:

> We have one of the world's largest reservoirs of technical personnel, but also the world's largest number of illiterates; the world's largest middle class, but also the largest number of people below the poverty line and the largest number of children suffering from malnutrition. Our giant factories rise from out of squalor; our satellites shoot up from the midst of the hovels of the poor.[5]

The educated and skilled individuals in India's middle class do not think it is their responsibility to lend a hand to help run India's democratic institutions, not even from outside political and public office. Nor, barring a few who have a variety of motivations to join the *political class*, do the middle class members want to give a few years of their lives to public service and bring to bear the standard of their integrity and efficiency. They are so deeply disenchanted with the selfishness and corruption of the present political class that they do not want to have anything to do with public life. Some have even written off India as a possible place where their children should stay and bring up their families. Consequently, their entire effort is focused on one goal and that is to send their children to the United States and let them make a life for themselves there.

Ironically, some of the parents of the contemporary middle class were touched by the Indian national movement itself, and they also played a role in making that movement a *mass movement*. Mahatma Gandhi and other national leaders in fact depended on them to carry their message, and Constructive Programme in general, to the towns and villages of India. For such a group to have changed so radically was nothing short of a severe blow to democratic India. Only a few members of this group currently pursue nongovernmental organization (NGO) activities during or after a lifetime of professional work. The rest of this huge resource remains untapped to strengthen India's democracy and make it perform effectively. If and when members of this group do precisely that, they will have a large impact on India's democracy. As of now they retain a strong preference for liberal democracy and are highly critical of the corruption and crime the political class has introduced, but do not want to help to improve the quality of governance. Consequently, if there is any segment of Indian society that needs a lesson in civic activism, it is this educated, and able, middle class. At the moment it is content with the attention that it has received nationally and internationally. In the words of an American observer, Stanley A. Weiss:

> The World Bank and the International Monetary Fund estimate that India will be the world's fourth largest economy in this century. It has the second biggest pool of English-speaking, scientific manpower after the United States. Its software exports should increase from $4 billion today to $50 billion by 2008, revolutionizing India's balance of payments position and allowing an even more liberal attitude towards trade.[6]

The Problems of Ethnopolitical Development

One of the major problems that has come from the Indian democratic experience is how does a country grow in political capacity to transact the business of democracy and also make it produce intended results? Among emerging countries trying to make a transition to democracy, India was the first to realize that there is much more to democracy than the setting up of legal and political institutions, underlining of normative principles which lie at the root of liberal government, holding of free elections, writing of procedural manuals for conducting the business of elected bodies, etc. After that the more difficult tasks follow. And these consist of telling the people, on both sides of the electoral divide, about the dos and do nots of democratic behavior, without which its fragile institutions and procedures would remain on insecure foundations. But more than that, how do you tell the voters that it is *their* responsibility to monitor constantly and not only at the time of elections whether or not the political power exercised by their elected deputies and ministers is in accordance with the established policy and law? It is here that we come into the arena of maturing citizens' political capacity to be able to secure responsibility and accountability from people they elect to public office. Such a process of maturing in political capacity was not shortened in the case of Western countries, which had two to three centuries of political evolution to arrive where they are today. In developing countries, on the other hand, participatory institutions were created and adult universal suffrage was put in place in *advance* of the growth of a commensurate political capacity to use them effectively. Such a problem was thus not present in the democratic development of Western countries. There democratic institutions grew, by and large, in response to, and along with, the growth of the citizens' capacity to transact political business with them. Participatory institutions in major liberal democracies of the world such as Britain, the United States, and France grew along with their citizens' urge and relentless demand to participate it the formulation of public policy. Various reform bills had to be passed to enable the new and politically conscious groups to share the power of policy-making. Thus at every stage a demand, followed by an agitation, sometimes prolonged and ugly, had to occur before new categories of citizens were admitted into the power-sharing arena.

For the first time in history, that was not the case in a major political society. In the case of India, during the colonial administration, the right to vote was insisted upon by those who led the national movement. And it was conceded in small installments, grudgingly and with all kinds of qualifications, to a fraction of India's population. Consequently, there was not much prior experience in the use of such a right. The constitution of the Indian Republic literally foisted on its citizenry the universal adult franchise by which all its public institutions at the state and union levels had to be constituted. A few years later it extended that principle to authority at the village, subdistrict, and district levels.

The Indian baptism in political empowerment thus affected two groups: those who were touched by the Indian national movement and, thereby, overcame their fear of and hesitation in public participation; and those who subsequently benefited from their actual involvement in a participatory democratic process. At the rural level, particularly, the middle-caste agriculturists, who often emulated the higher castes, also learned to involve themselves in the participatory process and make demands for either advancing their interests or protecting them. Nevertheless, those who were left out were the bulk of rural and urban dwellers who had neither any experience with political involvement nor someone who could guide them into it. Those who got involved in the participatory process *grew*, as it were, in their political capacity to be able to influence public policy or even to demand accountability from those who were involved in making it. But those who remained outside became politically less developed and even continued to have a fear of government and public authority. Fifty years after the arrival of democracy in India, the bulk of its educated middle class often feels embarrassed to subject an electioneering politician to a session of political scrutiny. The idea of carrying placards in the streets is just unthinkable for members of this class. They would rather throw up their hands than perform what they think are unruly acts. Nobel laureate Gunnar Myrdal once remarked that one of the problems with India's educated middle class is that it does not get angry enough with its politicians and administrators.

So now there are two huge nonfunctional components in the democratic society of India: one that has not been touched either by India's national movement or subsequently by its participatory process and the other, the middle class, that has decided to pass *moral judgments* on how very terrible India's democratic process is without any corresponding sense of obligation to do something about it. These very same individuals are otherwise well-informed about how educated people get involved in such processes in Western democracies and then make their politicians pursue economic and social goals that they think are desirable. They would not let such knowledge disturb them. As a result of these imposed and self-imposed inabilities, those in power, both elected and appointed, at the state and national level, took advantage by using and abusing the resources of society and powers of office completely.

The opposition political parties in the states and the center have often done a reasonably good job of questioning the accountability-dodging politicians who come from all political parties. But they are so deeply focused on electoral benefits to them by such criticisms that the public outside those legislatures rarely takes them seriously. Then there is the uneven role of the Indian judiciary, which ranges from total inertia to activism in some cases. The institution that has acted most admirably in making the democratic process more effective is the print and electronic media whose members routinely grill highly placed politicians.

We need to explore the theoretical implications of this problem of what I called *ethnopolitical development.*[7] This phenomenon is further complicated in India because of the deeply ingrained hierarchical nature of its society and its far reaching influence on democratic politics. While the upper- and middle-caste rural and urban dwellers, with their education and contacts, develop their own savvy in manipulating the democratic process to their advantage, those below them often depend on the leaders of political parties and, more recently on their own caste leaders who, in turn, have their eyes firmly set on how to turn their caste cohesion into an electoral *vote bank.*

How to Make Democracy Produce Results

Pride in Being the World's Largest Democracy

Apart from its classical civilization, there are two other things that the Indians are proud of: their success in building and operating the world's largest democracy; and how well their kith and kin have done in competition for technical, scientific, managerial, and educational jobs abroad. Right down the line, the Indians do not entertain the thought of trading their highly imperfect democracy for any other form of government. On the contrary, they maintain that they should have been given due credit for having successfully built the world's largest democracy in one of the poorest countries, with its mind-boggling diversity. This democracy not only has survived but also has increasingly given a better account of itself. When Indira Gandhi tried to rule the country with the help of emergency laws, the Indians threw her out in the following election; when towering leaders disappeared, the Indians allowed those who were next in line to grow in office; and when national political parties started losing their hold, the Indians gropingly learned to work with coalitions. The Indians have thus become collective learners from their own democratic deficiencies. And nothing can ensure the survival of democracy more than such a process of learning.

Talking of the largest democracy, just think of 600 million people on the electoral role, registering a voter turnout of nearly 60 percent in the general election of 1996! The sheer logistics of conducting such an election required three weeks and a large number of security personnel. With the Cold War context gone, there is now a growing appreciation of this achievement in Western countries and, in particular, in the United States. When an American senator recently described India as "a vibrant democracy," the accolade-hungry Indians were delirious. At last the world's strongest democracy had discovered the world's largest. What kept them apart for so long? Should the discovery of one democracy by another have taken half a century?

Increasing Degree of Criticism and Consultation

Any visitor to India is struck by the quality of its newspapers and, in particular, the articles based on current topics, national and international. But more impressive is the responsible public criticism they engage in. Equally impressive and enlightening is the public scrutiny of programs offered by the electronic media. Nothing is sacrosanct any more when it comes to public office or the highest institutions in the country, namely, the Lok Sabha, the Supreme Court, and the President. Criticism of their conduct is undertaken with eager participation from the readers and the audience. Before long this is bound to influence the quality of governance and democratic performance in general.

Also gone are the days when government did things in a hush-hush fashion. Prime Minister Vajpayee, unlike his predecessors, consults with diverse political parties, industrial and business houses, union leaders, academics, the media, NGOs, and others who are active in public life. Even the framing of the budget now involves a wide consultative process. A major newspaper reported this as follows:

> The Finance Minister will begin consultations with various segments of the economy. Starting off with representatives of the agricultural sector and noted economists, over the next few days consultations have been scheduled with trade union leaders, representatives of small scale industries, consumer organisations, industrialists, financial institutions, scientists, representatives of the entertainment and media industry and, finally, with economic journalists. The exercise would constitute the widest consultations that any Finance Minister has held as part of pre-budget exercises.[8]

More and more Indians are thus given an opportunity to participate before any major decision—domestic, financial, or international—is made.

Increasing Volume of Nongovernmental Activity

Despite their aversion to contesting for public office, the educated middle class, the NGOs, and the cooperative institutions are increasingly involved in social and economic activities and issues that have deep repercussions on India's public life in general. Contemporary urban and rural India is full of individuals from professional, religious, and secular organizations who quietly get involved in helping with educational, environmental, medical, feminist, and social problems, or in areas where there are natural disasters. The most common among these are the mature professionals who after a lifetime of work want to do something for others. They work in the neighborhood or adopt a village or join voluntary work camps.

In this area, the most distinguished and effective work has been done by India's rapidly developing cooperative movement and within it the dairy cooperatives. The dairy cooperative movement is a year older than Indian independence and, in half a century, it has succeeded in making India the largest milk-producing country in the world. Out of roughly 450 districts in India, it has now spread to nearly half of them. It has organized approximately 100,000 milk cooperatives in different parts of India and touched the lives of nearly 10 million milk producers and their families; these are either small or marginal farmers or landless agricultural laborers. This has been, truly, an organization of the little guy in rural India, who had been bypassed by many development projects.

Because land is limited it cannot be given to everyone, but, to a point, everyone can be given a milk-producing animal to supplement his or her income. That is what has started happening in contemporary rural India. Through the dairy industry, some of the poor in India have now found an escape route from poverty. As a result of veterinarians looking after animal health, members of dairy cooperatives have also started grasping the significance of human health care and hygiene. As the milk economy in grassroots communities is almost entirely run by women, their economic involvement and participation have also given them added status. Finally, these milk cooperatives at the village and district levels are run on democratic lines. They elect their officebearers, appoint professional people at the district level to help them with modern dairy processing and marketing, and closely supervise their work. In a genuine sense these *economic* democracies, which are run on hardheaded economic lines, also have repercussions on their *political* counterparts, namely, the panchayats, run by the same people. Unlike the broader democratic picture of India, which is under review here, these economic democracies are genuine policy-implementing democracies with very little or no corruption in them. The more they prosper, the more they ensure an effective democratic future for India.[9]

Global Norms and Definitions

Views of Democracy Theorists

As stated earlier, the theories of democracy that we have in scholarly works so far are almost entirely based in the social and historical experiences of a few Western societies. None of those theories could have been timeless or of universal significance in their entirety because in the social sciences, unlike the natural sciences, one cannot totally avoid the accretions of time and place in which theories were formulated. To be universally valid in their claim, therefore, they will have to face continually the challenges of research, including that in areas in which they originated. Unfortunately, there is a widespread tendency to either ignore such challenges or select those aspects of non-Western democratic experience that support the Western theory. In the latter approach, in particular, there is an assumption that because a number of those theories stood the test of time, they do not need to be refined or replaced and that scholars who insist on such a refinement are either too parochial or just lack good theoretical training. The theorization of the Indian experience of democracy, however limited, has thus met with indifference and even anxiety that once one admits its uniqueness, one will be condemned to a profusion of non-Western particularisms and democratic relativism. Then where would you stop?

In that connection, the works of three major political theorists can be cited. Robert Dahl moved toward an extrapolated ideal type of democracy, which has universal significance and validity. Samuel Huntington spoke of the shifting perception of what scholars regarded to be the major characteristics of democracy. And Arendt Lijphart extended the validity of his theory of democracy to India without engaging in what Earnest Gellner, after Karl Popper, would have called "the ethic of falsification."

Robert Dahl argued that the term "democracy" should be used only as an ideal type. This is because no form of government can secure for its citizens total accountability on the part of those they elect to public office. What most countries of the world have, at best, is "poliarchy" or "near democracy."[10] Dahl had reached that conclusion after an empirical scrutiny of the conduct of elected officials in America. He had, thus, moderated the claim of Western countries to have become true democracies.

An equally moderated position was put forward by Samuel Huntington. Periodizing various "waves" of democracy and their significance to international politics, Huntington was clear about two issues. The first is that along with each wave bringing more countries within the orbit of "democracy," there were also, historically speaking, "reverse waves" which took them away from it. Second and more significant, these distinct waves also changed the perception of scholars on what "democracy" in its operational contexts should refer to. Here Huntington was deeply influenced by the definition given by Joseph Schumpeter, who referred to "democracy" as something that operationally refers to "democratic method" or "institutional arrangement," rather than bringing in a fuzzy concept like "the will of the people" to explain it. Once its normative content was played down, it helped Huntington to define "democracy" to mean a form of government, its sources of authority, and the procedure of constituting it.[11]

The position of Lijphart was different. He was in search of a universally valid theory of democracy in which Indian exceptionalism or deviancy could not be permitted. He maintained that "India is not a deviant case for consociational (power-sharing) theory but, instead, an impressive confirming case."[12] To Lijphart, India has been able to remain a democracy despite being a highly divided society because it has held on to what he sees as the four important elements of power-sharing: "(1) grand coalition governments that include representatives of all major linguistic and religious groups, (2) cultural autonomy for these groups, (3) proportionality in political representation and civil service appointments, and (4) a minority veto with regard to vital minority rights and autonomy." Simultaneously, it has successfully avoided the "majoritarian winner-take-all democracy," which leads often to instability in divided societies.[13]

Writing in the tradition of grand theory, Lijphart certainly missed the opportunity to rework it in the face of new challenges. He may have taken the "consociational" aspects of power-sharing far too seriously while exploring why India, a deeply divided and even fractured society, was also able to sustain democracy. The mind-boggling diversity and division in India go much deeper than those in Dutch, Austrian, and Canadian societies. When divisions and conflicts based on caste, class, religion, and region go through the mill of the democratic process, they do not always follow the route of a prior sharing of power, based on consensus, but remain on a shifting sequence of strife and accommodation. The more the Indians accumulate the experience of strife sequentially resulting in accommodation, the more they expect such accommodations in advance, and the more they are able to tone down the anticipated virulence of oncoming strife.[14] At the other extreme one can also cite a number of major events when the center and the states have made decisions that had nothing to do with powersharing.

Even in the highly divided Indian society, those out of power wait for their turn at the polls. And their wait, in between elections, did produce results not only for themselves but also for the stability of Indian democracy.

Indian Democratic Experiences and Implications for Theory Construction

Finally, let us have a glimpse of where the Indian democratic experience has implications for theory construction.

Plurality and Diversity of Democratic Experience

The significance of the Indian democratic process suggests that since different societies come through different social and historical experiences, such experiences also become vital aspects even of their democratic practices, visions, and ideals. Because societies that sustain democratic polities are different, the fact of their being different must also be recognized as contributing to the plurality of democracies. Simultaneously, India's regional, cultural, and linguistic diversity exercises a powerful influence on the way its development and democratic processes work or the way in which its entire "ethnic federation" works.

The theories of democracy that we have so far are based largely on the emergence of the nineteenth- and twentieth-century societies in most of the Western European and North American countries, where their internal differences became less pronounced, or they had indeed found settled ways of incorporating such differences. Such a parallel does not do justice to the continuing diversity of Indian society. The Western societal picture, which is at the root of some of our theories of democracy, often makes us less sensitive to the persisting plurality or internal diversity of different societies in the non-Western world, which influence and shape their democratic process.

Socially Oriented Democratic Process

Unlike Western democracies, any attempt to understand the Indian democratic process independently of the extraordinary role played by the values, the cohesions, and the manners of transacting business at the level of *society*, will deprive us of any understanding of democratic *actualities* at the ground level. We need to look at the Indian democratic process as a continuing society-polity interaction until such time as the rules governing democratic practices of dos and do nots come to acquire a widespread legitimacy and adherence of their own or until such time that a civil society establishes a matrix within which democratic business is transacted regardless of one's social background.

Ethnopolitical Development

One of the arguments in this chapter has been that the Indians came to acquire universal suffrage and the right to political participation in advance of their commensurate preparation for it. Another is that elected and appointed officials, soon after independence, came to occupy the institutions of government, and it was not possible for all the segments of Indian society to influence them or to seek their response or their accountability. This asymmetrical political relationship created a unique problem for the fledgling democracy. There was no parallel for this in the evolution of Western democracies, in which it took 200 to 300 years of demand, agitation, and near rebellions to obtain, incrementally, the right of participation for the average citizen. In such a process of demands and commensurate pressure generated to support them, the citizens of Western democracies became politically mature enough to transact their political business with elected or appointed officials.

At the Indian end, the ethnopolitical development of its citizens had to wait for their political maturity through their own involvement in the democratic process. The more they involved themselves, the more they evolved politically, and the more they were able to narrow down the distance between themselves and their rulers. There was no simple or shortened way to hasten that process. This aspect of Indian democracy requires a lot of theorization.[15]

Normative-Pragmatic Balance

Finally, it is not enough to have a political ritual of periodic elections and plurality of political parties competing for political power to deepen the faith of citizens in democracy, as is often mistakenly believed. Democracies must also be made to produce results that are in keeping with citizens' expectations of them. And it is here that we find that citizens take too long to discover that at the root of the democratic process there is the principle of trial and error. If a democracy does not succeed in evolving policies that it expects will deliver desired results, then it should be able to force a course correction, with or without replacing elected personnel, but without destabilizing the society. This also means that the citizenry will have to put into office those who continually discuss with them the needed balance between what is normatively desirable and what is politically or realistically possible. The ability or inability within different societies to strike such a balance from time to time also needs theoretical exploration and analysis.

These, then, are some of the broad areas of Indian democratic experiences that could be explored in theory construction. Such explorations will have to take its democratic experience seriously.

Endnotes

1. A. H. Somjee, *Democracy and Political Change in Village India* (New Delhi: Orient Longmans, 1971).

2. See in this connection A. H. Somjee, "Caste and the Decline of Political Homogeneity," *American Political Science Review* 67, no. 3 (1973).

3. From Prem Shankar Jha's presentation at the Shastri Indo-Canadian Institute Conference on "Managing Change in the 21st Century: Indian and Canadian Perspectives" (New Delhi, January 1996).

4. See in this connection, *Vohra Committee Report: Nexus between Crime and Politics* (1995).

5. Celia W. Duggar, "Rich-Poor Gap Endangers India, President Warns," *Intenational Herald Tribune* (January 26, 2000).

6. Stanley A. Weiss, "Develop Separate Policies for India and Pakistan," *International Herald Tribune* (January 28, 2000).

7. A. H. Somjee, *Political Capacity in Developing Societies* (London: Macmillan, 1982): 29–59.

8. *The Hindu* (January 5, 2000).

9. A. H. Somjee and Geeta Somjee, "Milk Cooperatives and Profiles of Social Change in India," *Economic Development and Cultural Change* (April 1978). Also see Geeta Somjee and A. H. Somjee, *Reaching Out to the Poor* (New York: St. Martin's Press, 1989).

10. Robert Dahl, *Polyarchy, Participation and Opposition* (New Haven: Yale University Press, 1971): 2–8.

11. Samuel P. Huntington, *The Third Wave: Democratization in the Late Twentieth Century* (Norman, OK: University of Oklahoma Press, 1991): 6.

12. Arendt Lijphart, "The Puzzle of Indian Democracy: A Consociational Interpretation," *American Political Science Review* 90, no. 2 (1996).

13. Ibid., 258.

14. A. H. Somjee, "Party Linkages and Strife-Accommodation in Democratic India," in *Political Parties and Linkages: A Comparative Perspective*, ed. Kay Lawson (New Haven: Yale University Press, 1980): 204–21.

15. A. H. Somjee, *Development Theory: Critiques and Explorations* (New York: St. Martin's Press, 1991): 153–73.

Suggested Readings

Ayesha, Jalal. *Democracy and Authoritarianism in South Asia: A Comparative and Historical Perspective*. Cambridge, UK: Cambridge University Press, 1995.

Beteille, Andre. *Caste, Class and Power*. Berkeley: University of California Press, 1965.

Dahl, Robert. *Polyarchy: Participation and Opposition*. New Haven: Yale University Press, 1971.

Diamond, L., J. Linz and S. M. Lipset, eds. *Democracy in Developing Countries*. Boulder, Colo. L. Rienner, 1988-91.

Gellner, Ernest. "Civil Society in Historical Context," *International Social Science Journal* 129 (1991).

Gould, H. A. and S. Ganguly, eds. *India Votes: Alliance Politics and Minority Government in the Ninth and Tenth General Elections*. Boulder, Colo.: Westview, 1993.

Huntington, Samuel P. *The Third Wave: Democratization in the Late Twentieth Century*. Norman, Okla.: University of Oklahoma Press, 1991.

Huntington, S. P., and Joan Nelson. *No Easy Choice: Political Participation in Developing Countries*. Cambridge, Mass.: Harvard University Press, 1976.

Kohli, Atul. *India's Democracy*. Princeton, N.J.: Princeton University Press, 1988.

Kumar, Krishna. "Civil Society: An Inquiry into the Usefulness of Historical Terms," *British Journal of Sociology* 44 (Sept. 1993): 375-95.

Lijphart, Arendt. "The Puzzle of Indian Democracy: A Consociational Interpretation," *American Political Science Review* 90, no. 2 (June 1996).

Sen, Amartya and Jean Dreze. *India: Economic Development and Social Opportunity*. New Delhi and New York: Oxford University Press, 1999.

Somjee, A. H. *Political Capacity in Developing Societies*. London: Macmillan, 1982.

Somjee, A. H. *Parallels and Actualise of Political Development.* London: Macmillan, 1986.

Somjee, A. H. *Development Theory: Critiques and Explorations.* New York: St. Martin's Press, 1991.

Srinivas, M. N. *Social Change in Modern India.* Berkeley: University of California Press, 1969.

Weiner, Myron. *Party Building in a New State.* Chicago: Chicago University Press, 1967.

7

Democracy and Islam: Are They Compatible?

Anwar H. Syed

Western democratic theory asserts that people have the right to be governed by their consent, usually given through representatives, chosen in free and fair elections, who constitute themselves as legislative assemblies that make laws and authorize taxes and the disbursement of their proceeds. Individuals may express themselves freely, form associations, criticize and oppose the government of the day, and dismiss it if they do not approve of its performance. Political parties normally exist to organize elections and the legislature's business. We look for these elements in examining the status of democracy in the Muslim world.

The Muslim World

The area of our concern consists of some two scores of countries that contain large Muslim majorities. It is not feasible to deal with each one of them. I shall make some general observations about the Middle East and then examine the status of democracy in Egypt, Pakistan, Iran, and Turkey in greater detail. I shall then attempt to relate the strength or weakness of democracy in these polities to Islam and to their native political cultures.

The winds of democratic change would appear to have stayed away from much of the Muslim world, and where they have come, they have been received with considerable ambivalence or even skepticism. Iraq and Syria are cruel one-party dictatorships, backed by their respective military establishments, and therefore nothing need be said of them in the context of democracy. Saudi Arabia is a monarchy with no political parties, elections, or legislature. It does not allow freedom of speech or that of the press, and its security agencies keep their eyes open for dissidents. The king consults his family members, keeps himself accessible to tribal chiefs, other notables, and to an extent even to ordinary people. The same holds, more or less, for the Persian Gulf emirates except Kuwait. They have appointed advisory bodies whose recommendations do not bind the Amirs (kings). Rule in the emirates, however, is not as stern as it is in Saudi Arabia.

More often than not, Kuwait has been a democracy of sorts, It has had several elections since 1961, and these have been reasonably fair, except for a certain amount of gerrymandering to favor the Amir's tribal allies over the usually less cooperative townspeople. Debate in the Kuwaiti assembly is often vigorous, and members feel free to criticize the government's policies and officials. But, in the past, when they were too loud, the Amir suspended the assembly and restricted the freedom of the press as he did in 1976. There are no political parties in Kuwait, but the notables meet in "clubs," discuss issues, and convey their views to appropriate officials or quarters.[1]

Democracy worked well in Lebanon until its deep religious and ethnic divisions erupted into a long and devastating civil war starting in 1975. Parts of the country have been under Israeli and Syrian occupation for many years. The civil war has ended, but the political landscape in Lebanon is still much too unsettled to allow a useful discussion of the state of democracy in that country.

Jordan has been partly authoritarian and partly democratic since the early 1950s. Political parties operate, elections are held, and a parliament functions as a fairly vigorous forum of debate. On occasion, it has overridden the king's veto. Once, in 1976, the king dismissed it but restored it later, and it has been in place since then.

Egypt

In 1952 a group of army officers executed a coup, abolished the monarchy, and made Egypt a republic. In 1954 they chose one of their more dynamic members, Gemal Abdel Nasser, to be the country's president. He dissolved the legislature and banned political parties. But then he established a party of his own, first the "National Union" in 1956 and later the "Arab Socialist Union" (ASU) in 1962. These parties were formed to select candidates for elective office and to maintain contact with the masses, not so much to know what they desired but to tell them what the government expected from them. In 1956 a constitution was promulgated, which gave the president extensive executive and legislative powers. Nasser was elected president. The ASU managed the elections, but the resulting legislature exercised little power.

Nasser did not tolerate opponents. The Muslim Brotherhood was banned, and its leaders were arrested in 1954 and, again, in 1956. Its leading intellectual, Sayyid Qutb, was executed. The press was kept under scrutiny. Intelligence agencies looked for the regime's critics and also watched one another. Nasser's government closed down the Sharia, or Islamic courts, nationalized Islamic endowments, and abolished the sufi brotherhoods. A constitutional revision in 1964 made Islam the state religion, more to control Muslim institutions than to let them guide the government.[2]

Nasser died in September 1970. His successor, Anwar el-Sadat, toyed with the idea of a multiparty system. But then, instead, he divided the Arab Socialist Union into three sections to represent the leftist, rightist, and centrist political positions and to compete with one another in the elections of 1976. The centrist section, led by Sadat himself, converted itself into a political party, called the National Democratic Party. Other political groups also functioned. The parliament became freer to criticize, debate, and modify the executive's legislative proposals.

Sadat wanted to befriend the ulema (Islamic scholars and clergy). In 1980 he agreed to treat the *Shariah*-meaning the law and injunctions of Islam contained in the Quran and the Prophet's traditions, called his Sunna—as the main source of legislation, but this did not satisfy the Islamic groups. They wanted the regime to enforce the *Shariah*, not merely treat it as a source of inspiration. Excluded from overt participation in politics, the Muslim Brotherhood remained influential, nevertheless, and continued to oppose the un-Islamic Egyptian state and government. Sadat was killed in October 1981, and Hosni Mubarak, his vice president, took his place. Mubarak continued Sadat's policy of increasing freedom of the press and the role of political parties and parliament. Elections during his rule have been freer than they were in the 1970s. It would appear that, with the passage of time, democracy has made some noticeable progress in Egypt.

Pakistan

Pakistan has gone through three periods of parliamentary government (1947-58, 1972-77, and 1988-99). For the other twenty-five years or so, it has been ruled by military dictators or presidents supported by the military. I shall limit myself here to a statement of how democracy functioned in Pakistan when it did.

During its first eleven years (1947-58), Pakistan was a democracy but only in a manner of speaking. Members of the National Assembly, which also acted as a constitution-making body until 1956, had been elected in 1946, a year before independence. The assembly took nine years to adopt a constitution, and it did not hold a general election, with the result that its legitimacy became questionable. Even so, members came to the assembly well prepared and debate on important issues was both lively and competent. The press was relatively free. Numerous political parties existed; some of them had a religious or regional orientation and some were secular-minded. One of the major parties, called the Pakistan Muslim League (PML), ruled at the center and in the provinces until 1956. This party, as well as several others, was divided into cliques and factions, each revolving around a particular notable. The parties were not cohesive, and the members' loyalty shifted from one faction or party leader to another.

Consequently, prime ministers and their governments were often weak and indecisive, subject to manipulation by members of the assembly and also by the head of the state. The latter dismissed a prime minister in 1953, and the following year he dismissed the assembly itself. His successor, President Iskandar Mirza, intrigued with factional leaders in the assembly and forced several prime ministers out of office.

General elections were held in Pakistan for the first time toward the end of 1970 and returned the Pakistan People's Party (PPP), led by Zulfikar Ali Bhutto, to power in areas that now compose Pakistan. The National Assembly framed a new constitution providing for parliamentary government, in March 1973, after which Bhutto became the prime minister. His party soon fell prey to factionalism and violence and weakened at the provincial and local levels. Other parties existed and functioned, but not without considerable harassment and even persecution. Preventive detention laws and states of emergency, during which fundamental rights were suspended, remained in effect for periods of time. Critics and opponents were manhandled, tortured, and imprisoned in many instances. Representatives of the press were seduced or intimidated, and those who would still not submit were penalized in other ways.

Mr. Bhutto came to the National Assembly only rarely and, as he stayed away, so did many of his ministers and party members. Debate was usually dull when it was not frivolous and flippant. Bhutto's government held a general election in March 1977 and rigged it on such a large scale as to have instigated a massive protest movement, which encouraged General Ziaul Haq, the army chief, to overthrow Prime Minister Bhutto in a coup on July 5, 1977.[3]

The third parliamentary regime (1988-99) saw two prime ministers, namely, Benazir Bhutto (Zulfikar Ali's daughter) and Nawaz Sharif, a wealthy industrialist. Their rule was as personal and authoritarian as was that of

Mr. Bhutto, but it was more incompetent and corrupt. The press was free, but both prime ministers were vindictive and oppressive toward their political foes. The president of Pakistan dismissed Miss Bhutto twice and Nawaz Sharif once for corruption, incompetence, and misuse of official authority. Sharif was ousted the second time (October 1999) by the army chief on similar grounds.

During this period elections were held in 1988, 1990, 1993, and 1996. The 1988 elections were believed to have been fair but not the ones held in 1993. The other two were said to have involved some "irregularities" but not blatant rigging. Of the two major parties, the PML was somewhat better organized than was the PPP. The PML has seen numerous changes in its top leadership and, in spite of factionalism, it has retained considerable popular support. Top leadership in the PPP has remained in the Bhutto family, and recently Miss Bhutto's appointed executive committee elected her the party's chairperson for life. During the last several years the party has been in a shambles.

The National Assembly has been just as sedate and ineffective as before. Individuals contest assembly elections not because they wish to discuss issues of public policy, but to gain prestige in their respective areas, to exact rewards for their support of party leaders, and to have leverage with government officials in their respective constituencies. The reason why democracy has not worked as well in Pakistan as it might have done is not that the politicians are incompetent, but that their commitment to the public interest is weak.

Officially, Pakistan is an Islamic republic. Each of its three constitutions—those of 1956, 1962, and 1973—contained the provision that no laws repugnant to the Quran and Sunna would be made. In 1985, acting on his own authority as a military ruler, General Ziaul Haq inserted numerous Islamic provisions in the constitution of 1973. But many of them have not been enforced and, generally speaking, Pakistanis do not take the Islamic character of their state seriously, while the ulema regard it as hypocritical.[4]

Iran

From 559 B.C. when Cyrus the Great ascended the Persian throne until the end of Pahlavi rule in January 1979, kings have ruled Iran. Iranians have traditionally wanted a strong king capable of maintaining order, preserving their territorial integrity and freedom from foreign domination, and, above all, providing justice. But they were blessed with such a king only rarely. For the most part, monarchical rule in Iran (both Zorastrian and, after 661 A.D., Muslim) was personal, absolute, arbitrary, arrogant, corrupt, and often weak.

After the middle of the nineteenth century, as European diplomats and businessmen came to Iran and as Iranian young people went to study in

Europe, especially France, a group of intellectuals and professional persons, who admired not only Western technology but also Western social and political ideas and institutions, emerged. They desired popular participation in politics and limits on the king's authority. Note that at this time the Iranian kings were politically weak, profligate, and indebted to and subservient to foreign powers, mainly Britain and Russia. An unexpected alliance between the Westernized intellectuals, some of the more liberal ulema, and their followers among merchants and ordinary people forced the king to accept, in principle, a constitutional democratic system. Their efforts in the pursuit of this goal between 1905 and 1911 are known in Iranian history as the "constitutional revolution."

In 1906 the ailing Qajar Shah, Muzaffaruddin, agreed to the election of a Majlis (parliament) to draft a constitution, which it did, and which he signed as he lay on his death bed in January 1907. But with some support from Britain and Russia, his two successors declined to implement it. On October 31, 1925, the Majlis deposed the Qajar dynasty and, in a moment of thoughtlessness, offered the throne to Reza Khan, an army officer of some distinction, who then became Reza Shah Pahlavi.

The constitution of 1906 was never formally repudiated nor was it ever implemented. Both of the two Pahlavi kings ignored the Majlis and manipulated it when they did call it to session. Elections, when held, were rigged. The Shah appointed prime ministers and other higher-ranking civil and military officials.

The two Pahlavis thought of themselves as modernizers, and their concept of modernization included the Westernization of Iranian culture. Both of them were convinced also that they knew best what was right and good for Iran. They had no tolerance for those who differed with them or opposed them. One of Muhammad Reza Shah's numerous intelligence agencies, the notorious SAVAK, is believed to have tortured tens of thousands of Iranians to death. They disallowed or discouraged political parties. A loose alliance of liberals, called the National Front, existed but it had no mass following. The Tudeh (a communist party) operated covertly, but while it had some following in urban centers, it had little influence in rural areas. In 1975 the Shah created a party of his own, called the "Rastakhiz" (National Resurgence Party), and outlawed all others. The Rastakhiz got nowhere and did nothing for him.

Mohammad Reza Shah, as well as his father, professed to be Muslim but regarded Islam as an obstacle to Iran's modernization and progress. He thought of its exponents, the ulema, as a nuisance who should be mitigated as much as possible. He, even more than is father, persecuted them. A few of them were seduced or intimidated to stay quiet or cooperate with him, but many remained hostile. He seized the endowments, which they had managed to support their schools, mosques, and charitable activities, and exiled, imprisoned, and tortured some of them.[5]

The Shah's hostility toward the Islamic establishment, his indiscriminate rush to modernization, his importation of tens of thousands of American and European managers, advisors, and technicians, his promotion of Western culture, his own and his family's huge misappropriation of public moneys, and his subservience to the United States generated a massive revolt against his rule, led by Ayatollah Ruhollah Khomeini. He fled, followed by many thousands of his supporters. The revolutionaries abolished the monarchy, declared Iran to be an Islamic republic, and placed Ayatollah Khomeini at its head in February 1979.

The Islamic Republic of Iran

The vast majority of Iranians subscribe to the Shia version of Islam. The Islamic republic follows a model presented by Ayatollah Khomeini in one of his writings, titled "Velayat-e-Faqih." It calls for an Islamic state in which the *Shariah* would be supreme. The ayatollah ordered a referendum, and more than 90 percent of those who responded said they wanted Iran to be an Islamic state. Toward the end of 1979 he approved a constitution prepared by an elected body of "experts." It established a legislature, called the Majlis as before, to be elected every four years by universal adult franchise, and an elected president who would have his own council of ministers.

This constitution also created two religious authorities entitled to veto any legislation and acts of the executive that they might find to be repugnant to the *Shariah*. These authorities were a Council of Guardians (consisting of a dozen higher-ranking clerics) and, at the very top of the governmental system, a functionary called the Faqih (pressumably the most distinguished jurist available). He could veto legislation, the government's domestic and foreign policies, and appointments to various public offices, and he could disqualify individuals who wished to run for elective office. The Assembly of Experts, referred to above, elected Ayatollah Khomeini as the Faqih.

After his death in 1989 the political ulema chose Ali Khamenei as the new Faqih. He had been much more of a political activist than an Islamic scholar. He was only a "hujjat-al-Islam," a position lower than that of an ayatollah. Departing from the customary way of advancement in the Shia clerical hierarchy, the political clergy designated Ali Khameini an ayatollah. Thus, they transformed the office of the Faqih, making it more political than religious.

Since 1980 several presidential elections have been held, most recently in 1997, in which a moderate cleric, Muhammad Khatami, won nearly 70 percent of the 29.7 million votes cast. It may be useful to note, as an indication of a trend, that his predecessor, Ali Akbar Hashemi Rafsanjani, was also a moderate, even pragmatic, cleric. Six elections to the Majlis have been held between 1980 and 2000. The conservatives dominated the Majlis following the first four elections, but they won only a plurality in the fifth one (held in 1992), which showed a decline in their popularity.

In the sixth election, held on February 18, 2000, the liberal reformists won a clear majority (170 of the 290 seats), even while a second round of polling remained to be held in 65 electoral districts when these first reports came in, meaning that eventually their victory would probably become even larger. Taking only 45 seats, plus a few more that they might gain in the second round, the conservatives would appear to have suffered a humiliating defeat. I should add that the liberal reformists are those who would lift, or at least soften, the current restrictions on persons, organizations, and the press. Some of them want to restrain, or even abolish, religious authorities such as the Council of Guardians and the Faqih. They want their governments to represent the three important elements in their national psyche, namely, the old Persian tradition, Islam, and, more recently, a degree of Western thought and culture—not any one of them to the exclusion of the other two.[6]

Soon after the establishment of the republic, the clergy formed a political party, called the Islamic Republican Party (IRP), and banned all others. The IRP itself was dissolved in 1988 and replaced by smaller groups, cliques, and factions. The government changed its mind before the elections of 1996 to allow parties to emerge and contest elections if they would undertake not to oppose the republic's basic Islamic character.

The state of human rights would appear to be precarious in the Islamic republic. During its first two years or so, "people's courts," presided over by clerics, summarily tried and executed hundreds of persons, including politicians, military officers, and bureaucrats, deemed to have been loyal to the Shah. The more militant opponents of the regime, notably the leftist Mujahedin-e-Khalq, possessing a large and seasoned guerrilla army, were suppressed. All kinds of other "dissidents" were detained. They must have been quite numerous, for political prisons are just as full under Islamic rule as they were under the Shah.

By way of implementing its version of the Islamic ethic, the new government imposed the "hejab" (covering for hair and the body except the face and hands) on women; banned or discouraged romantic themes in novels, movies, and television shows; forbade drinking, gambling, and all other activities of which Islam disapproves; and toward these ends it restricted freedom of expression. Notwithstanding this great concern with ethics, corruption is rife in the Islamic republic, not only among bureaucrats who will do nothing for a citizen without a bribe, but also among a great many of the ulema. The ordinary Iranian's life and liberty are no better or securer now than they were during the Shah's despotic rule. The trend of election results suggests not only that the revolution is mellowing but also that it is mellowing because the people are becoming increasingly disenchanted with the Islamic republic and the ulema as its overseers.

Turkey

Since the end of World War II, democracy has worked more effectively in Turkey than anywhere else in the Muslim world. But it has not been unblemished as we will see. Mustafa Kemal Atatürk, elected president of the Turkish republic in 1923, made no pretense to being a democrat and admitted that he was an autocratic ruler, but claimed that he did what he did to advance Turkey's interests, not to appease public opinion. He dominated the National Assembly, elected every four years under a constitution adopted in 1923, which consisted largely of Westernized former military officers and civil servants who supported him. He launched the Republican People's Party (RPP), banned all other parties, and toyed with the idea of a two-party system but abandoned it. Turkey remained a one-party state until a few years after Atatürk's death in 1938. He had no desire to politicize the peasantry, kept the franchise limited to the propertied and educated classes, and was content to rule with the help of elites working under his direction.

Atatürk was skeptical of religion generally and saw Islam as a great impediment to Turkey's modernization which, he thought, included Westernization of Turkish culture. He forbade the "fez" (traditional Turkish cap), ordered his people to wear Western hats and adopt surnames, and encouraged women to discard the veil. He changed the Turkish language script from Arabic to Latin and made Sunday, instead of Friday, the weekly holiday. He disestablished Islam as the state religion, abolished Islamic law and courts, reduced the number of mosques, and discouraged prayer and fasting. He seized Islamic endowments, banned the sufi orders, and closed down their houses. Atatürk was a fierce nationalist and a secularist. His reforms, so to speak, may have appealed to other Westernized, secular-minded Turks, but as Turkish politics after his death demonstrated, they had not gone well with the Turkish masses, especially those in the rural areas.[7]

Atatürk's successor, Ismet Inonu, allowed a multiparty system to emerge in Turkey in 1945. One of the new parties, called the Democrat, won a landslide victory over the RPP in two elections in the 1950s. Led by a charismatic leader, Adnan Menderes, it reversed some of the late Atatürk's anti-Islamic measures to enhance its popularity. Soon Menderes and his colleagues became dictatorial. They imposed restrictions on the press and public meetings. They subjected the RPP to severe repression, confiscated its property, shut down its newspaper, and tried to oust its adherents in the bureaucracy, army, universities, and economic public enterprises.

The military overthrew the Menderes government in 1960 and, later, two other governments in 1971 and 1980 on the grounds that they were violative of the constitution, oppressive, corrupt, and, in some cases, too weak and unstable to control urban violence. The military amended the constitution to enhance the president's authority, secure the independence of the universities and the judiciary, and safeguard individual rights. In each case, soon after the military rule ended, political parties, which had been outlawed, returned to the scene under different names. New parties also surfaced, such as the Motherland Party and the National Salvation Party, an Islamic party which later changed its name to the Welfare Party.[8]

On occasion a single party has won a majority in the assembly and formed the government, as was the case with the Democrat Party in the 1950s and with the Motherland Party in the early 1980s. But more often governments have been formed by coalitions of two or more parties and groups and, as in many such cases, they have been unstable, weak, and indecisive. This continues to be the case. One still hears of victimization of political opponents and stern measures against the advocates of Islamic rule perceived as prone to violence. But generally speaking, individual rights in Turkey are fairly secure.

An intriguing but difficult question concerning Turkey confronts us, which I should mention even if I cannot answer it satisfactorily. Why has democracy worked better here than anywhere else in the Muslim world? One reason may be that certain forms of social organization which inhibit democracy, discussed below, are not present in Turkey. It has never had landowners, each possessing hundreds, even thousands, of acres of land, with the result that it is not plagued by feudalism. Second, except for a relatively small area in eastern Anatolia where the Kurds live, Turkey is not, and was not, a tribal society.

A substantial part of the population in western Anatolia is descended from people who emigrated there from the Balkans after the overthrow of Ottoman rule in that region and, thus, they have a European origin. A small part of Turkish territory is still located in Europe. The elites in the military, bureaucracy, universities, professions, business and industry, and some even in politics, are Europeans or of European extraction. Even more important is the fact that they think of themselves as Europeans (regardless of what the Europeans may think of them). They want to be like Europeans, and in looking for models to follow they look to Western, not Eastern, Europe. I venture to suggest that this state of mind on their part is a major reason for their inclination to secularism and for their desire to be seen as successful in operating a democracy. This was the case with the Young Turks toward the end of the nineteenth century, with Kemal Atatürk and his colleagues, and it may be the case with the elites even now. But I doubt that the Turkish peasantry has the same state of mind and inclinations. As its participation in politics grows, the functioning of democracy in Turkey may undergo changes.

Interpretations

At this time, democracy in its Western version is working reasonably well in Turkey; it is struggling to go forward in Egypt, Jordan, Kuwait, and Pakistan;

it is absent from the other emirates and Saudi Arabia; and its status in Iran since the Islamic revolution of 1979 is problematic. How do we explain this state of affairs? Because the great majority of people in these countries are Muslim, it is unavoidable to ask whether Islam and democracy are compatible. It is also important to emphasize that the words "Islamic" and "Muslim" should not be used synonymously, for not everything that Muslims actually do is Islamic.

Let me first submit that the Quran and the Prophet's Sunna have little to say about governmental organization. The Quran asks Muslims to settle their collective affairs by mutual consultation ("shura"), and it requires them to obey those from among themselves who are rulers. But it does not specify how shura is to be conducted or how anyone may become a ruler. Sunni Muslims regard the Prophet's rule in Medina (622–32 A.D.) and that of the first four "pious" caliphs (632–61 A.D.) as genuinely Islamic. But the precedents of this period do not provide clear guidance.

The Prophet never said how his successors were to be chosen. Each of them came to office in a different way. An elective element operated in three of these cases in a small way, but we would not equate it with a popular election as we understand that term today. Neither during this period of Islamic rectitude, nor at any time later, was succession to rule institutionalized. The Prophet did occasionally consult his companions in settling affairs of state, and so did his four pious successors. But they did so on an ad hoc basis and did not feel bound by the advice they had received. No known body of the consultees with an established membership list and schedule of meetings existed. The shura was also never institutionalized.

Issues such as the consent of the governed and their right to choose those who would govern them did not engage the medieval Muslim jurists. But they were concerned with the ruler's pledge of following and implementing the *Shariah*, which he normally gave in return for the allegiance promised to him by the notables and others. The jurists took up the issues of accountability and political obligation. What were the Muslims to do about an unrighteous ruler?

The issue of accountability came to a head only once in Muslim history, in 656 A.D., during the rule of the third pious caliph, Uthman bin Affan. Groups of Muslims accused him of nepotism in the allocation of public funds and offices. They asked him to step down, which he declined to do, arguing that God had given him his office and only He could take it away, that he was not accountable to his critics, and that they had no right to remove him. They rejected his reasoning and killed him. This event became one of the reasons for civil war among Muslims during the rule of the last pious caliph, Ali ibne Abu Talib (656–61 A.D.).

Returning to the medieval Muslim jurists, they agreed that the people's obligation to obey ceased if the ruler's conduct violated the *Shariah*. But they were divided over whether the people might then revolt. Abu Hanifa (d. 767), regarded as the greatest of jurists in Sunni Islam, financed a revolt against an unrighteous caliph of his own time, but did not join it, because he thought it would fail, which it did.[9] Later, Ibne Taimiya, a jurist in the tradition of Imam Hanbal (d. 855), also upheld the right of popular revolt against a wicked ruler. On the other hand, al-Baqillani (d. 1012), al-Baghdadi (d. 1037), al-Mawardi (974–1058), and al-Ghazali (1058–1111) maintained that the community could withdraw its loyalty from an unrighteous ruler and transfer it to a successful rival. But they did not favor revolt, for they feared that it would divide and disrupt the community. Some of them quoted the "sages," who had counseled that forty years of tyranny were preferable to one day of anarchy.[10]

The jurists took this position reluctantly, invoking a "doctrine of necessity" in its defense. Al-Ghazali observed that "the concessions made by us are not spontaneous, but necessity makes lawful what is forbidden." Earlier, al-Mawardi had asserted that "necessity dispenses with stipulations which are impossible to fulfill." In this connection, it may also be useful to recall one of the Prophet's traditions, which says:

> Whosoever sees evil, let him undo it with his hand; if he cannot do this, let him speak against it; and if he cannot do even this, let him despise it in his heart, and this is the lowest degree of faith.[11]

In actual practice, while rivals have overthrown kings, Muslim masses, until recently, remained content with despising tyrants in their "hearts."

Setting aside the medieval jurists' reservations, more recent and contemporary Muslim thinkers have not only endorsed revolt against tyrants but also supported modern democratic ideas and institutions. Basing themselves on the Islamic concepts of man's status as God's vice-regent on earth, mutual consultation, consensus, and "ijtehad" (right of independent judgment in interpreting the *Shariah*), some of the ulema as well as lay scholars of Islam have argued that Islam not only allows but also requires a democratic polity, so long as it works within the limits prescribed by God and his Prophet. Abulala Maududi, a well-known Islamic scholar, notes that an Islamic state, in which all have equal rights, is not to be governed by the ulema but by the entire community to whom God has delegated a part of His sovereignty. The community, through the expression of its "general will," elects executives whom it may depose if it finds their performance to be unsatisfactory.[12]

Professor Fazlur Rahman observes that shura means mutual discussion in which all participate as equals; it does not mean merely that the ruler consults some of his subordinates or companions. He adds that those who would deny a Muslim community its right to democracy make Islam "null and void." Professor Muhammad Hamidullah notes that the modes of consultation (shura)— electoral rolls, form of election, and duration of representation—may be determined by community leaders according to the needs of their country and age. Baqi as-Sadr, an Iraqi political theorist, says that the people have a right to participation in governmental decision-making and they may do so through an elected representative assembly. Earlier, Muhammad Iqbal (one of the founding fathers of Pakistan and a renowned poet and philosopher) had suggested that the individual's right to ijtehad might be transferred to a representative assembly. The concept of ijma (consensus) would justify majority rule.[13] It seems to me that while Islam may be interpreted to allow rule by a pious few, it does also leave the door open to democracy. It is concerned primarily with righteousness: a people may prefer a corrupt democracy to a corrupt dictatorship, but their choice in this regard is made outside the framework of Islam.

A word should now be said about the Shia persuasion, which has prevailed in Iran since the early sixteenth century. The Shia believe that following the Prophet's death, the rulership belonged to his "house," meaning his descendants through his daughter, Fatima, and her husband, Ali ibne Abu Talib. This chain of descendants consisted of eleven others after Ali. They were, according to the Shia, the most authentic interpreters of the *Shariah*, innocent of sin and even error, and therefore truly entitled to lead and rule the Muslim community. Ali ruled for five years, and his older son, Hasan, for about six months. The rest of them suffered extreme persecution at the hands of the rulers of their time. The twelfth of them, known as Mehdi and also as the "hidden imam," is believed to have ascended to heaven in 879 A.D. He remains there and continues to be entitled to rule the world. In his absence all governments are essentially illegitimate; Muslims may remain aloof from them, obey them if essential, and revolt against them if possible.

Khomeini changed this outlook significantly. He maintained that in the hidden imam's absence, the ulema, who presumably knew his mind, could rule and that their government would be legitimate. Moreover, the ulema, led by the Faqih, could reinterpret Islam to the extent of modifying even such basic requirements as the duty to pray, fast, and perform the pilgrimage to Mecca. Islam would guide the state, but the state could remake Islam.[14] It should, however, be noted that none of the other "grand" ayatollahs (six or so) accepted Khomeini's innovation and, instead, continued to adhere to the traditional Shia view.

Some Western students of Islam caution that Muslims will have democracy only if they reinterpret Islam and their historical tradition, because these inhibit democracy more than encouraging it. This, in fact, has been happening. Muslim intellectuals generally reject the kingship that emerged and prevailed after 661 A.D. As we have seen above, reinterpretation of Islam with regard to several matters, including those relating to governance, has been going on for more than a century. Sir Syed Ahmad Khan, Muhammad Iqbal, and Maududi in South Asia, Ali Shariati, Jalal Ale-Ahmad, Khomeini, and some of his fellow ayatollahs in Iran, and Jamaluddin Afghani and his numerous disciples in Egypt, notably Muhammad Abduh, have all been reinterpreters.

In actual practice, most Muslims follow Islam only selectively. They are guided also by their native traditions which, interestingly enough, have nativized their Islam. We must then ask how their native traditions affect their receptivity to democracy.

The native tradition in all of the Muslim countries has been authoritarian, not only in government but in almost all other relationships. This continues to be the case, albeit to a lesser degree: A disposition to defiance is developing among the subordinate parties in these relationships. In the native political cultures of some, though not all, of the Muslim countries—notably Pakistan, Iran, and Egypt—a related element is feudalism. Great landowners get peasants and tenants to work on their lands, not on a contractual but on a customary basis. Peasants and tenants, even their wives and children, do errands for landlords and their families, beyond their work on the land, without compensation. They are meek and servile toward landlords and their agents, and any sign of disobedience or independence of action on their part will bring forth the landlord's wrath.

The relationship between landlords themselves is hierarchical: larger landowners expect deference from the smaller ones and will use violence against the latter if deference is not forthcoming. They pay homage and tribute to the higher powers—let us say, rulers and their agents—when they are strong. But they will not be submissive to them if they see that the higher powers have weakened. Loyalty will cease or shift from one overlord to another, depending upon whose power is ascendant. In the context of democratic politics, the same holds for loyalty to parties and interaction with party leaders.[15]

Next we should consider tribalism which, in a strange way, mitigates the impact of feudalistic authoritarianism. Pakistan, Iran, Saudi Arabia, and all of the emirates are tribal societies in varying degrees. The tribes may be nomadic or settled. The former are, for the most part, beyond the government's reach because they keep moving from place to place. Their chiefs and notables, acting together, settle disputes, if any are brought to them, and punish those who commit crimes according to their customary law. Substantial equality prevails among their members even if some of them own more goats, sheep, or camels.

Settled tribes operate in a similar fashion. They do accept some government regulation but attempt to exact advantages from it in exchange for their cooperation. Like the nomads, they too are largely self-governing and well disposed toward the values of individual freedom and equality. But, wishing to maintain their own separate identities, they have little interest in politics at the national level even if it is democratic. Another factor, unfavorable to democracy, is the tribal inclination for violence. Intertribal warfare has been a fact of life throughout history. And, within a given tribe, enmities between individuals and families, which erupt into violence, continue for generations. Resorting to the arts of peace for settling disputes, essential to the successful functioning of democracy, is not common in tribal societies.

Patriarchy and it next of kin, patrimonialism, prevail in all Muslim countries. These terms are well understood, but I should still mention, even if briefly, a few aspects of patrimonialism. Rule is personal. Decisions are justified not on "merit" but on the ground that they have emanated from the ruler. He may be influenced by those who have his ear and there is, therefore, intense rivalry among the elites to get close to him. On his part, he keeps them in a state of conflict so that they may not be able to form alliances against him. This pattern characterizes not only the man at the top but also his lieutenants in their relationship with their own subordinates.

Neither Islamic nor native cultural traditions have brought democracy to the Muslim world. It has appeared where it has because of the Muslim elites' increasing exposure to the West. This has gone on for more than a hundred years. The aspiration for democracy is becoming a part of the Muslim political cultures. Muslims, increasingly, want democracy regardless of what anyone may say about its compatibility with Islam. They cherish Islam, even when they do not practice all of it, and they want democracy. Reinterpretations of Islam, referred to above, make it possible for them to have both. Neither Islam nor their native traditions are rigidly fixed; both are undergoing change. Given the present ease of communication, their nativity is absorbing aspects of Western culture.

A Muslim democracy need not be regarded as a "contradiction in terms," if it makes certain symbolic concessions to Islam or even implements parts of the *Shariah*, if that is what the people concerned want. Israel is not a secular state, but it is a democracy. The United Kingdom is a democracy despite the facts that, at the symbolic level, the Queen is Queen by the grace of God, defender of the faith, and head of the Church of England, that the Lords Spiritual sit alongside the Lords Temporal in the House of Lords, and that, in actual practice, no Catholic or Jew has ever been prime minister. The connection between secularism and democracy would seem to have been overstated.

Considering the current trends, it seems that the prospects of democracy in the Muslim world will improve with the passage of time. Its absence in Saudi Arabia and most of the emirates may be due to the fact that these are "rentier" states with enormous revenues and very small populations. They provide subsidized food and housing and jobs for those who want them. Their people pay little or nothing in taxes. Their desire for participation in government is therefore not great, but it will probably increase considering that tens of thousands of their young people have received education in the West and consider their governments to be anachronistic. They will eventually want political participation, and when they do, democracy may begin to emerge in this region also.

Endnotes

1. James A. Bill and Robert Springborg, *Politics in the Middle East* (Glenview, Ill.: Scott, Foresman, 1990): 245–46, 283–87.

2. For an account of Nasser's rule and that of his successors (Anwar Sadat and Husni Mubarak), see M. E. Yapp, *The Near East Since the First World War* (London: Longman, 1991): chap. 8. Also see Bill and Springborg, 208–27.

3. Anwar H. Syed, *The Discourse and Politics of Zulfikar Ali Bhutto* (New York: St. Martin's Press, 1992): chap. 8.

4. Anwar H. Syed, *Pakistan: Islam, Politics, and National Solidarity* (New York: Praeger, 1982): 142–52.

5. Sandra Mackey, *The Iranians: Persia, Islam and the Soul of a Nation* (New York: Penguin/Plume, 1996): chaps. 7–9.

6. For a good account of liberal and conservative trends in Iran today, see *The Economist* (February 19, 2000): 19–20, 26–28. A fuller statement of the same, and an account of Khatami's election as President in 1997 and the Majlis elections of 1992 and 1996 may be seen in Mackey, *The Iranians*, 393–410.

7. Yapp, *The Near East*, chap. 5.

8. Yapp, *The Near East*, chap. 12.

9. Hamidullah, *Khutabat-e-Bahawalpur* (Lectures in Bahawalpur), (Islamabad, 1988): 101.

10. Syed, *Pakistan*, 16–18.

11. Syed, *Pakistan*, 16.

12. John O. Voll and John L. Esposito, "Islam Has Strong Democratic Traditions," in *Islam: Opposing Viewpoints*, ed. Paul A. Winters (San Diego, Calif.: Greenhaven Press, 1995): 115.

13. Ibid., 116–18.

14. Mackey, *The Iranians*, 349.

15. Syed, *Discourse and Politics*, 257–59.

Suggested Readings

Baker, Raymond W. *Egypt's Uncertain Revolution under Nasser and Sadat.* Cambridge, Mass.: Harvard University Press, 1978.

Enayat, Hamid. *Modern Islamic Political Thought.* Austin: University of Texas Press, 1982.

Esposito, John. *Islam: The Straight Path.* New York: Oxford University Press, 1989.

Farah, Tawfic E., ed. *Political Behavior in Arab States.* Boulder, Colo.: Westview Press, 1983.

Hourani, Albert. *Arabic Thought in the Liberal Age.* London: Oxford, 1962.

Ismael, Jacqueline. *Kuwait: Social Change in Historical Perspective.* Syracuse, N.Y.: Syracuse University Press, 1982.

Khuri, Fuad. *Tribe and State in Bahrain.* Chicago: University of Chicago Press, 1981.

Layne, Linda L. *Elections in the Middle East: Implications of Recent Trends.* Boulder, Colo.: Westview Press, 1987.

Mackey, Sandra. *The Saudis: Inside the Desert Kingdom.* Boston: Houghton Mifflin, 1987.

Noll, John O. *Islam: Continuity and Change in the Modern World.* Boulder, Colo.: Westview Press, 1982.

Peterson, J. E. *The Arab Gulf States: Steps Toward Political Participation.* New York: Praeger, 1988.

Sharabi, Hisham. *Neopatriarchy: A Theory of Distorted Change in Arab Society.* New York: Oxford, 1988.

Springborg, Robert. *Mubarak's Egypt.* Boulder, Colo.: Westview Press, 1989.

Sullivan, Earl L. *Women in Egyptian Public Life.* Syracuse, N.Y.: Syracuse University Press, 1986.

8
—

Democracy in Africa: Does It Have a Chance?

Yohannes Woldemariam

Introduction

The post–Cold War era has given rise to the greater promotion of liberal democracy by the European Union, the International Monetary Fund (IMF), the World Bank and the United States. Before the end of the Cold War, Western governments, with one eye on Cold War geopolitics and the other on protecting their own economic and political interests in Africa, openly supported a succession of friendly dictators. However, now is a time of transitions to and consolidations of democracy, not only in Eastern Europe and the former Soviet Union, but also in Africa and elsewhere. Northern governments and financial institutions are urging moves toward political liberalization and pluralism as a condition for continued foreign aid.

Toward this end, African countries have been divided into four categories. At the top of the pyramid are a handful of states with strong commitments to laissez-faire and democratic governance but which are not yet considered consolidated democracies. Benin, Botswana, Mali, Madagascar, Mauritius, Namibia, and South Africa fall in this category. Second are those that have shown modest promise by reforming their economies and have carried out multiparty elections.

Burkina Faso, Kenya, Malawi, Mozambique, Senegal, Tanzania, Uganda, and Zambia fall in this camp. In the third category are countries such as Burundi, Eritrea, Gabon, Gambia, Niger, Ethiopia, and Rwanda. These countries have embraced macroeconomic reform and seek to develop without democracy. The last category of countries encompasses those that either resist both economic reform and democratic rule or are unable to exercise authority across their territory due to civil war or state collapse. Angola, Cameroon, Chad, Congo, Nigeria, Sierra Leone, Somalia, and Sudan are in this group. More recently, events in Ethiopia indicate that it seems to be on the verge of joining the last category of countries. None of these categories can be assumed to be stable as events in Africa are in constant flux and recidivism or stagnancy occurs frequently.

Scholars are also increasingly endorsing the trend toward liberalization. Leading Africa specialist Crawford Young has argued that what is taking place is a broad form of political as well as economic liberalization that can possibly provide a pathway beyond perpetual crisis. And just as there is little way out of political crisis except through democratization, Young maintains: "The liberal market economy for the moment has no credible competitor."[1] In a similar vein, according to Africa scholar Larry Diamond, economic and social pluralism constitutes the most powerful source of democratic energy, initiative, and pressure in Africa. In fact, Diamond sees throughout the world "the most widespread diffusion of democratic forms of governance since the inception of the nation-state," largely thanks to economic liberalization, because "a society energized and transformed by liberal economic growth demands and requires liberal politics as well."[2] Others believe that capitalism can exist under a wide variety of regimes such as liberal democracy, fascism, or military dictatorship. There is a connection between democracy and free markets but no clear causative relationship.

Nevertheless, the "democratic project" is becoming the dominant issue in African politics, not only because of the insistence of outsiders, but also because there are indications that peasants, workers, and intellectuals in Africa are no longer prepared to put up with being victims of despotic regimes. They are exiting the public realm and creating new private spaces in which they hope to construct their own independent and parallel systems of survival. Such an exit symbolizes their rejection of the existing forms of authoritarian governance and their desire for a new deal embedded in more democratic structures of accountability.

But how can such democratic structures emerge from the authoritarianism so prevalent in Africa today? Is liberal democracy the appropriate model for Africa? Can democracy be simply dictated or wished into existence? The latest move for liberalism and democracy is really nothing new; it has been the language of comparative politics since the 1950s and 1960s and was rekindled in the 1990s in the form of neodevelopmentalism. In the 1950s and

1960s, prominent scholars such as Seymour Martin Lipset and W. W. Rostow argued for the universal implementation of liberal democracy without due consideration for the necessary contextual prerequisites and contingencies such as history, demography, ethnicity, religion, kinship, viability of civil society, political culture, patrimonialism, and authoritarianism. Rostow suggested that given the single motor force of national economic development, a viable democracy would emerge. It would be established through a process of gradual evolution.[3] But his model ignored important constraints such as ethnicity, culture, and local and regional differences that often inhibit and prevent the realization of liberal democracy.

There are also ironies in neodevelopmentalism as prescribed for Africa. As foreign policy specialist Howard J. Wiarda states: "Western foreign assistance programs, largely based on the older ethnocentric understandings, have seldom been successful . . . because Western policy makers . . . lack the comprehension and knowledge base to understand the Third World on its own terms, its own language, and in its own cultural and institutional terms."[4] Western history cannot be used as a guide for the developing world. The international context and landscape are quite different from those of earlier developmental periods. The influence exerted by Northern governments, the World Bank, and other development agencies hinders the continent's ability to creatively experiment with alternative innovations and has often harmed Africa by trampling on independence and indigenous thought. It is impossible to understand the struggle for democracy in Africa without considering the role of the international financial institutions and Northern governments.

An important step in creating African democracy is to find a democratic tradition within Africa and adapt it to universal democratic ideals. The transition to democracy cannot be assumed to be a uniform process always having the same social classes, the same types of political issues, or even the same methods of solution. Nor does a model of transition need to maintain that democratic evolution is a steady process that is homogeneous over time. Many African countries have not enjoyed the prolonged economic development, civic culture, institution building, and social consensus necessary for democracy's effectiveness. Hence, discussion and evaluation of some important constraints are in order, followed by some recommendations.

Historical Factors and Political Cultures

The basic requirements of national unity and a sense of identity that some scholars have presented as necessary for a transition to democracy have been largely absent in Africa. The literature says that the vast majority of citizens in a democracy-to-be must have no doubt or mental reservations about the political community to which they belong. Decolonization and independence do not necessarily bring a sense of national community. The new nations of Africa had borders defined in the Berlin conference of 1884–85 by rival colonial powers but not necessarily corresponding to cultural, ethnic, or political boundaries. Africans entered the nation-state system just as the operations of that system were being challenged in Europe itself. Basque separatism in Spain, the dissolving of Yugoslavia, and the coming into existence of the European Union are just three examples. The problem in Africa is that almost all of the countries on the continent still have not sufficiently developed the basic characteristics of nationhood. One of the leading scholars in West European nationalism, Hans Kohn, observed that nationalities are

> . . . Products of the living force of history (most of them possessing) certain objective factors distinguishing them from other nationalities like common descent, language, territory, political entity, customs and traditions, or religion . . . the most essential element is a living and active corporate will . . . ."[5]

The citizens of most African states lack the psychological commitment to their fellow citizens that emanates from the widespread sharing of language, religion, ethnicity, history, culture, and traditions. Moreover, trust, consensus, and unity are not easily developed in societies that have experienced numerous coups and a succession of authoritarian leaders. Africans are often traumatized from authoritarian leaders, mass privation, brutal police and secret services, and in some cases human rights violations of particular ethnic, religious, racial, political, or occupational groups. A European nationalizing elite could capitalize upon a widely shared commitment to use of a particular language, the existence of social links and moral values based upon a shared religious tradition, the absence of severe cleavages based upon ethnic differences, and a perceived common history. Mazzini, Bismarck, Paderewski, and other nineteenth- and twentieth-century leaders of European nationalist movements had relatively little difficulty in finding citizens who had already identified themselves as members of the Italian, the German, or the Polish "nation." African governing elites, by contrast, have inherited the political apparatus of the colonial state but have yet to establish those bonds which effectively orient a diverse people toward each other and toward the nationalizing elite.

The European diplomats who divided the continent in the nineteenth century did so on the basis of inadequate knowledge of and concern for the human, cultural, economic, and environmental realities faced by the African inhabitants. Their actions led to the creation of political, social, and economic absurdities such as Gambia, a territory 200 miles long and roughly 30 miles wide. Such arbitrariness created considerable barriers to the continuity of social, political, and religious ties among a given people. Far from being "natural national entities" or cohesive nation-states, the nations of modern Africa must make do with borders created to satisfy European power-brokering in the "scramble of Africa"—borders that often violate rather than reinforce units of culture or ethnicity. It is important to understand the single most significant fact of political existence in Africa: the artificiality of the national borders and the consequent problem of cultural and linguistic disunity.

The mere existence of electoral systems, a multiplicity of political parties, and legislatures and courts do not, by themselves, indicate very much about the extent of real democratic change. Stable democracy has rarely occurred by the reformist mode of transitions in which the masses mobilize from below and impose a compromised outcome without resorting to violence. Britain, France, Belgium, and Portugal all decolonized Africa rapidly, without properly putting in place liberal democratic institutions. Generally, in the last decade of their rule, the colonial powers instituted patchwork reforms of what essentially had been institutions of oppression and exploitation. African societies thus went from colonial despotism to the presumed liberal democracy without parallel changes in the economy or polity. The African commitment to liberal democracy was therefore half-hearted and short-lived. This is due to the absence of the necessary prerequisites in the structure of African societies for a successful implementation of liberal democracy.

Civil Society versus Ethnic Fragmentation

Following popular uprisings in Eastern Europe in the late 1980s, the notion of civil society gained widespread currency among Western intellectuals. Democracy, many argued, meant the liberation of civil society, as in Eastern Europe. But what are the constituent elements of civil society and what is the state-society nexus in Africa?

Although all democratic political philosophers have used the concept of civil society, there is no uniform definition of what it means. However, the dominant liberal theory sees it as an autonomous sphere existing between the state and the family or the individual, which sets limits on government's inherent tendency to expand. Forged in the annals of Western social theory, the concept of civil society is anchored in a dichotomy central to modern sociology, that between community and society. The clearest explanation of this dichotomy is to be found in the writings of the great German sociologist Max Weber, as he seeks to contrast "communal" action with "associative" action. According to Weber, community relations are based on various types of affectual, emotional, or traditional bases, whereas relations in a modern society turn around either a rational fixed market or voluntary associations. Although communal relations have natural or primordial bases, societal relations are historically constructed. In this distinction between community and society was anchored the postwar edifice of modernization theory, constructed around the dichotomy of tradition and modernity. In sum, the stronger the articulated interests in civil society outside of the state, the more likely democracy becomes.

Most political scientists believe that strong democracy is related to strong community associations and institutions, with roots stretching back hundreds of years, creating a civic spirit that became instrumental in the establishment of more effective modern democratic governance. Nowhere in Africa is there a clear line of demarcation between state and society. The notion of civil society providing instruments of countervailing power that would force the African state to become accountable to the governed is either poorly developed or nonexistent in Africa. In such circumstances it makes little sense to look for definitions of civil society grounded in social, economic, and ethical arrangements considered as separate from the state. A system of liberal democracy infused with a Lockean conception of state-society relations, based on the supremacy of the individual, is incompatible with conditions in Africa. In rural societies, strategies of withdrawal and engagement, peaceful or violent, religious or secular, are seen as the only avenues of moral and physical salvation in the face of a predatory state.

What there is of civil society in Africa is generally locally based, stronger at the grassroots than as a centrally organized national phenomenon. Such local groups include age groups, ethnic groups, religious congregations, women's self-help groups, and groups that focus on particular local issues such as water or educational provision. According to long-time Africa specialist Rene Lemarchand, in the space occupied by civil society in Africa are to be found religion, spirit possession, sorcery, witchcraft, and magic, which provide a source of spiritual power, potentially convertible into a political and economic power.[6] But the civil society that forms a vital component of capitalist democracies relies upon total integration of all groups into a commoditized economy. In Africa, this is not the case, as subsistence production and self-reliance are real options. Indeed, the demise of an effective capability to deliver goods and services by the nation-state in Africa has, in most cases, encouraged a withdrawal by rural families and communities. People are generally only partly engaged in a commoditized economy and in the social and political relationships associated with such an economy. The rest of their existence rests upon a different economic, social, and inevitably political logic.

The contacts between interethnic groups resulting from increased urban migration and the incompatibility of values and interests of the various groups are enormous challenges for the postcolonial African state. The fundamental problem in Africa has been the prevalence of modern tribalism. The spread and reinforcement of kinship were dominant modes of political life in Africa during the early phases of colonialism. As the enslaving state became increasingly a predator, kinship systems were strengthened, providing protection against the dangers of the violence created by the slave trade.

The predatory nature of the postcolonial or neocolonial state in Africa has also provoked self-defense by kinship ties or their bureaucratic equivalents and with this a corresponding subversion of the state by smuggling and related kinds of economic crime. Matters have come to such a point that in present-day life there is no doubt that kinship connections are what generally count for the most in everyday life. Tribalism, ethnicity, and kinship organizations cannot produce a democratic state, whether or not they are disguised as political parties. Instead, the resorting to tribalism and kinship suggests the collapse of civil society or what exists of it. The evidence for this is visible in Ethiopia, Sudan, Uganda, Chad, Burundi, and quite a few other countries. These are submerged in chronic violence which reveals time and again that tribalism, ethnicity, kinship, and their equivalents could act as agents of instability that nothing seems able to contain.

Modern tribalism has become the single most enduring reality of contemporary Africa. For example, the multiparty state proclaimed in Zaire in 1990 had fostered overnight no fewer than 230 "political parties," not a single one of which had any of the national organizational and mobilizing capacity that a political party is supposed to have. This was clearly a reversion to tribalism under the thinnest guise and was going to solve precisely nothing. For social transformation to take place, the emergence and growth of a middle class free from tribal politics are required. But in Africa, there is no middle class or civil society because social groups are co-opted into what the Ghanaian scholar Ayittey calls the "Vampire State," (a parasitic or bloodsucking state). African intellectuals are often also part of the Vampire State as they are corrupted and co-opted. Hence the emancipation of the intelligentsia to serve as a midwife of social transformation in Africa is essential according to Ayittey, if Africa is ever to make the transition from the current state of chaos to democratic governance. Ayittey does not specify what he means by emancipation in this context and how it would lead to democratization.

Socioeconomic Basis of Democracy

Democracy is a system to ensure the responsible use of power by guaranteeing accountability. In the modern nation-states of Africa, a majority of the population is still living widely dispersed in rural areas. Literacy and educational levels are low; communication and transport systems are poor. News is still spread predominantly by word of mouth about local issues, rather than about provincial, national, or international concerns, conveyed through the television, radio, and press. In the modern nation-state, for citizens to be able to make their governments accountable, they must have a level of education and consciousness as a citizenry. Specifically, a conscious citizenry must be able to define what is and what is not in the public sphere, that is, determine the legitimate scope of government's action and have redress if that mark is overstepped.

Both liberals and neo-Marxists agree on the positive correlation between democracy, literacy, economic growth, and industrialization. The pioneering work of Lipset, drawing from Weber, emphasizes the role of economic development, increased literacy, urbanization, and industrialization in creating favorable conditions for democratic governance. Traditional values are anti-modernization and antidevelopment and foster ascriptiveness, whereas modern values and ethics promote achievement and modernization.[7] Some theorists saw the persistence of royal absolutism or, more generally, of a pre-industrial bureaucratic rule into modern times as creating conditions unfavorable to democracy of the Western variety. The demise of feudalism and the landed aristocracy and the presence of an independent class of town dwellers were essential for the achievement of democracy in Britain, France, and the United States. In these countries, there were highly developed civil societies of organized interest groups, professions, and other economic forces.

By contrast most Africans are still pastoralists or depend on subsistence farming to survive. Their values are still traditional and are not oriented toward liberal democracy. Incompatible values, which are not easily subject to change, become a serious problem for nation building. Among the Masai, the Somali, and other cattle-raising people in East, Central, and Southern Africa, one does not change occupation according to preference. Rather, one is born into a pastoral society and all males at the appropriate age are expected to begin acquiring cattle. The ownership of cattle is associated with the allocation of respect within society. Resistance is encountered when agricultural development schemes intrude upon the land, which the pastoral people regard as essential for the grazing of their herds.

Different traditions for family relationships such as rules on incest, polygamy, and inheritance of property are also difficult to reconcile between ethnic groups. In the United States, for example, when the Mormons adopted the institution of polygamy, it presented a challenge to the basic commitment to monogamy within the American social system. The situation in Africa is far more complicated. Attitudes toward polygamy versus monogamy had been an issue where Christianity presented a standard that differed from Islam and most other African traditional social systems. For example, in both the Sudan and Nigeria, the religious bifurcation roughly corresponding to regional divisions of the two countries between north and south has created a serious challenge to the democratization process by the effort to introduce and universalize the *Shariah* (Islamic law). In both cases the southern regions of the countries concerned are predominantly Christian or practicing a mix of traditional African belief systems, whereas in the northern regions of both countries, Islam is the anchor of culture, political thought, and general orientation. To a large degree, such religious divisions are responsible for national fragmentation, reinforcing ethic and regional tendencies. Religion is not compartmentalized or separated from political beliefs in traditional societies. It sustains the social relationships among generations in a community and between members of an extended family and it sanctifies economic activities. For instance, the contacts between diverse cultures in the postcolonial African state complicate the formulation of a national code of family law, in holding parents accountable for the discipline of children, or in deciding issues of inheritance where members of two ethnic groups are involved.

Moreover, the global historical record clearly illustrates that without sufficiently high levels of economic development, democracy becomes nearly impossible. The poor are too concerned with survival to engage as active citizens, and those who occupy public office bring with them the same concerns of their own material insecurity; corruption thus becomes rampant. In terms of their per capita income, most Africans are no better off now than they were at independence. The economic conditions are not more hospitable for democracy now than they were before.

Africa has suffered from having the lowest rates of gross national product (GNP) per capita and of food consumption per capita while being cursed with the highest rate of dictators per capita in the world. According to the World Bank, real annual GNP growth per capita in sub-Saharan Africa (population-weighted average) was as follows: 1965–73, 2.9 percent; 1973–80, 0.1 percent; and 1980–7, −2.8 percent.[8] Recent data show that the economic situation in sub-Saharan Africa is improving significantly. Real gross domestic product (GDP) growth has averaged 4.25% annually from 1995 to 1998, while annual inflation has fallen from 47% in 1994 to just 10% in 1998. The overall fiscal deficit has also dropped from nearly 9% of GDP in 1992 to less than 5% in 1998.[9] Do the recent economic growth and improvement, which result largely from IMF-sponsored implementations of structural adjustment programs, herald good news for democratization in Africa? Using loans and the threat of default as levers, the IMF has pushed 16 countries in Africa to accept its brand of free-market shock therapy: lowering trade barriers, raising interest rates, devaluating currencies, privatizing state-owned industries, eliminating subsidies, and cutting health, education, and welfare spending. These structural adjustment programs attract foreign investment and stimulate the business climate. But the programs also drive up the cost of living, rip holes in already tattered safety nets, and help kill small farms and businesses.

Consider the case of Tanzania. After 15 years of IMF-imposed structural adjustment carried out effectively since 1995 under President Benjamin Mkapa, Tanzania's inflation has fallen below 7%, the GDP is growing 4% a year, and imported goods fill the shops of the capital. It would be nice were it not for the 15 to 18 million people—more than half the population—living in dire poverty, with 12.5 million of them unable to afford the most basic needs. Fifty-one percent of Tanzanians now survive on $1 a day or less, down from 65 percent in the mid-1980s; but these statistics miss the fact that everything in a farmer's life costs more today. According to a study by the Evangelical Lutheran Church, currency devaluation and the elimination of agricultural subsidies raised fertilizer prices to between two and four times their normal price. Farmers could not borrow because short-term interest rates in rural areas reached 100 percent. Yields also fell, and thanks to global oversupply and greedy middlemen, farmers were often paid less for what they could grow. As a result, famine remains a persistent threat for 40 percent of the country.[10]

A similar scenario holds for IMF/World Bank "showcases" in Africa such as Ghana, Zambia, and Ethiopia. The failure of development is not in its inability to combat poverty, but in the inability to enter into a dialogue with the people who are most in need. The intervention instigated by IMF/World Bank planners ignores the reality of complex socioeconomic structures operating contrary to Western industrial capitalism. This results in several unintended negative side-effects, which could have the cumulative outcome of destabilizing social relations within the populace and concentrating power in the hands of the elite, the military sector, and the state.

Democratization in Africa inevitably has to be seen in relation to the continent's pressing development needs. What is more certain is that unless a fairly rapid degree of development takes place, democracy will be hard to sustain. All the talk of a wave of democracy sweeping the continent and thereby ignoring the many constraints such as economic underdevelopment may only serve to undermine the process. It is also important not to fall into the simplistic trap of believing that Africa's problems are all the fault of Africa's own internal shortcomings. They are not. Neither are Africa's problems all the result of external factors such as the unequal and unfair workings of the global economic system and a colonial legacy, which left fragile economies reliant on the export of a handful of raw materials. The reasons for the existence of dictators in Africa, the absence of democracy, and the economic crises in many countries leading to hunger and poverty are a complex mixture of external and internal factors.

Major challenges for the new democratization process lie in the seemingly intractable problem of Africa's lack of development, the huge debt, and increasing marginalization from the global economy. A democratic system may be introduced and new parties may come to power; yet in the absence of economic growth they will probably face the same old problems and in all probability will generally fall into the same old patterns of behavior. Moreover, whatever party may be elected to power, it will be obliged to follow virtually the same economic policy because this is dictated by the Structural Adjustment Programs of the IMF. Hence, the industrialized countries of the North, which determine IMF and World Bank policies, are insisting on democracy while at the same time that they are denying any choice of economic policy. The economically powerful states in the North set the rules of the international economy and political system for their own benefit, and this inevitably undermines the short-term prospects for democracy at the level of the African nation-state. A permanent state of economic crisis does nothing to enhance democracy. As Africa scholar S. N. Sangmpam writes: "Pseudocapitalism, because of its distorted core relations, repudiates the fundamental rules of the capitalist democratic game, especially the equalization of opportunities, which is the necessary ideological requirement for liberal democracy."[11] This "pseudocapitalism" results from the inability of capitalism to overcome the dynamism of the mode of production of precolonial societies. Africa lacks the attributes that have historically been associated with the development of liberal democracy. Moreover, current international policy does not allow agencies such as the IMF and World Bank to address issues in the internal politics of sovereign countries. Thus we see the IMF and World Bank imposing austerity measures to control inflation and currency flows caused by these countries' flawed internal practices rather than demanding reforms leading to transparency and accountability in political and financial structures.

While looking into the effects of mistaken IMF/World Bank policies, we also need to address other major causes of failure by these agencies to require honesty and accountability in national and local governments as a prerequisite for financial assistance. This will require a new attitude toward national sovereignty and further erosion of the untouchability of ruling groups when those rulers are not promoting the sell-being of their countries' populations.

Patrimonial Rule versus Institutional Changes

The European model that Africans inherited disintegrated rapidly. What emerged from the debris of the colonial European model were varied forms of personal rule that achieved varied degrees of successes with varied degrees of coercion. Where there was success, it was precarious, temporary, and crippled by ethnic limitations; where there was failure, it was usually massive and tragic.

There was also the trend and rapid move to single-party rule. But of greater significance is the personalization of power, to the extent that in many cases the leader's thought was elevated to the status of ideology, such as rule under cruel and bloody dictators such as Idi Amin, Mengistu, Meles, Mobutu, Banda, Bokassa, Habre, Mugabe, Campore, and Abacha. They used the state as if it were their private fiefdom that they could plunder and abuse with impunity. Since independence, there have been over eighty successful coups and countless more unsuccessful ones. The rapid disintegration of the inherited parliamentary model during the 1960s quickly degenerated, giving rise to personal rule shaped more by the ideas of the ruler rather than by effective political institutions and regulations. As Africa scholars Robert H. Jackson and Carl G. Rosberg assert:

> Personal rule is a system of relations linking rulers not with the "public" or even with the ruled, but with patrons, associates, clients, supporters, and rivals, who constitute the "system." If personal rulers are restrained, it is by the limits of their personal authority and power of patrons, associates, clients, supporters, and—of course—rivals. The system is structured not by institutions, but by the politicians themselves. In general, when rules are related to the ruled, it is directly by patron-client means.[12]

Precisely because the whole system depends on personalities, it lacks the institutionalized coherence required for long-lasting viability. Being an unpredictable and arbitrary type of political rule, patrimonialism has a strong anticapitalist effect. Democracy is problematic in states that lack institutional traditions of political competition. As Max Weber stated:

> . . . the patrimonial state lacks the political and procedural predictability, indispensable for capitalist development, which is provided by the rational rules of modern bureaucratic administration . . . . It is quite possible that a private individual, by skillfully taking advantage of the given circumstances and of personal relations, obtains a privileged position that offers him nearly unlimited acquisitive opportunities.[13]

In the African context, such patterns have created conditions for the "bloodsucking" state as well as for its violent and coercive maintenance. In those countries where cosmetic elections are held, rulers have become quite adept as using, rigging, and manipulating the electoral process to legitimize their rule and appear acceptable to their benefactors in the West. The political game is to have just enough democracy to avoid the decreasing or withholding of aid by donor countries and lending institutions, but not enough to allow the opposition to win. To be sure there are some exceptions to this rule. For example, Senegal has often been described as a quasi democracy: no election since independence in 1960 had ever resulted in a change of government. But when President Abdou Diouf gracefully conceded defeat on march 20, 2000, he became only the third elected African head of government to do so in four decades. That, by itself, is a victory for African democracy, but the norms in most of Africa remain nonconducive for democracy.

Toward a New Paradigm: Rooting Democracy in Africa's Own Past

The European project in Africa, as it developed and consolidated, was based on denying Africa's past, a ruthless severing from Africa's roots, and an acceptance of imported European models. If modernization is believed to come only from outside and not from inside the continent, two difficulties arise. First, there is no possibility of building upon existing foundations; instead, these can only be seen as an obstacle to progress, not as an untapped development resource. Second, dependence on the outside will continue for an unnecessarily long period because development will essentially have to rely on external rather than internal resources.

Africans must rediscover their roots and build upon them their own indigenous political, economic, and social order. Britain's democratic system draws its strength precisely from its historical roots and evolution—no less the American system. Why should this be any different for Africa? Yet the dominant thinking at present denies the validity of precolonial Africa's political culture as a vital input to its political systems and processes. The Japanese experience is relevant for Africa in modernizing the indigenous system rather than relying exclusively on an imported version of liberal democracy. What would have happened in and to Japan if the Western world made Japan a target for colonial possession in the second half of the nineteenth century? The Meiji reforms that brought Japan into the modern world were built on the strength of existing indigenous institutions, adapted progressively to modernization. It is a legitimate question whether Africa has the same development potential in its existing institutions that moved Japan from the Third World into one of the leading powers in the First World in less than a century. For Africa, this option was negated by colonization. This suggests that a new approach that takes internal conditions as the primary point of departure is essential.

Precolonial African society had a political culture based on widespread participation and strong moral codes. Moral codes and participation are currently absent in the conduct of affairs of many, if not most, African polities. For instance, if we examine the political history of the precolonial Asante system in Ghana, we derive from the experience the following principles: first, a unifying force; second, a system of participation that must not only work, but must publicly be seen to work; and third, a systemic distrust of power. The myth about the arbitrary and unpredictable nature of precolonial African political communities is not supported by historical evidence. Africans depended in part, like the British system, on the accepted manipulation of the symbols of institutional power, with the Golden Stool of the Asante fulfilling a role similar tot hat of the Crown of England. The symbolism of the culture has to resonate with the symbols of democracy and accountability (e.g., the Stool of the Asante).

For democracy to become firmly established, it must both build upon the traditional system, yet at the same time challenge its antidemocratic aspects such as the lack of participation of women in the decision-making process. Democracy must become part of the social and cultural fabric of society. Traditional authorities, which reinforce democracy, must be incorporated while incompatible ones such as patriarchy should be discouraged. If we look at one of Africa's rare cusses stories in the continuation over time of a democratic system, then Botswana provides just such a model. The success of Botswana's democracy rests in no small measure upon its grounding in the traditional system of local-level democratic consultation, which has in turn made Botswana enjoy the highest economic growth rates of any African country. In Botswana, an indigenous institution such as the chieftaincy is coexisting with democracy and some would say has even strengthened it. Even allocating parliamentary seats based on ethnicity can also help sustain a functioning democracy as in Mauritius. The relationship between traditional indigenous institutions and democracy is complex. Some traditional institutions such s those that deny citizenship to women are clearly incompatible with democracy, whereas others such as the Eritrean Baitos (village assemblies) are democratic. To be sure, democracy has to become rooted in the indigenous cultural system to work.

Conclusion

Democracy should be taken for what it is, that is, an instrument consisting of an institutional arrangement to achieve goals judged valuable and desirable in any society such as justice and respect of human rights. There is no "African democracy" as such, just as there is no "European democracy." France, Britain, and Sweden have different political systems but are still democratic. "African democracy" then is about having different institutional arrangements to achieve democracy. For instance, a parliament can have one chamber, as in Sweden and Benin, or two chambers, as in the United States and France.

A broad theoretical framework that takes into account African exceptionalism, history, culture, and economic status, on the one hand, and the imperative to learn from advanced democracies, on the other, is indispensable. Democracy must be seen as a process. The first and most important step should be encouraging the emergence of civil society by guaranteeing civil liberties and a free press and judiciary to investigate abuses. This means constraining the power of the state to control all economic, social, and political activity. Encouraging activity independent of the state is therefore important for building democracy. The liberation of civil society and the economy from the patrimonial state is an essential precondition for democracy. The ability of the patrimonial state to own and operate economic institutions, generally dubbed parastatals, must be dismantled so as to eradicate official corruption and a bloated state bureaucracy. A case can be made that Tanzania's well-intentioned experiment of Ujamma (familyhood), under the centralized rule of Julius Nyerere, failed among other reasons because of its overreliance on parastatals. To make the case differently, political democracy presupposes not only economic growth but some degree of economic democratization and the establishment of an autonomous sphere of civil society. The fact that there e 2,000 ethnic languages and 20,00 dialects in sub-Saharan Africa points to the complexity and persistence of tribal organizations. The violence and ethnic hatred that has plagued Africa are largely due to competition for resources. In the words of Africa specialist Naomi Chazan, "what colonial administrators previously grouped together as tribal identities for administrate purposes became the urban-led demands in the post-independence reality."[14] These demands forced groups to view each other as enemies in competition for the same resources.

In sum, the promotion of democratic governance in Africa must overcome at least four immediate problems, namely ethnic fragmentation, demographic explosion, containment of environmental degradation, and rehabilitation of African agriculture. These four aspects are interrelated. Democracy presupposes a certain level of economic development. The example of Rwanda illustrates the intrinsic relationship between the demographic and environmental contingencies. In 1950 Rwanda had 2.5 million people. Then Rwanda was relatively self-sufficient in food and its population density was within the limits of the carrying capacity of the environment. The land distribution in the country today is less than half a hectare per head as its population has grown to 8.5 million. It was this organic disconnection between population and the environment made worse by ethnic cleavages that resulted in the 1994 genocide. Unless the four interrelated problems of growing ethnic cleavages, overpopulation, growing environmental degradation, and agricultural rehabilitation are effectively dealt with, democracy in Africa cannot be securely stabilized.

This discussion of democratization in Africa has not reached a series of firm conclusions about the future prospects. The liberal democracies, the IMF, and the World Bank generate their own ways of defining Africa's problems, usually using categories derived from and applicable to their own histories and political cultures. There is thus disjunction between the Western perception of Africa's problems and Africa's self-perception. An analysis suggesting that the causes of poverty in Africa are multiple and complex, rather than technical and geographical, is needed.

The West tends to have a monolithic view of Africa as if it is one society, with one set of problems. The reality is that several quite different trajectories are discernible in the histories of African states, with different potentials for the future. For example, in the case of Sierra Leone and Somalia, civil society is clearly not integrated with a centralized state, whereas in South Africa, there is a relatively vibrant and developed civil society. In Africa, democratic institutions have not yet been fully established in most cases. But even here there are exceptions such as Botswana, Senegal, Mauritius, Tanzania, and South Africa.

it seems that democratization in Africa is emerging in at least two ways. The first is formal participation that involves the establishment of state-sanctioned processes of organization, election, decision-making, and security. The second is informal participation, which involves the establishment of patterns of participation outside the state, at the level of society and economics. These can involve novel forms of nongovernmental cooperative organizations. This kind of informal participatory democracy operates not at the level of the state but at the level of civil society, challenging the clientist- and patronage-based postcolonial African state. This trend creates an opportunity to move away from state centrism and dictatorship toward a more open polity and economy. In such a situation, it is conceivable that a structured and decentralized state could provide needed essential services such as education, health, and security. Perhaps, the best way the West can help Africa move to democracy would be to help build infrastructures at both the state and local levels that would promote literacy, technical expertise, and, last but not least, health.

Endnotes

1. Crawford Young, "Democratization in Africa: Contradictions of a Political Imperative" (paper presented to the annual meeting of the African Studies Association, St. Louis, Mo., November 23–26, 1991) 1–2, 26.
2. Larry Diamond, "The Globalization of Democracy," in *Global Transformation and the Third World*, Robert O. Slater, Barry M. Schutz, and Steven R. Dorr, eds. (Boulder, Colo.: Lynne Rienner Publishers, 1993): 31, 36.
3. Seymour Martin Lipset, *Political Man: The Social Bases of Politics* (New York: Doubleday, 1960, and W. W. Rostow, *The Stages of Economic growth* (Cambridge, UK: Cambridge University Press, 1960).
4. Howard Wiarda, "Ethnocentrism and Third World Development," *Society* (September/October 1997): 55.

5. Hans Kohn, *Nationalism: Its Meaning and History* (New York: Van Nostrand, 1955): 9–10.

6. Rene Lemarchand, "Uncivil States and Civil Societies: How Illusion Became Reality," *The Journal of Modern African Studies* 30, no. 2 (1992): 177.

7. Seymour Martin Lipset, "Values, Education and Entrepreneurship," in *Promise of Development: Theories of Change in Latin America*, Peter F. Klaren and Thomas J. Bossert, eds. (Boulder, Colo.: Westview Press, 1986): 39–75.

8. World Bank, *Sub-Saharan Africa. From Crisis to Sustainable Growth: A Long-Term Perspective Study* (Washington, D.C.: World Bank, 1989): 221.

9. Ernesto Hernandez-Cata, "Sub-Saharan Africa: Economic Policy and Outlook for Growth," *Finance & Development* 36, (March 1999): 10.

10. Eric Pooley, "The IMF: Dr. Death?" *Time* 155, no. 16 (April 24, 2000).

11. S. N. Sangmpam, "The Overpoliticized State and Democratization: A Theoretical Model," *Comparative Politics* 24, no. 4 (July 1992): 7.

12. Robert H. Jackson and Carl G. Rosberg, *Personal Rule in Black Africa* (Berkeley: University of California Press, 1982): 19.

13. Max Weber, in *Economy and Society*, Guenther Roth and Claus Wittich, eds. (Berkeley: University of California Press, 1978): 1095.

14. John W. Harbeson, Donald Rothchild, and Naomi Chazan, eds., *Civil Society and the State in Africa* (Boulder, Colo.: L. Rienner Publishers, 1994): 114.

Suggested Readings

Ake, Claude. "The Unique Case of African Democracy," *International Affairs* 69 (1993).

Bratton, Michael, and Nicolas van de Walle, *Democratic Experiments in Africa: Regime Transitions in Comparative Perspective.* Cambridge, UK: Cambridge University Press, 1997.

Harbeson, John W., Donald Rothschild, and Naomi Chazan, eds. *Civil Society and the State in Africa.* Boulder, Colo.: L. Rienner Publishers, 1994.

Holm, J. D. "Rolling Back Autocracy in Africa: The Botswana Case," in *Beyond Autocracy in Africa.* Atlanta: The Carter Center, Emory University, 1989.

Joseph, Richard. "Africa, 1990–1997: From Abertura to Closure," *Journal of Democracy* 9 (1998).

Mamdani, Mahmood. *Citizen and Subject: Contemporary Africa and the Politics of Late Colonialism*. Kampala, Uganda: Fountain, 1995.

Ottaway, Marina. *Africa's New Leaders: Democracy or State Reconstruction?* Washington, D.C.: Carnegie Endowment for International Peace, 1999.

Simone, T., and Abdou Maliqalim. *In Whose Image? Political Islam and Urban Practices in Sudan*. Chicago: University of Chicago Press, 1994.

Tripp, Aili Mari. *Changing the Rules: The Politics of Liberalization and the Informal Economy in Tanzania*. Berkeley: University of California Press, 1997.

Wamba-dia-Wamba, Ernest. "Beyond Elite Politics of Democracy in Africa." *Quest: Philosophical Discussions* 6, no. 1 (June 1992).

Young, Crawford. *The African Colonial State in Comparative Perspective*. New Haven: Yale University Press, 1994.

Young, Crawford, ed. *The Rising Tide of Cultural Pluralism: The Nation-State at Bay?* Madison: University of Wisconsin Press, 1993.

9

Conclusion: Democracy in Its One and Many Forms

Howard J. Wiarda

Democracy is both universal—in the senses both that all people (*almost* all) want it *and* that it has certain core requirements that give it global applicability—and particular—in the sense that all countries and cultural areas practice democracy in their own way.

Of the fact that most people, if they are able to choose, want democracy, there can be no doubt. Democracy and the political freedoms and basic human rights that it implies are well-nigh a universal aspiration. Public opinion surveys tell us that in country after country, 80, 85, or 90 percent of the population prefer democracy. Particularly with the decline, overthrow, and discrediting of authoritarianism on the one hand and Marxism-Leninism on the other—the two major alternatives to democracy in the twentieth century—democracy seems to have the global playing field all to itself. In the modern world, no other system of government enjoys the legitimacy that democracy has; indeed, one can go further and say that democracy is now the *only* form of government that has global legitimacy. Today, democracy has triumphed in the world; Winston Churchill's backhanded complaint that "democracy is the worst form of government except for all the others" seems to have been borne out.

Furthermore, there is substantial agreement on the core requirements of democracy: (1) regular, fair, competitive elections; (2) basic civil and political rights and liberties; and (3) a considerable degree of political pluralism. In Western Europe, as Eric Einhorn's chapter emphasizes, the definition of modern democracy has been expanded to encompass social and economic democracy, the welfare state, but in other countries that may not necessarily be the case: either as in a poor country that cannot afford all the elaborate and costly provisions of full economic democracy or as in the United States where such provisions are seen more as a matter of voter choice rather than integral to democracy.

Note that the definition and "core requirements" of democracy listed above apply largely to Western, developed democracies; they tend to assume and take for granted the culture, history, and overall high socioeconomic development of the West. They assume that a country has experienced the Renaissance, the Enlightenment, the Industrial Revolution, and the movement toward limited government, in fact, the *whole panoply* of Western experiences, history, culture, and high socioeconomic development. But in many poor and non-Western countries, this history, experience, and foundation for democracy have been lacking. That is why we suggest the need for a broader definition of democracy, one that encompasses some level of literacy and socioeconomic development, some degree of tolerance and civility, some degree of egalitarianism, military subordination to civilian authority, a functioning and independent legislature and judiciary, and a considerable degree of probity in the management of public funds. We use the terms "some level of" or "a considerable degree of" because no democracy is ever perfect, and we need to be realistic about the level of democracy we can expect—even in the United States!

Here we have at least a working definition of democracy. But then we also have all those distinct political, philosophical, religious, and cultural traditions surveyed in this book. Many of these are not only different from but at variance with the Western conception of democracy. And even *within* the West, as we have seen, both the practice and the philosophical basis of democracy may be quite different. The question is: Can these two every meet? That is: Can we find some concordance between our general definition of democracy (largely Western-based) on the one hand, and all those myriad and diverse cultural, regional, philosophical, and historical differences and distinct countries and regions, on the other?

Let us take the easiest case first. U.S. democracy is highly individualistic, grounded at least historically on Anglo-Dutch-Protestant conceptions, organized on the basis of separation of powers, and highly pluralistic. But can that be the basis for a universal model? European democracy tends to be based on solidarity and communitarianism more than individualism, does not have, in its parliamentary systems, the same conception of separation of powers as in the United States, is less oriented toward interest group lobbying, and has a broader sense of socioeconomic democracy. Even in the contrasts between the United States and its close allies and culturally related democracies in Western Europe, therefore, there are some major differences that require at least a certain degree of cultural relativism.

Russia, or at least those areas west of the Ural Mountains, is European in geography, but in its history, religion, sociology, politics, and culture it is only partly European. Since the collapse and overthrow of Communism in the period 1989–91, Russia has embarked on a democratic, more capitalistic or mixed-economy course, and it wishes to be incorporated into the prosperity, affluence, and consumerist culture of the West. But, as Steve Boilard's chapter makes clear, Russia is divided over its commitment to democracy and a Western-style economy. Particularly when the political and economic going gets tough, Russia ends to repudiate that, including democracy, which comes from the West. Instead, it emphasizes its "Slavic traditions," which is a code phrase for nationalism, authoritarianism, to-down decision-making, concentrated power, and even anti-Americanism. But because it is desperately poor and needs Western capital, Russia accepts Western influence even while resenting it at the same time. Russia now has institutions and public opinion supportive of democracy, and even its Slavophiles have no alternative *system* to offer, only carping at the existing system. So Russia is a mixed bag: a country that is formally democratic but with weak democratic institutions and a political culture that is still only partly democratic.

Much the same, interestingly, could be said of Latin America. Latin America is *partly* Western, a fragment of feudal, medieval Spain and Portugal circa 1500 that is still struggling to modernize and democratize. Beginning in the 1970s Latin America commenced an impressive transition to democracy that resulted in nineteen of the twenty countries (all except Cuba) now being counted in the democratic camp (defined in most cases as formal or electoral democracy). However, Margaret MacLeish Mott's chapter shows how Latin America is still, like Russia, only partially democratic; that its democracy, grounded in ancient and medieval Christianity, is quite different from U.S. democracy; and that Latin American democracy demonstrates a curious, often confusing, sometimes chaotic, blend of U.S., European, indigenous, and Hispanic traditions. Democracy in Latin America is also development-related: as socioeconomic modernization has gone forward, the foundations of Latin American democracy have also been strengthened. Latin America is, again like Russia, currently in transition, and its political institutions, therefore, often exhibit curious blends and hybrids of democracy and authoritarianism.

The discussion then moved to East Asia, the first of our non-Western areas, and the Confucian tradition. Here the political trajectories, traditions, and current situations are complex and varied, so complex that it may be difficult to generalize across countries. First comes Japan, which was defeated, occupied, and strongly influenced in its political institutions by the post-World War II U.S. occupation forces. It is formally a democracy, but with its culture, work habits, family system, and all-powerful bureaucracy still dominated by not-very-democratic Confucian traditions of order, hierarchy, and obligation. Second are Taiwan and South Korea, which may be treated together for our purpose. Both had long and strong Confucian traditions; both had authoritarianism for long periods, but then both democratized in the 1980s and 1990s. The reasons for democratization are significant: outside (United States and others) pressures, internal demands for greater freedom, the end of the Cold War, which made security issues less important, and developmental transformations. With regard to the latter, whereas in the early stages of their development (1950–70) Taiwan and South Korea felt they had to keep the authoritarian lid on to prevent social upheaval and disintegration, in the last two decades they had become affluent, secure, and self-confident enough that they felt they could loosen up—democratization.

The Philippines had four centuries of Spanish colonialism followed by a half-century of U.S. occupation on top of a long but fragmented indigenous tradition; its democracy is a mix of all three of these influences. China is, of course, the paradigm case: *the* center of Confucianism, a powerful, autocratic, and authoritarian tradition, then a communist revolution, and now a gradual loosening up. China, at least in the coastal trading areas, is becoming more capitalistic, but its political system is still Marxist-Leninist totalitarian, and it shows few signs of gravitating in a democratic direction. But the possibility exists that China, as well as other Southeast Asian nations, will follow the South Korea/Taiwan model: economic development first, followed by a gradual liberalization that leads to democracy. Meanwhile, we also need to wrestle with our chapter author Peter Moody's injunction that *all* of Asia is becoming *post*-Confucian: more affluent, more pragmatic, globalist, and less shaped by its ancient traditions and more by interdependence.

Our analysis then shifted to South Asia, specifically India. India is a big and important country (one billion people) and an emerging world power, with (like its neighbor and rival China) a long history and rich cultural heritage (mainly Buddhist), but also great diversity of its own. It was colonial master Great Britain that brought democratic institutions to India and, unlike other former colonies, once independent, India did not feel compelled to repudiate everything from its colonial past. Rather, its democracy has proved to be healthy and vigorous, although (rather like Japan) practicing democracy in its own special fashion. However, India's economic system for a long time remained autarkic; only in recent years has it begun to liberalize. So here we have a case that is the opposite of the East Asian examples: in India it is political democracy that has come before economic liberalization and growth rather than the other way around. The result is the paradox emphasized in author A. H. Somjee's chapter: the absorption of Western democratic theories but a non-Western democratic experience.

We next moved on to the Middle East. Of all the areas surveyed here, the Middle East has been among the least hospitable to democracy, with only five or six governments out of forty that could be termed even partially democratic. Recall also Professor Samuel P. Huntington's conclusion from his study of "the clash of civilizations"[1] that it was Islamic civilization with whom the United States was most likely to clash in the twenty-first century. It *is* true that there is much in Islam, a in Confucianism, that can be used to justify autocratic, authoritarian, despotic government and that has certainly been the predominant practice so far. On the other hand, one can also find in Islam justification for democratic consultation between ruler and ruled, for pluralism, and for a government limited by social norms and popular values. Additionally, we must take seriously author Anwar Syed's statement that there is nothing in Islam, neither in the *Koran* nor in the *Shariah*, that expressly prohibits democracy. So is it something inherent in Islamic culture and religion that has proved inhospitable to democracy, or is it instead frustration, a feeling of powerlessness in the face of Western (United States, European, and Israeli) power or perhaps—as in China or, earlier, as in Taiwan and South Korea—underdevelopment? The answer: It is probably some combination of all of these.

Finally, the analysis moved to Africa. Despite the optimistic official rhetoric coming out of Washington recently, Africa seems to be on the edge of a precipice. War, pestilence, diseases such as acquired immunodeficiency syndrome (AIDS), colonial legacies, starvation, underdevelopment, corruption, bloodshed, natural disasters, dictatorship, thuggery, ethnic conflict, bad government, donor fatigue, Western indifference—all these and other ills plague Africa. In almost every country the situation seems well-nigh hopeless. And yet in a handful of countries there are some rays of hope: democratic elections, a reduction of the corrupt state sector, greater transparency in the management of public affairs and funds, a nascent civil society, and decentralization of public services and their administration through local or indigenous agencies. Africa is also the poorest area surveyed, so again the question arises: if Africa were more economically and socially developed, would its chances for democracy by improved? Our author, Yohannes Woldemariam, thinks so; on the other hand, he also advocates a distinctly African model of democracy and governance. Africa's problems are presently so overwhelming and the conditions so bad that no amount of economic pump-priming is going to do the trick anytime soon, nor can we hold out much hope for an indigenous African model of democracy if war, revolution, disease, and the myriad other problems listed above constantly wipe out or threaten to eliminate the gains made.

This brief survey supports several conclusions. The first is that the desire or aspiration for democracy is well-nigh universal, particularly since the other main alternatives, authoritarianism and Marxism-Leninism, have declined, collapsed, or lost legitimacy. The second is that this universal drive for democracy runs up against an incredible diversity of countries and societies that have very different histories and cultures, mean different things by democracy, or accord it different priorities. Matching people's aspirations for democracy, therefore, with these distinct cultural traditions is a real problem if our goal is the advancement of democracy.

But we have also seen that the frequent mismatch between democratic aspirations and the realities of political culture can change over time. East Asia is a prime example: a Confucian tradition that in the past often supported authoritarian or autocratic rule has now been transformed in several key countries into support for stable democratic government. What accounts for such changes" We identify five factors: (1) war and military occupation, (2) the changing balance of international forces and power, (3) social and economic development, (4) globalization, and (5) changing political culture. We take up each of these factors below, but first we need to examine more closely the argument over whether democracy is universal or not.

There is a growing consensus, at least in the West, that democracy and human rights are universal.[2] Those universal goals are incorporated in the United Nations charter, to which all member states are signatories, and in the Universal Declaration of Human Rights. No one wants to live under dictatorship or suffer torture or abuse under tyrants, either from the left or right. Instead, if given a choice, all peoples everywhere would opt for democracy. And, if one looks at the world over the last three decades, there is strong support for this position: quite remarkable transitions to democracy in many parts of the world, the collapse of both authoritarianism and communism paving the way for democracy, a sharp increase in the number of democracies globally, and overwhelming public support for democracy across cultures as *the* best form of government.

The contrary argument is also strong. It asserts that few things are universal and that all rights, values, and political institutions are defined and limited by cultural perceptions. If there is no universal culture, there can be no universally accepted criteria of democracy. For example, the United States has a strongly individualistic culture, but how can one talk about individual rights or one-person, one-vote in societies that are communitarian and emphasize group rights, not those of individuals? Similarly, in the Confucian and Indian traditions, the emphasis is on duties more than on rights; how can *that* be reconciled with an American or universal conception of democracy and human rights? Hence, the argument runs, it is both ethnocratic and self-defeating for the West to try to impose its definition and criteria of democracy on the rest of the world. Indeed, many in the Third World suggest that the concept of "universal" human rights or democracy is a smoke screen for the West to impose its values on them and to continue dominating them. Additional arguments are that democracy is too divisive and polarizing for poor and weak countries to afford and that authoritarianism is more efficient in establishing stability and achieving economic growth, particularly in its early stages.

The viewpoint and conclusion of this book are that there are certain *core principles* that all countries, regardless of culture, need to have to qualify as democracies: honest and competitive elections, basic political and human rights, some degree of pluralism and egalitarianism, military subordination to civilian authority, and honesty and transparency in the administration of public funds and programs. But beyond that our authors argue that there is a great deal of variety, depending on culture, history, tradition, and level of development, in the form, institutions, and practice of democracy. As long as a country has the core principles listed here, we are prepared to call that country democratic. The result is that not only are the *istitutions* of democracy often different as between the United States and Europe, for example, but the actual *practice* and *functioning* of democracy in diverse countries such as Japan, India, South Africa, and Argentina may be quite different as well. So long as we agree on the democratic basics, we are prepared to accept considerable variation on the particulars.

Moreover, we argue here for the acceptance of degrees, gradations, and "halfway houses" of democracy. Authoritarianism and democracy need not be seen as polar opposites but as involving a spectrum, a continuum; in this sense all countries including the United States are incomplete democracies on democracies in-process, with some countries further along on the journey than others. That also means we may have to settle on the fact that some countries are incomplete democracies or partial democracies, that they lack the foundations and infrastructure of democracy and, therefore, often blend some degree of democracy with some degree of authoritarianism. These are often the hardest countries to deal with in a policy sense, giving rise to the dilemma of whether you reward them for their democratic accomplishments or punish them for their democratic failures. For example, some African tyrants have held elections that are just democratic enough to avoid international sanction but not democratic enough to allow the opposition to win. Peru's Alberto Fujimori was democratically elected, but the election was tainted; he is an autocrat, but in terms of combating drugs, achieving economic growth, and eliminating a terrorist guerrilla threat, a particularly effective and popular one. For policy makers, these are the tough cases.

But even if we accept gradations, degrees, and varieties of democracy, we need not say that is the end of the story. For, in fact, countries change, evolve, and are transformed. We now take up the question raised and briefly outlined earlier of how countries do in fact evolve and how democracy may be established or enhanced in the process.

1. *War and military occupation.* In the mid-1940s the United States defeated and militarily occupied both Germany and Japan. During the occupation, the United States eliminated or abolished numerous older and authoritarian institutions, *forced* these countries to write new and more democratic constitutions, and oversaw the transition to democracy in both. More recently the United States and its NATO allies have militarily occupied parts of the former Yugoslavia and sought to instill democracy here. Haiti is another example of a country whose democracy was restored at the point of U.S. bayonets. Obviously one does not want to recommend this solution for very many countries of the world, but one must also admit that key countries such as Germany and Japan are democracies today in significant part because of wartime defeat and subsequently military occupation.

2. *The changing balance of international forces and power: diplomacy and pressure.* U.S. and international influence can often be decisive in pressuring countries toward democracy or in preventing a coup or backsliding in an already existing democracy. President Jimmy Carter initiated a foreign policy heavily influenced by human rights considerations; under President Ronald Reagan the emphasis was on democracy, both as a way of influencing wobbly authoritarian regimes and of undermining communism. And now, particularly since the end of the Cold War, the United States stands as a democratic beacon for many nations with unprecedented influence in world affairs. Obviously the United States has to be careful when, where, and how is promotes democracy (sanctions versus quiet diplomacy or overt pressure versus simple persuasion), but of the fact the United States can use its international force, power, and pressure to advance democracy there is no doubt. Some analysts want the United States to go so far as to use force to impose democracy on the rest of the world; others are skeptical of that tactic. Nevertheless U.S. diplomacy and pressure can be and is often used to advance democracy abroad.[3]

3. *Social and economic development.* A large body of literature suggests that there is a rather close correlation between levels of socioeconomic development and democracy. As literacy, education, urbanization, levels of economic development, and overall modernization go up, so do the odds for democracy. This is not to imply direct causation (economic growth does not *cause* democracy), nor is it to suggest that democracy requires rigid prerequisites (e.g., a fixed rate of literacy before democracy becomes possible). But it is to say that as countries become more affluent, middle class, and educated, the chances of their having and sustaining democracy increase. Other things being equal, if you want democracy it is better to be wealthy than poor. By the same token, while no country needs to be dismissed as hopeless, we must recognize, if we wish to be successful, that the odds of the United States successfully bringing democracy to poor, illiterate, underdeveloped Cambodia,

Haiti, or Somalia are pretty low. And from a foreign policy point of view where you need to point to accomplishments for the policy to succeed, be funded, and have popular support, it is better to notch successes on your belt than a string of failures. Hence, while we may *wish* for democracy to be successful everywhere, we also need to be realistic in deciding where and when the policy can be successful.

4.   *Globalization.* Globalization is a hotly debated topic these days: it has its effect on democracy in the following ways. First, with authoritarianism discredited and Marxism-Leninism having collapsed in most countries, democracy enjoys unprecedented, near-universal legitimacy and is 'the only game in town." Second, the spread of the mass media—the Worldwide Web, music, and television—and the freedom and choices they convey all enhance the possibilities for democracy. Third, large numbers of businessmen and governments, even if they are not necessarily enamored of democracy, recognize that, if they want capital, investment, and economic growth, they must put in place regular and honest elections, transparency in the handling of public funds and programs, pluralism, responsibility, and accountability—that is, democracy. Globalization is, therefore, not just an economic or Internet phenomenon; instead, it has profound and generally positive implications for the spread of democracy as well.

5.   *Changing political culture.* We have learned in this book that some political cultures (Russian, Confucian, Islamic, and Latin American) have not historically been very supportive of democracy. But political culture is not fixed forever and unchanging; there can be divisions over political culture, the evolution of political culture, and changing interpretations of the political culture's basic precepts. For example, Confucianism, which was once thought to stand in the way of democracy, is now thought to be an ally of democracy; similarly, both Russia and Latin America have long had powerful authoritarian political cultures, but these are now changing in favor of democracy or at least mixed forms of limited or partial democracy. The political culture of the Islamic countries has been less favorable to democracy, but recall that there are no express provisions against democracy in Islam; at the same time, African political culture(s) may prove to be malleable with the main problem being lack of economic development to support democracy. And, of course, in all countries political culture is often altered as a result of economic development, rising literacy, and changing social structures, as well as the global forces noted above. So while some countries and some regions have not *in the pat* had a political culture supportive of democracy, over time new interpretations and new forces may cause such attitudes to change as well.

Although democracy, therefore, is not necessarily universal, it is becoming increasingly more so. Moreover, the dynamic factors analyzed above—changing political culture, globalization, social and economic development, foreign policy influence and pressure, and sometimes even war and military occupation—are all pointing in a direction that makes democracy more likely. The organization Freedom House that charts democracy's progress on a daily basis reports that 118 countries are now democracies, a record high number. Democracy is the only system of government that presently enjoys global legitimacy.

Although democracy as a system of government now has near-universal legitimacy, it is also mediated, as A. H. Somjee's chapter stresses, through local, national, and grassroots organizations that make its form distinctive from country to country and region to region. Moreover, the meaning(s), the emphasis, the priorities, and the institutions, to say nothing of the practices of democracy, vary significantly around the globe. In addition, we must recognize the fusions, the halfway houses, and the crazy-quilt patterns that may exist. For instance, Japanese democracy with its emphasis on consensus and harmony is quite different from the partisan and adversarial democracy of the United States. Indian democracy, which is rooted in ethnicity, caste, and identity, is very different from West European continental democracy. And Latin America, with its centralized, organic, and corporatist traditions seems at present to be finding a set of new equilibria, with most countries strung out at various points between autocracy and authoritarianism on one side and democracy on the other. East Asia, Russia, Latin America, and Eastern Europe all seem to exhibit various of these mixed forms.

Yet over time these mixed forms are also undergoing transformation; meanwhile, local ways of doing things are themselves being changed. The mixed forms that exist in Russia, East Asia, Latin America, or Eastern Europe, for example, are by no means static; rather, they continue to change under the ongoing impact of internal and external pressures: the same pressures that pushed them in a democratic direction in the first place continue to pressure them toward *greater* democracy. Similarly with the argument concerning local institutions: although Indian caste associations, African ethnic groups, and Islamic tribal leaders are all performing political functions and delivering public programs that can be described as pre- or proto-democratic, the very local institutions that are often lauded as providing homegrown forms of democracy are themselves also undergoing modernization. Indian caste associations often operate as actual or would-be political parties, African ethnic groups deliver rudimentary public policy, and Islamic tribal leaders are performing consultative and representational functions. In short, while we laud these local and grassroots forms of democracy, they themselves are also changing in the process of overall modernization. Few things are static anymore and the direction of the evolution is mainly toward democracy or democratic openings.

We find both this variety and this dynamism of democracy to be healthy. After all, different cultures and different societies at different levels of development do practice democracy in their own ways, and we should celebrate this diversity. Few countries practice democracy in the same exact way as in the United States: first, because their histories and cultures are different; second, because their level of development only permits democracy at a certain level; and third, because they may actually prefer their own form of democracy and their own ways of doing things. Just as many cultures, societies, and economies are different, so we can also expect different forms and practices of democracy. As long as the *core ingredients*—elections, rights, pluralism, and the like—are present, democracy can encompass many different varieties.

All countries will continue to filter the concept, institutions, and practices of democracy through the lenses of their own social, cultural, historical, and political values, priorities, and understandings. At the same time, all countries will increasingly be influenced by U.S. and Western culture, which is rapidly becoming a global culture and, therefore, by U.S. and Western concepts of democracy. But some countries have stronger cultures and societies than others. Japan, China, India, Iran, Argentina, Brazil, and Mexico are all examples of countries with strong political cultures of their own. Their political systems, while clearly influenced from the outside and by the pressures of globalization, will continue to try to shape the outside currents, including those of democratization, to their own realities. Japan is perhaps the best example of a highly successful and developed country that has absorbed *some aspects* of Western-style democracy even while continuing to follow its own path. In other words, big and strong countries, with their own powerful cultures, are able to selectively absorb what is useful from the West and its form of democracy even while retaining their own distinctive ways of doing things and of practicing democracy.

Other smaller, weaker countries and cultures—for example, those of Central America and the Caribbean—are less able to resist the outside pressures. They may simply be overwhelmed by the pressures emanating from the outside, from the global culture, and from the United States. Their own cultures and institutions are often too weak to assert their independence and to perform the winnowing or filtering functions that the Japanese culture does. Some of these countries may be submerged under or destabilized by the pressures of globalization and by the insistence that they conform to U.S. and Western standards of economic and political practice. American-style democracy, or capitalism for that matter, may be "too rich" for these countries to absorb, certainly quickly and all at once; attempts to push them too rapidly toward democracy could result not in democracy but in destabilization, which would set back democracy still further. And yet, even small countries often have an amazing capacity for flexibility to absorb outside pressures (including democracy) while at the same time continuing to practice politics in their own ways, which may involve compromises with full or complete democracy.

That is why we need to recognize mixes, gradations, and distinct varieties of democracy and to acknowledge that democracy in many countries is not an either-or proposition but a continuum, a journey, an ongoing process. We need a set of categories—limited democracy, partial democracy, incomplete democracy, and the like—that enable us to comprehend and come to grips not only with the many gradations of democracy but also with the unique, culturally conditioned forms that democracy may take. Not only will that give us a useful and realistic way of measuring the condition and status of global democracy, but it also provides us with a base to encourage further evolution toward democracy in the future.

Endnotes

1. Samuel P. Huntington, *The Clash of Civilizations and the Remaking of World Order* (New York: Simon and Schuster, 1996).

2. The analysis here follows Shashi Tharoor, "Are Human Rights Universal?" *World Policy Journal* (Winter 1999–2000): 1–6.

3. Thomas Carothers, *Aiding Democracy Abroad* (Washington, D.C.: Carnegie Endowment for International Peace, 1999).

Suggested Readings

Each substantive chapter in this book has already included notes and suggested readings for that particular area. Readers are urged to turn back to the end of each chapter for additional readings on each geographic or cultural region. Here we include only some general, overall readings on democratization.

Baloyra, Enrique, *Comparing New Democracies*. Boulder: Westview, 1987.

Carothers, Thomas. *Aiding Democracy Abroad*. Washington DC: Carnegie Endowment for International Peace, 1999.

Dahl, Robert. *Democracy and Its Critics*. New Haven: Yale University Press, 1989.

——. *Polyarchy: Participation and Opposition*. New Haven: Yale University Press, 1971.

Diamond, Larry. *Developing Democracy*. Baltimore: Johns Hopkins University Press, 1999.

——, ed. *Political Culture and Democracy in Developing Countries*. Boulder: Lynne Rienner, 1994.

——, Juan Linz and Seymour Martin Lipset, eds. *Democracy in Developing Countries*. Boulder: Lynne Rienner, 1988.

——, and Marc F. Plattner, eds. *The Global Resurgence of Democracy*. Baltimore: Johns Hopkins University Press, 1996.

Fukuyama, Francis. *The End of History and the Last Man*. New York: The Free Press, 1992.

Goldman, Ralph M. and William A. Douglas, eds. *Promoting Democracy*. New York: Praeger, 1988.

Hartz, Louis. *The Liberal Tradition in America*. New York: Harcourt Brace, 1955.

Herz, John. *From Dictatorship to Democracy*. Westport, CT: Greenwood, 1982.

Huntington, Samuel P. *The Third Wave: Democratization in the Late Twentieth Century*. Norman: University of Oklahoma Press, 1991.

Lijphart, Arend. *Democracies*. New Haven: Yale University Press, 1984.

Lipset, Seymour Martin. *Political Man: The Social Bases of Politics*. Baltimore: Johns Hopkins University Press, 1981.

O'Donnell, Guillermo, Philippe Schmitter and Laurence Whitehead, eds. *Transitions from Authoritarian Rule: Prospects for Democracy*. Baltimore: Johns Hopkins University Press, 1986.

Ottaway, Marina and Thomas Carothers, eds. *Funding Virtue: Civil Society Aid and Democracy Promotion.* Washington DC: Carnegie Endowment for International Peace, 2000.

Schumpeter, Joseph. *Capitalism, Socialism, and Democracy.* New York: Harper, 1947.

Wiarda, Howard J. *Democracy and Its Discontents.* Washington DC: Rowman and Littlefield, 1995.

——. *Cracks in the Consensus: Debating the Democracy Agenda in US Foreign Policy.* New York and Washington: Praeger Publishers for the Center for Strategic and International Studies, 1997.

——, ed. *Non-Western Theories of Development.* Fort Worth: Harcourt Brace, 1998.

Index